JESSE LIBERTY'S

from scratch

PROGRAMMING SERIES

MSMQ

from scratch

Neil Crane

A Division of Macmillan USA
201 West 103rd Street,
Indianapolis, Indiana 46290

MSMQ from Scratch

Copyright © 2000 by Que Corporation

International Standard Book Number: 0-7897-2127-9

Library of Congress Catalog Card Number: 99-62894

Printed in the United States of America

First Printing: December 1999

01   00   99   4   3   2   1

Trademarks

Warning and Disclaimer

Publisher
Paul Boger

Executive Editor
Tracy Dunkelberger

Acquisitions Editor
Holly Allender

Development Editor
Hugh Vandivier

Managing Editor
Matt Purcell

Senior Editor
Susan Ross Moore

Copy Editor
June Waldman

Indexer
Sandy Henselmeier

Proofreader
Benjamin Berg

Technical Editor
Vincent Mayfield

Team Coordinator
Cindy Teeters

Media Developer
Michael Hunter

Interior Design
Sandra Schroeder

Cover Design
Anne Jones
Maureen McCarty

Copy Writer
Eric Borgert

Production
Dan Harris
Mark Walchle

Contents at a Glance

Table of Contents

Foreword

Welcome to Jesse Liberty's Programming From Scratch series. I created this series because I believe that traditional primers do not meet the needs of every student. A typical introductory computer programming book teaches a series of skills in logical order and then, when you have mastered a topic, endeavors to show how the skills might be applied. This approach works very well for many people, but not for everyone.

I've taught programming to more than 10,000 students—in small groups, large groups, and through the Internet. Many students have told me that they wish they could just sit down at the computer with an expert and work on a program together. Rather than being taught each skill step by step in a vacuum, they would like to create a product and learn the necessary skills as they go.

From this idea was born the Programming From Scratch series. In each of these books, an industry expert will guide you through the design and implementation of a complex program, starting from scratch and teaching you the necessary skills as you go.

You might want to make a *From Scratch* book the first book you read on a subject, or you might prefer to read a more traditional primer first and then use one of these books as supplementary reading. Either approach can work; which is better depends on your personal learning style.

All the *From Scratch* series books share a common commitment to showing you the entire development process, from the initial concept through implementation. We do not assume that you know anything about programming: From Scratch means from the very beginning, with no prior assumptions.

Even though I haven't written every book in the series, as Series Editor I have a powerful sense of personal responsibility for each one. I provide supporting material and a discussion group on my Web site (www.libertyassociates.com—click on Books and Resources), and I encourage you to join my support discussion group (on my Web site) if you have questions or concerns.

Thank you for considering this book.

Jesse Liberty

Jesse Liberty
From Scratch Series Editor

About the Authors

Neil Crane is a specialist in the development of enterprisewide applications and has almost 10 years of experience in using industry-standard middleware tools to solve the problems of application integration. Neil joined Level 8 in 1996 and was responsible for the development of the training curriculum for both MQSeries and MSMQ. At Level 8, Neil developed the architecture for several distributed, enterprisewide applications and supervised their implementation.

Before joining Level 8, Neil worked for IBM in the United Kingdom on tools to facilitate the development of distributed, loosely coupled, application components. He is an IBM Certified MQSeries Solution Expert, Developer, and Engineer. Neil has a degree in software engineering from the University of Lancaster, England.

Chris Crummer is an application integration specialist and has almost 5 years of experience working with message-oriented middleware products, such as MSMQ and MQSeries. Chris joined Level 8 in 1997 and has served as both a senior consultant and instructor. Chris has helped *Fortune* 500 companies design and implement distributed applications based around middleware tools.

Prior to joining Level 8, Chris worked for the Canadian government, where he built an application system to manage the documentation surrounding the processing of goods for import or export for the customs department. The MQSeries-based system relied heavily on electronic data interchange (EDI) for the integration of data formats. Chris is an IBM Certified MQSeries Engineer and has a diploma in business information and computer programming from Fanshawe College, Canada.

Daniel Miller is a middleware specialist and instructor with Level 8 Systems. Daniel teaches the MSMQ curriculum and assists Level 8's customers with the implementation of industry-standard middleware products, such as MSMQ, MQSeries, and Level 8's FalconMQ.

Prior to joining Level 8, Daniel served as an instructor in Microsoft technologies for New Horizons Computer Learning Centers. He is a Microsoft Certified Professional and holds a degree in industrial and organizational psychology from the University of Arizona.

Dedication

For our families: Lesley & Benjamin, Carolyn & Isabelle, and Miriam.

Acknowledgments

A book like this may be written over a period of months, but the effort and experience to prepare such a work come from the combined efforts of many people over a much longer time. We would like to take this opportunity to thank all of our friends and colleagues at Level 8, and the customers with whom we have been privileged to work, for the experience that has helped us to write this book. In particular, we would like to thank our teachers Jason Brome, Ari Colin, and Lee King.

And, of course, special thanks go to our new friends at Macmillan, without whose patience and guidance none of this would ever have been possible!

Tell Us What You Think!

As the reader of this book, *you* are our most important critic and commentator. We value your opinion and want to know what we're doing right, what we could do better, what areas you'd like to see us publish in, and any other words of wisdom you're willing to pass our way.

As a publisher for Que, I welcome your comments. You can fax, email, or write me directly to let me know what you did or didn't like about this book—as well as what we can do to make our books stronger.

Please note that I cannot help you with technical problems related to the topic of this book, and that due to the high volume of mail I receive, I might not be able to reply to every message.

When you write, please be sure to include this book's title and authors as well as your name and phone or fax number. I will carefully review your comments and share them with the author and editors who worked on the book.

Fax: 317-581.4666

Email: opsys@mcp.com

Mail: Publisher
          Que
          201 West 103rd Street
          Indianapolis, IN 46290 USA

Introduction

This book is different from any other reference on MSMQ. Here's why. All other messaging and programming books start by teaching you simple skills that build in difficulty, adding skill upon skill as you go. When you've learned all the skills, the books then demonstrate what you can do: a sample deployment followed by a sample application.

This book does not start with programming technique: It starts with a project. We begin by analyzing and designing the project, and then we implement that design. Programming skills are taught in the context of implementation: First you understand what you are trying to accomplish, and then you learn the skills needed to get the job done.

MSMQ and Messaging Don't Have to Be Difficult

Many people believe that messaging in general is difficult to grasp. With Microsoft's MSMQ, messaging is easy to conquer. Because messaging is somewhat new to the industry, it is still in the process of being accepted as a business solution. We focus on the solutions that messaging offers and on ways that you can implement MSMQ to solve those needs.

The book starts with an introduction to the common daily situations and problems that businesses face. We detail messaging and queuing and describe them in relationship to the business problems at hand. Once you have a basic feel for messaging and queuing (notably MSMQ), we introduce the programming aspect of MSMQ.

The ActiveX components outlined in this book take you step by step in learning the actions, properties, and methods for each component. First, we introduce ActiveX, explain what it is, and describe what it does for you. We then present fundamental messaging logic and show you how to program it, step by step. As we present more complicated scenarios, the application will start to grow. The book gives you an understanding of messaging and shows you how to program around business issues.

Compiling the Code

The application logic in this book was written in Visual Basic 6.0 Enterprise Edition. The machine configuration consisted of a Pentium II 366MHz with 128MB of RAM running NT Server 4.0 with SP4.

The book provides screen shots for the setup and configuration of the Visual Basic programming environment. The book is laid out in a fashion to be appealing to both the beginner and advanced ActiveX developer.

Conventions Used in this Book

Some of the unique features in this series include

 Geek Speak—An icon in the margin indicates the use of a new term. New terms appear in the paragraph in *italics*.

 An icon in the margin indicates code that can be entered, compiled, and run.

EXCURSION

What Is an Excursion?

Excursions are short diversions from the main topic being discussed, and they offer an opportunity to flesh out your understanding of a topic.

With a book of this type, a topic might be discussed in several places, depending on when and where we add functionality during application development. To help make this all clear, we've included a Concept Web that provides a graphical representation of how all the programming concepts relate to one another. You'll find it on the inside cover of this book.

 Notes offer comments and asides about the topic at hand, as well as full explanations of certain concepts.

Tips provide great shortcuts and hints on how to program in Visual Basic and MSMQ more effectively.

In addition, you'll find various typographic conventions throughout this book:

- Commands, variables, and other code appear within the text in a special `computer font`.
- In this book, we build on existing listings as we examine code further. When we add new sections to existing code, you'll spot it in **`bold computer font`**.
- Commands and such that you type appear in **boldface type**.
- Placeholders in syntax descriptions appear in an *`italic computer font`* typeface. In this case, you will replace the placeholder with the actual filename, parameter, or other element that it represents.
- This arrow (➥) at the beginning of a line of code means that a single line of code is too long to fit on the printed page. Continue typing all characters after the ➥ as though they were part of the preceding line.

Part 1

Overview of Messaging

Chapter 1

An Overview of Message Queuing and MSMQ

Introducing Message Queuing

Before we discuss Microsoft Message Queue Server (MSMQ) and what it does, it is important to talk about the features and benefits of message queuing in general. It is also helpful to understand the business operations that have created the need for message queuing: How have we arrived at MSMQ (or message queuing in general) as a solution to our business problems? For that matter, what are our business problems?

But first, what do we mean by *message queuing*. Message queuing is a process by which different application programs can communicate with one another in a manner that is independent of time. That is, one application has some data that it must send to another, but the first cannot guarantee that the second is immediately ready to receive the data. To facilitate this transfer, a message queue is used. The first application builds a message that it places in a queue. That application is then free to move on to other tasks or end work altogether. When the second application is ready, it retrieves the message and processes it.

The preceding description, of course, presents the simplest view. We can extend this communication paradigm to cover a very broad, global computing network. It is also possible to create scenarios in which the first application expects a reply, but does not wait for it. Instead it continues processing something else, handling the reply when the reply is available and when the application is ready.

In recent years businesses have recognized their need to distribute applications. Whether to increase the performance of applications in a remote location or to enhance the availability of such applications, the task of presenting information has increasingly become separated from that of managing the information. With this environment has come the need to ensure the safe, reliable transmission of mission-critical and often private information.

One recent example is the requirement for businesses to interact with their customers across the World Wide Web. Companies have realized a specific need to supply customer services over the Internet in near real time. This one seemingly simple trend has sparked a need felt deep and wide across all of industry, trade, and commerce. This process calls not only for accurate and reliable delivery of the information received from the Web but also for adaptability to legacy systems long since entrenched in the veins of business.

Before we go any further, let's be very clear on one thing: Message queuing is not the same as email. Although the principles are similar, the underlying structure is far different:

- **Message queuing assures the delivery of your message.** Does email make that assurance? We don't think so! How many times have you relied on email to deliver an important document only to have to send it again and again to get it to its final destination? For business-critical systems and communication, email is simply too unreliable.

- **Message queuing can assure that the message is not duplicated.** Imagine you are traveling, you're in a hotel room in the middle of downloading your email, and your system crashes. The next time you begin the download, you could receive the same message again. Now imagine that the message was a withdrawal from your bank account. You would not want the recipient to process the same message twice, would you? (Unless, of course, it was a deposit!) MSMQ can guarantee that the message will be delivered only once.

- **Email expects its messages to be constructed and applied to a specific format.** MSMQ is not so strict. A message can be anything you need it to be. The important word is *need*. MSMQ is not intrusive; it does not dictate the format or layout of a message—you do!

The Business Need

Several factors may drive a company to use message queuing. In this section we provide some examples of the business needs that drive organizational change toward message queuing.

Access to Distributed Data

One common feature of business development in the 1990s has been to improve and allow for ease of access to distributed data, thereby gaining a competitive advantage.

The desire to make information available to users of the Internet and to improve the ease of use of call-center type applications has driven business to reevaluate how data is stored and presented. Data is frequently stored on legacy systems that would be costly to change. In addition, changing reliable systems poses a significant risk to business. How then does a company maintain established and reliable legacy data stores while also allowing for technological advances at the user-interface level? Message queuing can provide an easy bridge between modern graphical user interfaces (GUIs) and legacy data.

Graphical user interface, or *GUI*, is a Windows-based application that allows you to "point and click." It presents the user with a pleasing interface for entering information.

Legacy systems refer to older systems that run on the mainframe or outdated databases. Companies invest lots of money to maintain these legacy systems; programmers have been adding patches to some mainframe applications for 20 years!

A query built at a workstation may result in requests to several host databases. Using message queuing, the functions necessary to locate and access this data are hidden from the users. All they see is the answer to their question.

In the example in Figure 1.1, an end user may be requesting data from several sources. Consider a travel agent booking your next vacation. Several elements combine to make a complete itinerary: airline, hotel, rental car, insurance, and excursions. Your travel agent needs to request services from each element in turn. To build a single itinerary would require the agent to interact with five systems, each with its own user interface, and possibly to provide the same basic information for each piece of the reservation. The various elements would then be contacted, one at a time, to complete the transaction.

Now consider a system in which each element is booked in parallel with the other. In this case the agent's application records the basic information about the traveler, including where he or she wants to go and when. Then parallel requests are made to each service provider, and the responses are composed into a single itinerary. Individual elements may be altered until the traveler accepts the itinerary, and then a single action confirms the entire trip. To build such an application with traditional distributed programming techniques would be extremely difficult, if not impossible. Managing multiple concurrent sessions to different services would be difficult in itself. Add the logic to ensure that retrying temporarily unavailable systems does not lose a confirmed booking, and you begin to get the picture.

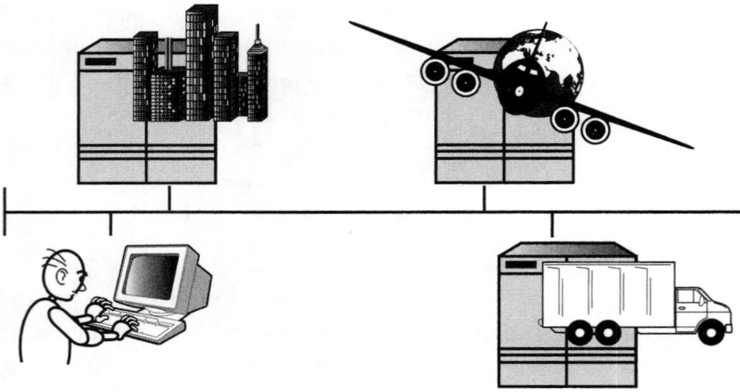

Figure 1.1

Access to distributed data.

Message queuing, as you can see from Figure 1.1, is a mechanism that can facilitate such business processes. By compiling the request into a message and fanning that message to each of the necessary systems, the client application is relieved of the responsibility to maintain connections with the remote systems. If one system is temporarily unavailable, the request is queued and resubmitted when that system *is* available. (Requests that naturally would expire in the real world can also be made to expire in this electronic one.) We take such features for granted in this discussion and discuss them in detail in subsequent chapters.

Integration of Heterogeneous Networks

As information technology (IT) grew as an enterprise in the 1980s, departments frequently commissioned and developed their own systems. These systems were often developed without regard for others in the enterprise, and "islands of automation" often developed. The challenge of the 1990s was to integrate these systems, along with those of customers and suppliers.

Mergers and acquisitions have extended the islands of automation challenge. In these cases the merged enterprises commonly have at least two different systems that perform the same function and need to communicate. Although having only one system to maintain may be a long-term goal, in the short term a simple connection between the two is more cost-effective than, for example, replacing a system within one company and retraining its users.

Cross-Platform Communication

For message queuing technology to be an effective solution to the problems we have outlined, it must be present on all platforms in use in the enterprise. MSMQ is available for Microsoft platforms and can be extended to other platforms such as UNIX and MVS with Geneva Message Queuing, available from Level 8 Systems. MSMQ messages can also be translated seamlessly to IBM's MQSeries using the Microsoft MSMQ-MQSeries Bridge.

➔ We discuss **Geneva Message Queuing** and the **MSMQ-MQSeries Bridge** in Chapter 14, "**Extending MSMQ to Non-Windows Platforms**" page 281.

Ease of Programming

Development of distributed applications has been a complex and highly skilled effort. Distributed programs typically devote large sections of the code to communication logic. Message queuing, and particularly MSMQ, simplifies this programming task significantly. Instead of the application having to manage a connection with a remote application, ensure the reliable transmission of the data, and handle any errors associated with the transmission, the application creates a message and puts it to a queue. (We explore this process in detail later. For now, consider this procedure no more complex than passing a block of data to a subroutine.)

MSMQ goes one step further by enabling this programming interface in a series of ActiveX components that may be used with Visual Basic, C++, and Java. MSMQ is fully COM compliant and can be managed by Microsoft Transaction Server (MTS) and/or Microsoft Distributed Transaction Coordinator (DTC).

Distributed Programming Paradigms

A lot of enterprise systems today consist of tightly coupled applications that depend on the availability of back-end or legacy systems. With applications depending on one another for completion (synchronous processing), the system environment is vulnerable to problems of time and the availability and reliability of networks and machines.

Traditionally, programs have communicated by passing information in files. This process is serial in nature so that one program cannot start until the previous program has completed. The length of a process is, therefore, the sum of the length of the individual programs' processes. The unit of data transfer is the file. Problems can occur when the connection between programs is broken, causing the length of the total process time to increase greatly and/or the data to become corrupted, lost, or duplicated.

Figure 1.2 demonstrates the traditional process flow with sequential processing. This type of business solution is both outdated and time-consuming.

Because most of these applications are several years (or in some cases decades) old, they are stressed to their maximum. With our current dependency on computers and their processing capabilities, today's information overload is causing these systems to falter.

Companies are scrambling to find viable solutions to either patch or replace these systems. Now, companies are faced with determining their business needs and requirements.

Figure 1.2

Traditional programs.

Time →

Prog 1   Prog 2   Prog 3

Seq File 1   Seq File 2

The following sections outline some approaches and implementations that exist in today's systems. The chapter continues with an overview of message queuing mechanisms and an explanation of how message queuing can solve specific business needs.

Synchronous Versus Asynchronous Processing

The remote procedure call (RPC) comes from a synchronous communication paradigm. Although RPCs share some features of messaging in terms of application transparency, the former rely on the network and the applications being available in real time. If any piece of the process is not available, the initiating program is responsible for trying again later or the request must be resubmitted.

RPC lends itself to many business problems, and messaging is not intended to replace RPC in all situations, just many of them! The application in Figure 1.3 has an extension, called a *stub*, added to it. This stub contains all the network smarts, like synchronization, error tracking, and application logic.

RPCs are the traditional way to allow applications to share information. RPC applications are very costly to develop and maintain. Error checking in these applications requires more code logic than is necessary for entire message queuing applications.

Figure 1.3

RPC process.

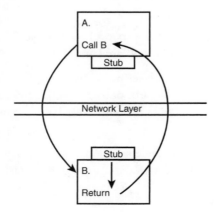

A.
Call B
Stub

Network Layer

Stub
B.
Return

Message queuing shields the programmer entirely from the complexities of the network and allows applications to communicate in a manner independent of time (asynchronous processing). The programmer doesn't care whether the receiving application runs on the same machine, a machine on the other side of the room, or one on the other side of the world. Message queuing allows an application to send a message and forget about it (store and forward). The message manager is responsible for the safe delivery of the message to its destination, as soon as a route to that destination is available. When the message reaches its destination, another application can, in a manner independent of time, retrieve the message and process it. If a reply is in order, it may be sent in the same way. In all cases, as shown in Figure 1.4, the program is unaware that the application even uses a network, let alone the location of the objects that are used. Additionally, the receiving application sets its own execution run time. Figure 1.4 depicts those applications sending and receiving the message at different intervals. The developer sets the execution of these, and the messaging layer imposes no restrictions.

Figure 1.4

Asynchronous processing.

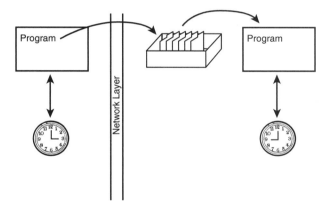

An everyday example of synchronous versus asynchronous processing involves the exchange of information over the telephone. When you make a phone call and someone answers, you begin a conversation. The event you have achieved is called a *sychronous connection*. If, instead, an answering machine answers, you can leave a message. This event is called an *asynchronous connection*. Some time later the person you called retrieves the message and may or may not reply. The answering machine acted as a queue, storing your information until the intended recipient of that information was available.

What Is Message Queuing?

Having reviewed the technical challenges facing businesses and the technologies that exist to help meet them, let's dig a little deeper into what exactly message queuing is and how it may be applied.

The concept of message queuing is nothing new. We use it everyday in just about everything we do. The idea of leaving a message in a queue for someone to collect and process later is something we use every time we mail a letter or leave voice mail.

In Figure 1.5, you mail your letter to a friend in New York, via the postal system. In message queuing terms, the letter is a "message," and the postal service is MSMQ. The postal service routes your letter from city to city and from state to state. Eventually, the letter will arrive at the intended destination. The person in New York can then retrieve the letter from a mailbox (in MSMQ terms, a "queue") at any time. There is no dependency on the sender for the receiver to get the message. The two actions are unrelated or *asynchronous*; that is, they occur independently of one another and of time).

Taking this illustration further, when you send the message, you can control the care that is taken with its delivery (as if you are using a special courier service): You can assign a high priority to the package, request confirmation of its arrival, or ensure that only its intended recipient gets it. Each of these features may also be applied to the electronic messages that we are considering.

Figure 1.5

Message store and forward.

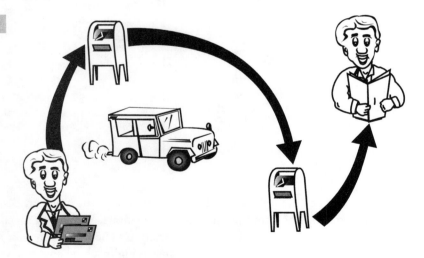

As we said before, the use of the telephone is another good analogy as we consider the difference between messaging and more traditional forms of program to program communication.

If you call someone and he or she answers the telephone, you conduct a conversation. This event may be thought of as synchronous, or *tightly coupled*, communication. The conversation takes place in real time. Commonly, however, when we call someone, that person is not available, so we leave a message. Later when that person returns our

1

call, we may take it immediately, or not. In this way a conversation may still be conducted, but in a manner independent of time.

Message Queuing in Action

A great way to utilize the power and flexibility of MSMQ is to process messages in a distributed environment. Allowing related (not dependent) messages to be processed on their own time and in their own direction enables us to have parallel processing.

The asynchronous model for message queuing leads to a network of asynchronous, event-driven, cooperative processes. Figure 1.6 shows the benefit of parallel processing in which two separate requests are processed on the their own and later reconstructed in a final response.

The programs in Figure 1.6 may or may not run on different nodes. These programs may even belong to different enterprises, as would likely be the case with the credit approval.

Figure 1.6

Distributed processing.

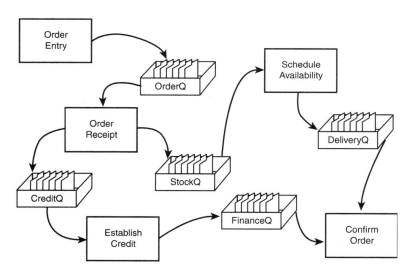

In Figure 1.6, a client wants to purchase something, for example, a new dining room suite, and requires instant credit.

1. Order Entry is a GUI application running in the store on the sales agent's desk. The customer's order is taken and passed to the OrderQ.

2. Order Receipt is the store's office server. It takes the order from the OrderQ and after some intermediate processing passes an inquiry to the warehouse's StockQ and to the credit bureau's CreditQ.

3. Establish Credit receives the customer's request for financing from the CreditQ, determines whether the customer's credit request may be approved, and sends the outcome to FinanceQ.

4. Schedule Availability receives the request from StockQ, checks the inventory to see whether the item is available in the warehouse, and determines the expected delivery date. The result is sent to DeliveryQ.

5. Back at the sales agent's desk, Confirm Order receives the responses from FinanceQ and DeliveryQ and enables the sale agent to complete the sale. If either the warehouse or the finance system is unavailable, the sales agent's system could apply some business rules to enable the sale to proceed anyway. For example, the delivery could be set for a predetermined worst case and later moved up when earlier availability is confirmed. This way the customer can leave satisfied that the order is complete, instead of wondering when it might be and, possibly, going somewhere else instead.

In this example, message queuing has allowed the developer of the system to break out parallel threads to speed up the processing of an order. It offers the opportunity for the business transaction to proceed, safe in the knowledge that the requests (or responses) will eventually reach their destinations intact.

Another example might be an online bookseller that needs to keep a very up-to-date and accurate inventory of its warehouse in order to keep overhead down and availability up. The online service experiences very little downtime, being available 24 hours a day all around the world. Therefore, an accurate picture of the inventory cannot be maintained merely by running an update once a day. The high-volume nature of the business also makes such processing expensive. Using message queuing, the business can update the warehouse continually, using small packets of information that do not depend on either a continuous connection or active machines.

Introducing MSMQ

MSMQ is Microsoft's message queuing platform for Windows, Windows NT, and Windows 2000. MSMQ provides a fast store-and-forward mechanism that enables applications running at different times to communicate across distributed networks. With Geneva Message Queuing from Level 8 Systems, this function may be extended across heterogeneous networks. MSMQ comprises several objects and components, but the two fundamental parts of MSMQ are the *queue* and the *message*. In the following sections, we'll talk about queues and messages and where they fit in the scheme of MSMQ.

The hierarchy of MSMQ is encapsulated in a GUI explorer called *MSMQ Explorer*. Figure 1.7 shows a high-level view of the MSMQ infrastructure. MSMQ Explorer is installed when you install any MSMQ Server. The program is also available when you install an independent client provided that you select the customized setup options. A typical MSMQ installation adds a MSMQ program group to your Start programs list. MSMQ Explorer is available as a member of the MSMQ program group.

➔ We expand upon the layers of this infrastructure one at a time in Chapter 3, "Sending a Message," see page 63.

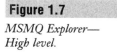

Figure 1.7

*MSMQ Explorer—
High level.*

The examples in the preceding section explained what message queuing is all about and, more important, what MSMQ is. The following section outlines some of the basic components of MSMQ; in the following chapters we talk about each object in greater detail.

The Elements Defined

Even before picking up this book, you had probably heard the terms *queues* and their *messages*, but in the context of MSMQ what do they mean?

The concept is very simple, and it all boils down to data and storage. We can pass data from application to application and from system to system in many ways. Message queuing and its components base themselves on accepted transaction flows. Whereas some applications rely on databases and some on flat files, MSMQ applications can now achieve the same desired results but with a superior infrastructure and a more flexible interface. To the programmer, sending a message is the same as creating a data structure and passing it to a subroutine with some parameters that indicate how to treat the data.

Messages

Simply put, a *message* is information or data being sent between computers. In the case of MSMQ, a message can contain text or binary data. MSMQ breaks a message into several parts or properties. This information can help to identify more than just the data's content.

➔ Chapter 3 details all the properties of a message and gives examples of ways to use them; see page 63.

The most important part of the message is the message body. The message body contains the data that you want to send between applications. The message manager does not care about the format. The message can contain numeric, character, or binary data in any combination.

You can also use MSMQ to transport preformatted messages. Such message data might include bitmaps, spreadsheets, or text-based documents.

One precaution must be taken to achieve the desired results: Both ends (sender/receiver) must agree on the expected format for the data.

Earlier we discussed the process of sending a letter to a friend in New York. In Figure 1.8, the information (such as a birthday card or a bill payment) is put into an envelope. MSMQ doesn't care what is inside the envelope; in other words, MSMQ doesn't care about the message data, or *body*, to use a MSMQ term.

Figure 1.8

Message diagram.

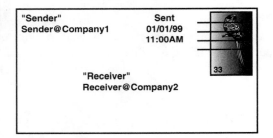

On the envelope, you specify details (or *properties*, another MSMQ term) that describe how the letter is to be delivered. The letter, of course, must include the name and address of the intended recipient. It might also indicate other important information, including your return address and any special delivery instructions. The postal system would then use these details to deliver the letter.

MSMQ behaves in a similar manner. Any message that is to be sent to another computer needs details surrounding the content to help MSMQ route the message. Again, MSMQ does not care what the message content is. You may want to add some additional protection to the letter, like registry authorization. MSMQ provides these much-needed capabilities. Some features include message encryption and authorization checks for specific objects.

Queues

Queues are simply holding areas for messages. Think of queues as mailboxes that hold your letters until you want to retrieve them.

1

In Figure 1.9, the queues are holding areas for invoices and orders. Applications can send and receive from these queues, provided the applications have the correct security permissions.

Figure 1.9

Queue diagram.

The MSMQ infrastructure comprises two types of queues: application queues and system queues. These represent the basic level of queues and certain message types they can possess. Applications use the application queue to send and receive their data (as generally noted in earlier examples). The message manager can also route administration messages to application queues. Such messages might contain information concerning the safe delivery of a message to its destination.

➔Administration messages are covered in greater detail later in Chapter 11, page 229.

The system queues are created only when MSMQ is installed on a computer. Some of the more notable system queues include the dead letter queue, the transactional dead letter queue, and journal queues.

➔ Further details and examples of **system queues** and **application queues** are provided in Chapter 3, page 63.

Technically, within MSMQ the definitions of queues are entries within the Microsoft Message Queue Information Store (MQIS). The content of the queues, that is, the messages themselves, may exist in memory or on the file system of the computers in the MSMQ network. Essentially, the MQIS is a SQL database that contains MSMQ's topology and like objects.

 Note With the release of Windows 2000, an Active Directory Service (ADS) will replace the MQIS. MSMQ's dependence on Microsoft SQL Server will be alleviated at that time.

Principal Features

So far we have explored ways that MSMQ can help meet many of today's business challenges. You can now begin to appreciate not only message queuing in general but also the strengths that MSMQ has to offer.

MSMQ has been designed from the bottom up for scalability, performance, and integration with modern distributed system architectures.

Its features include

- High availability
- Capability to prioritize different messages
- Asynchronous processing
- Dynamic message routing
- Guaranteed delivery
- Heterogeneous platform support
- Offline operation
- Tight integration with Windows NT, including such features as security, event monitoring, logging, performance monitoring, transaction support, cluster server support, and support for future Windows NT products
- A clear GUI administration tool in MSMQ Explorer
- Programming interfaces that include a C language Application Programming Interface (API) and ActiveX components for use with Visual Basic, C++, J++, and Active Server Pages (ASP)

Assured Once and Once Only Message Delivery

One of MSMQ's key strengths is its capability to ensure that data gets where it's supposed to go. MSMQ can assure that the message is delivered to the destination once, and only once.

Figure 1.10 shows how an application can send a message to the queue and terminate with a successful return code; in other words, MSMQ now has responsibility for the safe delivery of the message. Some time later an application can retrieve the message from the queue, thereby destructively removing the message. With a successful return code, MSMQ passes the responsibility to the receiving application.

A key point to consider when developing an application that assures message delivery is *who* has responsibility for the safe delivery of the message? If MSMQ has the message, MSMQ takes extensive measures to ensure that it retains a copy of the message until it can successfully deliver that message by use of MTS. If your application successfully retrieves the message, the responsibility lies in the hands of your application. If you lose the message, because of something like an unexpected application termination, the message will be lost from the memory of the machine that retrieved the message. The application logic must be built to handle such errors.

Figure 1.10

Assured delivery.

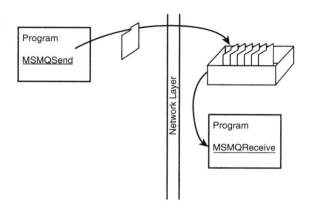

MSMQ provides transactional features that enable an application to manage a unit of work (UOW) to prevent the loss of data in case of a failure. MSMQ does so by sending and receiving *transactional messages*, or messages that are managed as part of a UOW. MTS or DTC coordinates the transaction. When messages are sent from one MSMQ node to the next, MTS takes responsibility for their safe delivery. When the message is delivered from point A to point B, MTS retrieves the message from point A under syncpoint control, and with a successful write (also under syncpoint) to the destination, MTS destructively removes the message from point A and makes it visible on point B.

➔ Details of these **advanced features** appear in Chapter 8, page 181.

A *syncpoint* is a synchronization point within a program. It is that point in the execution where a number of outstanding updates can be made available all at once. A syncpoint is like an invisible flag on a process thread. The transaction is usually under the control of a UOW, and a transaction coordinator (such as MTS) manages all the threads. If all the threads within the UOW are successful, they are committed. If one or more fail, then all the threads are aborted, rolling the resources back to the state they were in before the UOW was started.

High Availability

A key feature of MSMQ is its high availability. Applications running on MSMQ reside in a stable and robust environment. As the popularity of Windows NT servers grows, enterprise applications are working more closely with Windows NT. MSMQ helps facilitate the development of distributed, enterprisewide applications based around Windows NT. MSMQ has become the easy way to incorporate message queuing for the following reasons: MSMQ is tightly integrated with Windows NT, performs better than similar products on Windows NT, and is included with the operating system.

Message Processing and Prioritization

To treat some messages with greater urgency, MSMQ allows the programmer to set a priority for individual messages. Further, a queue may carry a specific priority, offering the system administrator the flexibility to control how messages flow through the network.

The processing of messages has traditionally been done in a *first in, first out (FIFO)* manner; this approach is also known as *sequential processing*. MSMQ has introduced the capability to deliver messages in a priority order. When the sending application gives a higher priority to messages that are more urgent, MSMQ processes these messages in a more timely fashion. In Figure 1.11, a sending application can set the priority of a message (ranging from 0 to 7, 7 being the highest). MSMQ still manages the message in FIFO manner, but the receiving application now receives the messages starting with the highest priority.

Figure 1.11

Message prioritization.

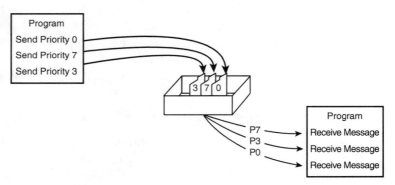

Like messages, queues can also be assigned a numerical value indicating their priority level. MSMQ routes and delivers messages based on a combination of the queue and message priorities. Messages are routed and delivered by queue priority first and by message priority second.

One part of MSMQ's processing capability is enabled via dynamic routing properties set by the MSMQ administrator. Used with MSMQ routing servers, messages are routed dynamically based on site link costs and processed in a store-and-forward manner. This capability gives MSMQ the power to do load balancing and/or to provide failover support when alternative routes for communication sessions must be found.

→ Chapter 13, "Advanced MSMQ Topics," provides details on these **advanced features**; page 257.

 Failover support is the action of having an alternative source process the transaction if the main flow is not available. Failover can also be viewed as a hardware requirement; for example, Microsoft's Cluster Server.

Performance

The performance of MSMQ can meet or exceed the performance of any other communications system designed for Windows NT. The exact performance of MSMQ on a particular Windows NT machine has a great deal to do with the settings on that computer and instance of MSMQ. In other words, the performance of MSMQ depends on many factors and variables:

- The speed and capabilities of the computers running MSMQ
- Whether the messages are recoverable or express messages
- Whether the messages are transactional
- The size of the messages
- The number of messages
- The location of the receiving queue (local or network)
- Whether the message demands an acknowledgment or journal entry
- The total cost of the utilized paths

All these pieces fit together to create the total performance of an instance of MSMQ.

Unplanned Outages and Mobile Support

"All this is well and good," you say, "but how can MSMQ guarantee delivery of the message when the connection goes down?" or "What happens when a user only connects once a day?" Guaranteed delivery in every circumstance is what makes message queuing so powerful. MSMQ basically has to deal with two kinds of outages: unplanned and planned.

Unplanned Outages

During a normal, connected session, MSMQ assures that any network outages are transparent to all executing applications (with the exception of applications running on dependent clients; this term is defined later in this chapter).

Assured delivery is the magic of message queuing and is all maintained within MSMQ. Remember that MSMQ assures the delivery of the message. If the network session is unavailable, MSMQ stores the message until the delivery is successful. This point strongly enforces the asynchronous processing logic. Shielding the applications (and their developers) frees them from dealing with unavailable session links.

Planned Outages

Mobile or offline operation refers to a planned connectionless operation of an application. In a connectionless operation, the MQIS is not available for the creation and opening of queues.

To allow for MQIS unavailability, MSMQ provides a unique direct format name for each queue that allows a mobile application to open the queue and send messages to it, regardless of whether or not the MQIS is available. The messages are stored on the local machine until the local machine is reconnected to the network. Upon reconnection, the messages are sent to the destination queue.

This capability gives message queuing capability to salespeople, delivery personnel, or any mobile client. Even though no communication sessions are available, the user, application, or workstation is transparent to the fact that the communication layer may or may not be available.

Tight Integration with Windows NT

MSMQ is integrated with all the major services offered by Windows NT, drawing on the strengths of each. MSMQ is coupled with the security manager, the event and performance monitors, the transaction managers (DTC or MTS), and the cluster server. Integration enables MSMQ to draw on the power of each of these services, taking advantage of new features as they become available.

Security

MSMQ is fully integrated with the Windows NT user access model. Security features are evident in all layers of MSMQ, from installation and topology construction to who has access to each object.

Security measures may be administered at many different levels. Security options are available at the enterprise, site, connected network, MQIS, computer, queue, and message levels. At the message level, security features are available for authentication, integrity, and encryption. Special access permissions are available from within MSMQ Explorer for the enterprise, sites, connected networks, computers, and queues. The MQIS security is most commonly maintained through the other security measures. By controlling the actions of certain clients, you can limit the access they have to change the MQIS.

1

Monitoring Events and Performance

MSMQ registers entries within Microsoft's Event Manager to record application, security, or system error and/or informational warnings. Snippets from the Event Manager are available from within MSMQ Explorer. The information in the Event Viewer relates specific information about MSMQ's involvement within the operating system. Use the Windows NT Event Viewer for problem determination and as a maintenance tool. Because of MSMQ's tight integration with Windows NT, the events that MSMQ generates are very useful when, for example, a problem with MTS causes a message to fail.

Performance measurement, which includes network message rates and transaction rates, is fully integrated with Microsoft's Performance Monitor. Again, like the Event Manager, specific information pertaining to MSMQ's performance statistics is relayed directly into MSMQ Explorer. Use the Performance Monitor to determine system load and the efficiency of message delivery.

Transactional Support

To assure, or guarantee, delivery of its messages, MSMQ relies on MTS. MTS assures delivery from one system to another for all recoverable and transactional messages.

➔ **Transactional processing of messages** is presented in Chapter 8, page 181.

 Note   If MTS not already present, it is installed automatically with any MSMQ server.

MTS has the ultimate responsibility for delivering recoverable and transactional messages. As shown in Figure 1.12, when an application sends a message to a MSMQ queue (UOW1), the application passes responsibility to MSMQ. To be more specific, the application passes responsibility to MTS. MSMQ is then tasked with delivery of the message from its own server to the next server within the loop, destination server (UOW2). Finally, the receiving application destructively removes the messages from the queue (UOW3). With the application successfully receiving the messages, responsibility is passed from MSMQ to your application.

➔ Further details on **transactional processing** appear in Chapter 8, page 181.

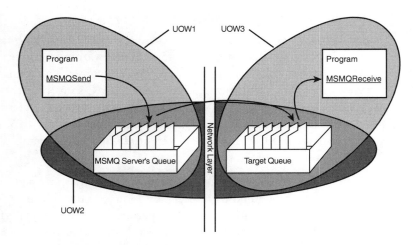

Figure 1.12

MTS's role in processing messages.

Administration Tools: MSMQ GUI Explorer

MSMQ Explorer is a full-featured GUI for the management of a MSMQ Enterprise.

MSMQ Explorer is a GUI tool that displays a logical view of your MSMQ Enterprise network. Using MSMQ Explorer, you can view and modify many of the properties of the following objects:

- The Enterprise
- Sites
- Connected Networks
- Computers
- Queues

Figure 1.13 shows a collapsed view of the MSMQ Enterprise; the view includes each object in the preceding list. A unique icon represents each object and is a quick way to identify the object and its function. To set or view properties on the enterprise, a site, a connected network, a computer, or a queue, right-click over the object and then select Properties.

➔ Appendix B explains the properties of MSMQ objects in greater detail, page 305.

MSMQ Explorer displays only those computers running the MSMQ service: independent and dependent clients, routing servers (RSs), backup site controllers (BSCs), primary site controllers (PSCs), and the primary enterprise controller (PEC). MSMQ connector servers (supporting foreign connected networks, foreign computers, and foreign queues) are displayed as well.

Figure 1.13

Collapsed view of MSMQ Explorer.

MSMQ Explorer displays different columns in the right pane when you click any of the following:

- Sites folder
- A specific site
- A computer
- A queue

You can reconfigure the right pane of the Explorer to display information appropriate to a particular administrator or administration function. To reconfigure the display, select Columns from the View menu item (see Figure 1.14).

Figure 1.14

MSMQ Explorer columns display.

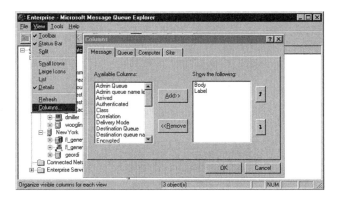

The currency of the information displayed by MSMQ Explorer is subject to MQIS replication delays. Changes you make from within MSMQ Explorer may not be displayed until replication takes place. For example, when you add a queue to a computer in site C from a computer in site B, you don't see the change in MSMQ

Explorer until the MQIS change has been replicated from site C to site B, regardless of which site contains the PEC.

 The MSMQ Explorer display is not updated automatically. To update the display, press F5.

Programming Interfaces

Two types of programming interfaces are available for the construction of MSMQ-based applications.

MSMQ offers a C language API, allowing application development in C or C++. MSMQ also offers ActiveX components (the main focus of this book) to support the languages C++, J++, VB, Java, or ASP. With the growing number of Web-based applications and COM-based architectures, ActiveX development is becoming more evident in organizations' programming environments.

 ASP stands for *Active Server Page*, and it is a development language used for Internet-based applications. When you enter information (for example, your address) on your Web browser, the underlying HTML is using ASPs to accept your information.

The function sets, offered by each of the APIs, allow for queue manipulation (create, modify, or delete), queue location (querying), and message manipulation (send, receive, or browse).

Architectural Features

So far we have looked only at the features of MSMQ and some of the available tools and techniques. Now let's look at the architecture of MSMQ and its functionality.

The infrastructure that provides the highway for messages to travel is almost as simple as message queuing itself. With the construction of a few elements, an enterprise can process messages from unlimited directions.

Layouts of the highway can be as simple as dirt roads in a small country town or as sophisticated as the interstates in a major metropolitan city.

MSMQ has taken over a lot of the manual construction in building your message queuing environment. Simple GUI-based tools enable you to complete the construction of your message queuing highway with a few mouse clicks. The following sections describe all the key construction materials used in building your message queuing highway.

Primary Enterprise Controller

Before you can start building a message queuing environment, you need to pour a foundation. The MSMQ *PEC* is that foundation, and as the name implies, it controls everything within the MSMQ infrastructure.

The MSMQ infrastructure has four main servers. The PEC is the first element that must be installed when building your MSMQ infrastructure. The PEC holds information about the enterprise configuration and the certification keys (used in authenticating messages) in a database known as the MSMQ Information Store, or MQIS. The PEC can act as any one of the other three servers.

The other main servers are the Primary Site Controller (PSC), the Backup Site Controller (BSC), and the Routing Server (RS). How scalable your enterprise is dictates which elements are necessary. You'll have to decide which kinds of MSMQ servers need to go where. Information about how to best make those decisions follows later in this chapter.

Primary Site Controller

The PSC is second in command, and you should install one for each additional site within your enterprise. Remember, the PEC is a PSC as well, so the PEC can manage the initial site.

Before we go any further, we should define the term *site*. A site is another way to interpret an organization's region or location of computers. It more or less comes down to what you define a site to be. As noted, it usually is a geographical location, but a site could also define a company's departments within the same building.

Figure 1.15 shows a site determined via the company's regions. The PEC can function as the headquarters, and PSCs are located at all the other office locations. The same would hold true if you broke down different departments in a company. Maybe administration is the PEC, and inventory, payroll, and accounting are individual PSCs.

The PSC holds information about the computers and queues of the site in a database. It can also function as a MSMQ RS. You do not have to install a PSC at every physical location, but if you don't, you may lose some of the benefits of MSMQ, such as the persistent and efficient routing of messages.

Backup Site Controller

A site does not require a BSC, but one or more BSCs should be installed at each site to provide load balancing and failure-recovery support if the PSC or PEC fails. The BSC holds a read-only copy of the PSC's and/or PEC's MQIS database.

Figure 1.15

Role of the PEC and PSCs.

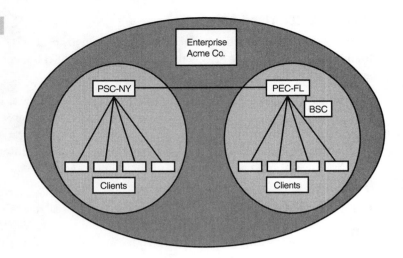

In the event of a PEC or PSC failure, the designated BSC takes over control. Applications can operate normally. The one exception is that because the MQIS copy is read-only, no queues can be created. When the PEC or PSC servers are available, their MQIS is available for further processing.

The BSC may also function as a RS. You must install a PEC or PSC before you can install any BSCs.

Routing Server

MSMQ Routing Servers (RSs) support dynamic routing, load balancing, and intermediate store-and-forward message queuing. This capability is one of the key benefits of MSMQ. The flexibility in building essential elements like this into your infrastructure adds incredible benefit to your business solutions.

Another feature of the RS is its capability to alleviate *session concentration*—a high volume of applications or clients accessing the same resource. The RS can disburse messages and connections through different servers.

With the other servers also providing RS capabilities, why have a RS in the first place? That's a good question! All the servers have a specific function. Every one is given a certain task to do, and if any one is distracted from its task because it is doing something else (that is, routing messages), you have the potential for a problem. Installing one or more RSs depends on your MSMQ connectivity requirements and the scope of your infrastructure: the number of dependent clients, independent clients, sites, connected networks, session concentration needs, and message volume. At a minimum, you should strategically install enough MSMQ RSs to allow messages to reach target queues through at least two servers.

Unlike the other MSMQ servers, RSs do not hold a copy of the MQIS database. You must install a PEC before you can install any MSMQ RSs.

Clients

We have mentioned already that MSMQ supports two types of clients: a dependent client (DC) and an independent client (IC). Clients are useful because they require fewer system resources than an MSMQ server on the machines that typically run applications. The programming interface is identical regardless of whether the application will run on either the clients or any of the servers. The differences lie in what happens to the application if the machine on which the application is running becomes isolated from others in the network.

Dependent Clients

A DC requires a connection to a MSMQ server to operate. If the connection is broken, the application cannot use any of the services provided by MSMQ. The DC is useful in corporate networks where applications run on a highly available network.

MSMQ DCs can be installed on computers running Windows 95/98 and on Intel-compatible computers running Windows NT Workstation or Windows NT Server. MSMQ servers can support up to 15 DCs.

Independent Clients

An IC operates in much the same manner as a server except that the IC does not have a local copy of the MQIS. ICs can also store messages in private and local queues. Private queues are not registered in the MQIS and can be addressed from other computers only by direct format name. Such queues are especially useful as reply queues. A client application creates a local, private queue and passes its format name in a request message. A responding application sends a message to the named queue (specified in the inbound message's properties), and when the response is processed, the receiving application can delete the queue.

If an IC becomes isolated from the network, applications that are running continue to run. The IC locally stores any messages that are sent. The disconnected IC will not be able to open new queues by anything other than their direct format name, as we discussed earlier in the planned outage section.

MSMQ IC software can be installed on computers running Windows 95/98, Windows NT Workstation version 4.0 or later, and Windows NT Server version 4.0 or later.

The MSMQ Information Store (MQIS)

The MQIS on the PEC is a Microsoft SQL Server database that contains a master copy of the definitions of the enterprise, site, site links, connected networks, and user settings, as well as a master copy of its site's computers and queue definitions (as seen in Figure 1.16). The MQIS database on a PSC contains a master copy of the local site's computers and queues.

Note   The MQIS does not actually contain messages. These are written to queues that are file system objects located on the local machine. The MQIS contains definition information only.

Figure 1.16

MSMQ Information Store (MQIS).

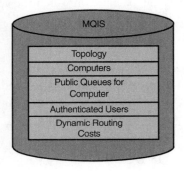

Each PSC MQIS (including the PEC MQIS) also contains a copy of the MQIS information owned by other sites. This information is maintained by means of data replication. Each BSC contains a replicated MQIS database from the PSC (and/or PEC) in its site. The PSCs and the PEC have write access to the MQIS information they own and read-only access to all replicated information that they receive from the PEC or other PSCs. Each BSC has read-only access to its replicated MQIS databases.

MQIS Replication

As we mentioned earlier, the MQIS is replicated to all the other servers within the enterprise. This feature allows administration to be handled from any location with a MSMQ Explorer. The MQIS is replicated in the event of changes to the infrastructure: new queues, queue property changes, and machine changes (hostname, site location, and so on). Figure 1.17 gives an example of the event chain in replicating the MQIS to other MSMQ servers.

Replication intervals are handled by user-defined time limits. There are two kinds of replication. *Intrasite replication* is the occurrence of changes being replicated within the same site. *Intersite replication* occurs between sites, such as one PSC to its PEC. Intrasite replication is quicker and cheaper than intersite replication and should therefore take place more often. By default, intrasite replication occurs every

2 seconds, whereas intersite replication occurs every 10 seconds. Regardless of how often the scheduled updates occur, the database is immediately replicated whenever the site topology changes.

Figure 1.17

MQIS replication.

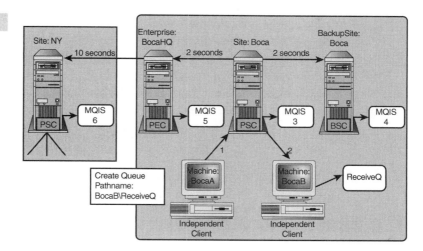

Examples

At this point, if you have already put message queuing into your application architecture, you are probably more confident than ever in your decision and are ready to optimize it in whatever manner possible. If you are still in the decision-making process regarding message queuing, perhaps you are still wondering how it can be applied to your particular business situation.

Here are a few examples of message queuing implementations to help you better understand its potential:

- A retail operation (as discussed earlier) uses message queuing to achieve parallel processing and reliable communications to simultaneously determine both an item's availability and a customer's credit potential.

- Two medical companies merge, and with each comes critical, and disparate, data storage and communication systems. While the Utopia may call for immediately combining the systems, the more realistic and workable solution uses message queuing to provide the communication between these two different, yet equally important, systems.

- Insurance agents are out of the office and away from a network connection all day. At the end of the day, they are available to connect to the network and update the company's central records with their day's activities. By implementing message queuing, however, all the agents with the company can send their information to local queues throughout the day. At the end of the day, when they log on to the network, message queuing takes care of the information, sending it to the appropriate destinations.

- Stock brokerages and banks have an especially acute need for accurate and reliable communication systems. Lost orders or misplaced funds have serious consequences. Message queuing prevents loss or duplication of records and allows for confident transactions and business processing.

- Automation systems in manufacturing plants require reliable communications between the applications that control the automation and the manufacturing floor itself. Again, message queuing can bring confidence and reliability to the process by guaranteeing the delivery of messages, once and once only.

- When someone orders phone service, many steps must be taken. Using message queuing and parallel processing, telecommunication companies can quickly and reliably set up customers' requests, even across unlike networks.

The Benefits to Business

We now can see how message queuing can greatly affect the way we see IT and how it relates to business effectiveness. Message queuing supports time-independent processing, allowing us to decouple our applications and free them up to do more work in less time. Message queuing allows for parallel processing, which helps applications do more things at once. It also provides assured delivery, something only message queuing can do. Assured delivery means that the integrity of our data stores is maintained and that our customers are better served with accuracy and confidence. Finally, message queuing allows for the integration of heterogeneous networks.

We may finally overcome the hurdle of having IT smokestacks rising throughout our organizations. Integration of the disparate systems that result from acquisitions and restructuring is much more straightforward. Communication between disparate systems no longer needs to be a long and tedious process.

MSMQ has arisen as an immediately competitive and viable message queuing solution. It is the clear choice for networks running Microsoft Windows NT. In the next chapter, we take a closer look at MSMQ—in particular, what makes it tick and in which specific situations it should be our choice for messaging.

Summary

This chapter started by explaining what messaging queuing is and by presenting scenarios to demonstrate how it can be deployed. We went on to discuss the principles of MSMQ and it's integral part in supplying the messaging layer between applications and servers.

Some of the main principles of messaging include

- Guaranteed delivery
- Once, and once only, message delivery
- Unintrusive format requirements

MSMQ incorporates these important requirements imposed on message queuing technologies. Guaranteed delivery ensures that your message arrives at the specified destination. Once, and once only, message delivery makes certain that the message is not duplicated. It's obviously important that the information traveling across the network not be replicated. The last point of MSMQ is that it does not impose any restrictions of the type of data you are sending. MSMQ does not care about the content of the message; it can be anything from a financial transaction to a bitmap of an x-ray.

We went on to describe some of the problems businesses are facing today. We described the following issues:

- Access to distributed data
- Integration of heterogeneous networks
- Cross-platform communication
- Ease of programming

Enterprises that are faced with some of these issues can use message queuing to alleviate some business problems.

We also started to introduce some of the elements that allow you to deploy a MSMQ infrastructure. Before we could begin to discuss the components of MSMQ, we needed to talk about some basic messaging elements. The two main pieces in message queuing are messages and queues.

Messages basically represent the data that is traveling between two points. We likened the process of sending a message to that of mailing a letter.

Queues are the holding areas for messages. The queuing concept allows for a *store and forward* mechanism. Queues can resemble mailboxes. When you mail a letter, you drop it in a mailbox. Some type of delivery mechanism (like MSMQ) retrieves the message and sends it to its targeted destination. Upon reaching the specified location, the letter is placed in a local queue for retrieval some time later.

In addition to presenting the basic components of the message queuing paradigm, we discussed the features of MSMQ and how they help to make it a robust platform on which to develop mission-critical applications. Such features include

- Guaranteed delivery
- Dynamic message routing

- Asynchronous processing
- High performance
- Strong security integration
- Tight integration with the Windows operation system
- Ease of use GUI administration tool and development API
- Offline operation

Having introduced the concepts, we looked at these specific elements of a MSMQ network:

- Primary enterprise controller (PEC)
- Primary site controller (PSC)
- Backup site controller (BSC)
- Routing server (RS)
- Independent client (IC)
- Dependent client (DC)

The PEC is our most important machine as it aids in providing the foundation to our hierarchy. Part of that responsibility allows the PEC to *act* like any one of the other MSMQ servers. A PEC must be the first machine that is installed in the MSMQ infrastructure.

A PSC allows for regional or departmental separation. The PSC allows for individual deployment of MSMQ but a PEC must be available during installation.

The BSC gives the deployment of MSMQ a failover point if you lose the MQIS from the PEC or PSC. The BSC provides a read-only copy of the MQIS and allows continual processing as long as no alternation is done to the entries in the MQIS (like adding a queue or changing a computer's property).

Some of the magic of MSMQ is provided by the RS, as it allows messages to be delivered over several delivery pathways. The RS delivers messages in a dynamic fashion, using site link costs. These site link costs also aid the load balancing of messages. Another feature of the RS allows us to provide session concentration between elements in our network.

The clients provide a smaller platform on which an application may operate. They do not have a MQIS or some of the other services. The main difference between the IC and DC is that the IC can have local queues, whereas the DC is a synchronous client. Thus it requires a server to be operational during the execution of an application so that messages can be stored on a queue hosted by the server. The IC also allows for mobile or offline support.

This chapter explains some of the elements that are necessary to understand message queuing in general and how MSMQ implements these features. The next chapter begins to talk about the case study you will be building throughout this book. Methodologies and design considerations are discussed for deploying MSMQ in a production environment.

Chapter 2

Introducing Our Example— Designing the Solution

Case Study Overview: e-books

This section outlines the application that you will be building as you read this book. This application, called "e-books," is used in a bookstore to place special orders. We're assuming that store employees use the application to place special orders while a customer is in the store. You will build this application from scratch, using the ActiveX components of MSMQ. We introduce the technology as we go.

In Appendix A, "ActiveX Component Reference," we've included a quick reference for each of the components. Complete reference material is supplied in the online help with MSMQ. The quick reference should help you find the appropriate material in the online help. We've selected Visual Basic (VB) as our development environment, but you could use any language that supports the use of ActiveX components.

On the Web site accompanying this book (go to www.mcp.com and search for the ISBN 0789721279), you will find sample code for each program that we introduce and downloads for our examples. This approach is like giving you the answers to a crossword puzzle! In our experience teaching in the classroom, we have found that the students who do the best are the ones who struggle through the basic principles and resist the urge to copy the example. We would encourage you to do the same, turning to the example only in the last resort.

As we work through the book, we will build component programs for the order-entry system, the order-processing center, the credit approval agency, and the warehouse.

The order-entry system is a graphical user interface (GUI) based application, built using VB. A simple form prompts for the customer's name, address, credit card information, and the title and author of the book he or she wants to order. When the form is complete, the clerk clicks the Submit button to submit the request to the order-processing center. For any one store, several instances of this application may be running. Figure 2.1 shows how this program might look like to the user.

Figure 2.1

The order-entry system.

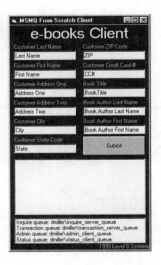

When the order-processing center receives an inquiry message, the center performs two operations in parallel, waiting for the result of each before replying to the order-entry system. The first operation obtains approval for the use of the credit card, and the second verifies inventory and price for the requested book. The first requires an exchange between the order-processing center and the credit approval agency; the second requires an exchange between the order-processing center and the warehouse. (In this example, all credit applications are approved, and all books are in stock, at one price; we are trying to demonstrate MSMQ programming techniques, not database management!) Figure 2.2 shows the basic elements of the e-books application and the order of the message flows.

A reply is sent to the order-entry system, indicating credit approval, price, and availability of the book. The order-processing system composes its reply from the replies received from the credit agency and the warehouse.

One or more instances of the order-processing application may be running in each store. There might be only one regional order-processing center. As the design fills out, you will see how to build scalability into an application based around message queuing.

Figure 2.2

Overview of the business process.

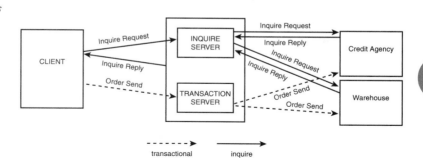

Overview of the Business Process

When the order-entry system receives the reply, the user has the option to confirm or cancel the order. Figure 2.3 shows the user display after the inquiry is complete.

Figure 2.3

Sample order-entry window after inquiry is processed.

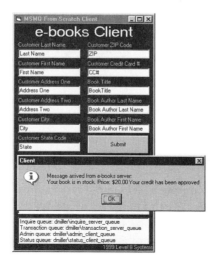

If a cancellation is requested, no further action is taken. If a confirmation is sent, the order-entry system forwards a message to the order-processing center that in turn forwards messages to the warehouse and the credit agency, requesting that the order be dispatched and billed, respectively.

Message queues will handle all interactions between the components. Figure 2.4 presents a complete logical workflow for the inquiry.

After the clerk has submitted the request and the response has come back, if the customer indicates that he or she wants to purchase the book, the request becomes an order. The first part of the request asks a few simple questions: Is the book in stock?

How much is it? Is my credit available? The response comes back to the clerk indicating that the book is in stock, it costs $20, and the credit needed is available. Now that the customer wants to complete the transaction and purchase the book, an order is submitted.

Figure 2.4

Logical workflow for inquiry.

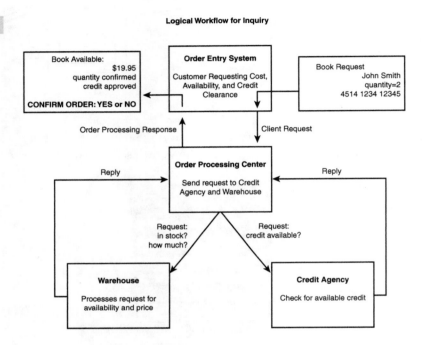

The application now behaves in much the same way. The main difference is that now the information requires a guarantee of delivery. By enabling a property on the message and the queue, the message now becomes (in MSMQ terminology) *transactional*. Before, if the message was lost, it was not a big deal to resend it. An inquiry message does no destructive action to the databases, such as removing a book from inventory. When someone purchases a book, the inventory database changes and a charge is applied to the customer's credit card. If one or more of the actions fail, everything needs to roll back, essentially acting as one atomic unit of work.

Figure 2.5 shows a logical view of the actual purchase. Notice that no customer interaction is necessary at the end. Once a customer indicates that he or she wants the book, the order confirmation server is guaranteed to process the request.

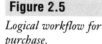

Figure 2.5

Logical workflow for purchase.

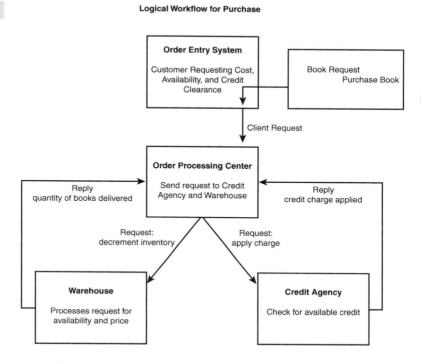

Logical Workflow for Purchase

Design Considerations and Methodologies

You should be aware of several models when you design middleware applications. We will briefly discuss a few scenarios and later apply these to our example. Picking the right methodology depends on the business problem at hand. It boils down to the behavior of the data: Where it is going, who gets it, and how it gets there.

Request/Reply

In the request/reply model a message is like a question that needs an answer. The request depends on the reply; the requester needs the reply to continue processing.

MSMQ enables the requesting application to state the name of the queue to which the reply should be sent. Thus the server can receive and process requests without needing to be aware of the routing of the message. Later we use message identification and correlation to pair up messages.

An example would be a request for information, such as your bank account balance, from an ATM machine, as shown in Figure 2.6. You would enter the information pertaining to your request, like your PIN and desired function (balance inquiry), and click OK. That request may be sent as a message to a central server to be processed. The information requested is extracted (via database lookup and so on), sent back to the original sending location (your ATM), and displayed on the screen.

Figure 2.6

Request/reply model.

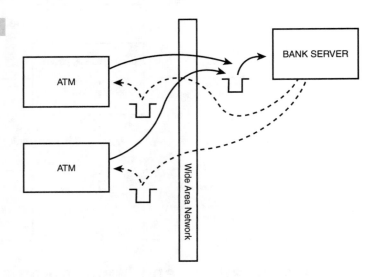

Publish/Subscribe

The publish/subscribe (also known as pub/sub) model is simply the process of publishing information to a general server process. Applications that want to view or process this information can subscribe to the server process, noting that they want to receive this specific information.

The architecture of the model is very similar to a hub-and-spoke topology. The central hub in Figure 2.7 is the main receiver and distributor of information. The hub receives the inbound information (published data) and notes which applications have subscribed for receipt of this data.

An example of this topology might be information that various agencies put onto the international news wires. As events occur, they are written about and published. Individual journalists watch the wires for different kinds of information, receiving items that relate to the area of interest to which they are subscribed. Information is pushed in one direction, and the publisher is unconcerned about who is receiving the information.

Figure 2.7

Publish/subscribe model.

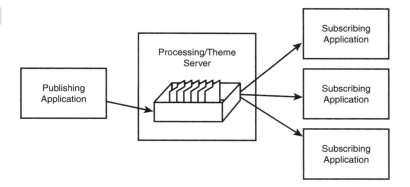

Programming Techniques

Whichever model is appropriate to your application (and you will probably use elements of both), programs must operate in a time-independent manner to group a collection of messages and correlate requests with replies. MSMQ makes available to the programmer a series of message properties that facilitate this step. We introduce the topic here and illustrate it in detail as it becomes relevant to the implementation of our distributed application.

Correlating Replies

MSMQ offers two message properties that are used together to match requests with response messages: the message ID and the correlation ID.

MSMQ sets the message ID property of every message when a message is created. The message ID is always unique. The correlation ID, however, can be set by a program and has the same format as the message ID. Both are, in fact, globally unique identifiers (GUIDs). A GUID, pronounced "Goo ID" is a 128-bit (16 byte) constant that is guaranteed to be unique across space and time. It appears in this format: EDFF2BD1-1FAF-11d0-8B7B-9493759B380C. It is used so that items such as components or messages can be uniquely identified. Microsoft has GUID-generation utilities that use a sophisticated algorithm to help ensure that the GUIDs generated on your computer are unique across every computer on the planet. This algorithm uses a combination of counters, the current date and time, and the address burned into your network card to generate a unique ID for your component, interface, or, in the case of MSMQ, your message.

Visual Basic 6.0 ships with several utilities that you can use to generate GUIDs. The UUIDGEN program is a command-line program, and GUIDGEN is a graphical utility. Both are a cinch to use. Make sure that you always use one of these utilities to generate new GUIDs. Never (never, *never!*) make up GUIDs. Use the tools provided. Remember that GUIDs need to be globally unique and that duplicate GUIDs can wreak havoc within the COM subsystem. Do your part and practice safe GUID generation.

Some GUIDs, for example, the message ID property, are actually generated by the MSMQ Subsystem.

Figure 2.8 shows how replies might be correlated.

Figure 2.8

Correlation ID model.

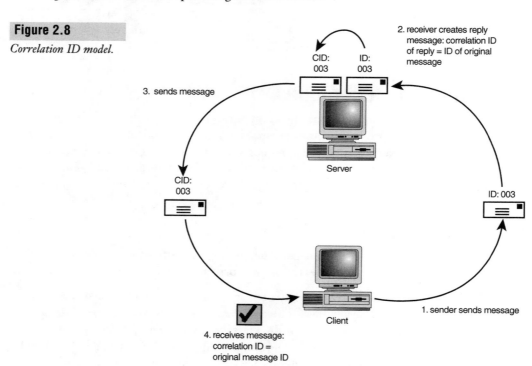

1. When a request is built, the requesting application leaves both the message and correlation ID fields blank (step 1 in Figure 2.8).

2. MSMQ receives the message from the application, generates a unique ID for the message, and returns the ID to the application. This ID must be stored for future use when processing replies.

3. The responding application receives the request and begins to build a reply. MSMQ generates a unique message ID for the reply also, but the responding application must copy into the correlation ID property of the reply the message ID of the request (step 2 in Figure 2.8). The reply message is then sent to its intended destination (step 3 in Figure 2.8).

4. When the requesting application receives the reply, the application can immediately determine to which request the reply correlates by comparing the received correlation ID with that of its log of message IDs (step 4 in Figure 2.8).

Grouping Messages

Occasions arise when one message does not encapsulate all the data relevant to a transaction. This situation might occur when a single message has too much data, when you need to collect data from several sources, or when you want to send a small amount of data as soon as it is available, knowing that a detailed response will follow.

We can use the correlation ID property to assist with the grouping of messages. For example, the first message in the group would be sent to MSMQ, and the resulting ID would be placed in the correlation ID field of all the subsequent messages in the group. If we want to indicate an order to the messages, we can use the AppSpecific property. A receiving application would search its input queue for any message with an AppSpecific value of 1 and use the retrieved message ID to search the queue for messages with a corresponding correlation ID. Messages can be grouped in other ways as well. For example, they may be grouped by using either different queues or the message label property. Different techniques are better suited to different applications.

As you work through the e-books example, you will be able to apply some of these techniques.

Detailed Design of e-books

A good place to start when designing a distributed, message-driven application is to consider the data and the actions that must be performed on it. Our example starts with a request to buy a book.

The first message is the request itself. It contains the customer's name, address, and credit card information, along with the name of the book the customer wants to purchase. The order-entry system builds the message and sends it to the order-processing system.

At this point the concept of *data persistence* becomes important. We've already talked about assured, once-only delivery, but is that type of delivery really required here? This message is a request message; no commitments have been made. If the system breaks down while the message is being processed and the information is lost, it probably doesn't matter. So what type of messages should we use in our e-books applications? MSMQ supports three classes of messages: express, recoverable, and transactional.

An *express message* is stored in memory only and is processed very quickly. Because it is only in memory, no guarantees are made that the message will be delivered. However these messages are delivered very quickly because they require the least amount of overhead.

A *recoverable message* is written to disk. In the event of a system failure before the message is delivered, MSMQ, which has safely stored the message, will resend the message to the destination. Because the delivery process quite possibly worked the first time and only the acknowledgment was lost, recoverable messages can be delivered more than once, but they will always be delivered.

Transactional messages are guaranteed to be delivered once, and only once. They are the only type of message that can be used in a unit of work. The overhead for processing these messages is clearly higher than the overhead for the other types of messages, but transactional messages are necessary when the data cannot be re-created and the integrity of the unit of work is threatened if any message is lost. (For example, although we might not mind if a message to credit our bank account is posted twice, we would certainly object to a debit being applied a second time!)

So returning to our example, what kind of message would you use for the initial request? We suggest using the express message class because this data can be easily re-created in the event of a system failure. In addition, in this case the customer is unlikely to wait for reinstatement of the service and so the inquiry would become irrelevant anyway.

So we've identified the data and the type of our opening message flow. Next let's look at the nature of the transaction. This message expects a response. The order-processing system will reply that the book is in stock or not, provide an anticipated delivery time, how much the order will cost, and whether the credit card was approved for the purchase. We'll be working with the request/reply model described earlier. Finally, let us consider the necessary queues. Clearly, we require one for the request and one for the reply. But who will create them? And if the programs are running on different machines, where will the queues be located? We have some background already in that we have decided that the messages can be express, so the physical location of the queues makes little difference to the design at this point. We need to consider the final size of this application. After all, it will run at several customer service stations in each store, and many stores will be in each region. Scalability is a big issue affecting our design.

The most important aspect of the design is that it is flexible, allowing us to add parallel elements as the demand for the application service increases. For the sake of argument, we've made a series of assumptions. (Note that there is not usually an obvious right or wrong answer to how the elements of the application are run.)

In this case each store has four or more client stations, each of which processes only one customer order at a time. In addition, each store has one order-processing center. All the stores use the same credit approval agency, and distribution is handled from several regional warehouses. Later in this chapter we discuss how this application architecture is mapped to our MSMQ network.

The store-based order-processing system has a queue onto which it receives Request messages. The order-processing system creates this queue when starting up with a queue type that identifies itself as an Inquiry Queue. (You will see in later chapters how the system actually creates the queue.) Each of the store-based client applications sends messages to this queue.

Each order-entry system creates its own queue onto which it receives the replies to its requests. This approach makes reply processing very efficient because the systems do not have to search through the replies to other requests. When the initial request message is sent to the order-processing system, the reply queue name property is set to identify this dedicated queue. The order-entry application searches the MQIS for queues with the type Inquiry Queue before sending the request. This request normally returns only one queue, but because the exact destination queue is determined when the application is run, we can use a backup order-processing system if the primary system fails or becomes overloaded. Figure 2.9 shows these queues and how they are used in our system.

Figure 2.9

Queues for the inquiry workflow.

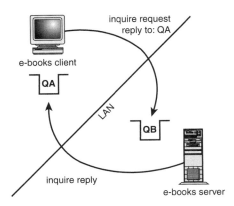

Next we must consider how the order-processing system handles the data it receives in order to produce the reply that we expect.

Again, let's consider the data first. We receive a single message containing the potential customer's name, address, credit card number, and book that the person wants to purchase. We reply with whether the credit card transaction was authorized, estimated delivery time, and cost. To handle the single customer request, it must be turned into two more.

The first is a message to the regional warehouse to check on the price and availability of the book. The only information that needs to be contained in this request is the name of the book and the author. That reply contains the delivery time (in days) and the price of the book.

The second is a message to the credit approval agency in which we submit the credit card number and an amount. The reply is a yes or a no. Now we have another design choice. We could execute each of these steps serially, waiting for availability information before getting credit card approval. Alternatively, we could submit a credit approval for an arbitrary amount that we consider will cover the cost of the book, only going back for further approval if the requested book was particularly expensive. The latter approach allows us to build some parallel processing into our workflow and reduces the time that we keep the customer waiting. We will adopt that approach.

We are using the request/reply model again for each of these transactions. The credit approval agency and the regional warehouse have independent input queues identified by a unique type, and each inquiry has a unique reply queue. As with the initial request, these messages are transient: If the message is lost, it will signal a network error and the total inquiry will time out. We can again consider these to be express messages.

Figure 2.10 shows the queues that are used for the processing of the inquiry workflow between the order-processing server and the back-end systems.

Figure 2.10

e-books inquiry workflow—Queues for back-end processing.

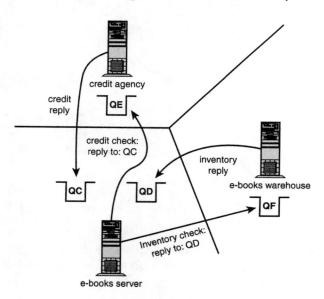

After the reply is sent back to the customer, we are ready to begin our second workflow and commit or cancel the order. The display in Figure 2.3 shows the message box displaying the price and delivery time for the book. Figure 2.11 displays the message box displayed by the order-entry system which allows the user to then submit an order for the book.

Figure 2.11

Sample panel to complete order.

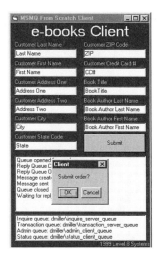

If the customer chooses to cancel the order now, no further processing is required. If, on the other hand, the customer chooses to proceed with the purchase, more messages must be sent to complete the order. This time, data will be sent that updates the state of the inventory and credit systems. Such messages cannot be lost, and we must ensure the integrity of the whole update. The individual elements must be coordinated, which requires the use of transactional messages.

→ For more information on **how to coordinate the elements**, see Chapter 8, "Order Confirmation Workflow: Client to Server," page 181.

For now, it is enough to understand that when a message is put in a queue, delivery is guaranteed once and once only.

Returning to the data, our order-entry system submits a message to the confirm queue of the order-processing system. This system contains the name and address of the customer, the credit card information, and the title and price of the requested book.

The order-processing system receives the confirmation from the queue and in the same unit of work sends a Charge message to the credit agency and an Order message to the warehouse. The Charge message contains the credit card number and the price; the Order message contains a description of the book, the agreed to price (in case it changed in the meantime), and the delivery address.

→ For more information on the concept of **unit of work**, see Chapter 8, page 181.

Because MSMQ is guaranteeing the delivery of every message, no return flow is necessary. The customer can receive a Confirmed notice as soon as the Order button is clicked.

→ In Chapter 10, "Delivery Confirmation and Audit," we consider how the MSMQ features for tracking and acknowledging messages provide a mechanism for handling any exceptions that occur. See page 215.

Figure 2.12 provides an overview of the message traffic that flows from the order-entry system to the order-processing system. The order-processing system then forwards the appropriate messages to the credit agency and the warehouse.

Figure 2.12

Book-order workflow.

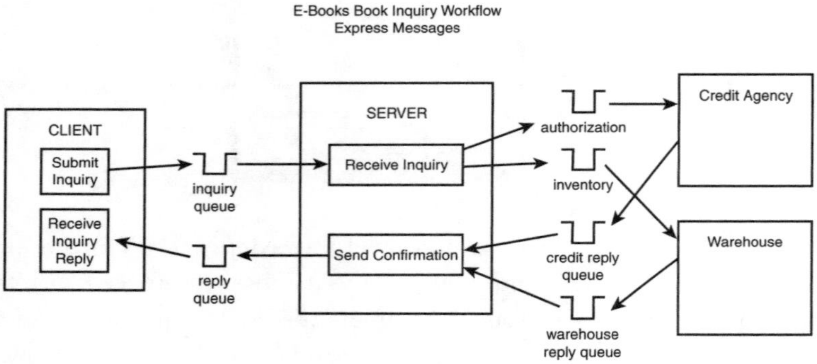

MSMQ Network Design

Let's take some time to discuss what our enterprise might look like in a real "e-books" production environment. In this section we examine the architecture of the entire workflow from the top down.

First we consider the general duties of the different MSMQ architectural objects. The primary enterprise controller (PEC) holds the master copy of the MQIS and is responsible for the replication of the data. Although the PEC may contain queues and perform regular server functions, it is better that it doesn't.

Attached to the PEC are other MSMQ servers such as primary site controllers (PSCs), backup site controllers (BSCs), and routing servers (RSs). The most used is the PSC. The PSC holds a copy of the MQIS and as such contains a record of all the public queue definitions known in the enterprise. PSCs typically house the server components of an application or provide regional or departmental access to the enterprise for MSMQ dependent or independent clients. Independent or dependent Clients understandably house client, or front-end applications, that require user interfaces. These independent and dependent clients have a smaller MSMQ footprint, do not have a copy of the MQIS, and are not responsible for any routing. Dependent clients require a synchronous connection with a MSMQ server and cannot have local queues.

Now let's look at how this information applies to our e-books enterprise. First, on the enterprise level, we have two companies involved in our workflow and therefore two enterprises: the e-books enterprise and the credit agency enterprise. As the e-books developers, we do not need to concern ourselves with the overall layout of the credit agency's enterprise. We only need to know about one of its machines: the one we connect to. This machine is most likely a PSC. This PSC may be acting as a router for clients that actually do the credit processing, but this behavior is not really our concern because any work on the credit agency side will be transparent to us.

The e-books enterprise, however, is our concern, and its breadth is quite wide. We have one central PEC. We are not going to concern ourselves too much with this PEC, however, because we are going to have PSCs for each of our locations. These locations are as follows: each store location, each office location (possibly call-in centers and so on), and each warehouse location. The diagram in Figure 2.13 shows these three sites.

On each PSC, we can have multiple clients. For example, at a store the PSC resides on a server machine in the back office, and each independent client resides on a workstation, either at the checkout counters, the information desk, or the customer service desk. Figure 2.13 shows multiple clients connected to the store and office site controllers.

So where do our applications reside? Well, the credit agency application resides on the credit agency site controller, and the warehouse application resides on the warehouse site controller, obviously! Each instance of the server application is connected to an instance of the warehouse application and to an instance of the credit application, each back-end system being able to handle requests from multiple server applications. Likewise, each server is able to process requests from multiple clients. To achieve load balancing, we may have several instances of the server application on our site controllers. For example, if we have many inquires relative to orders, we could run multiple instances of our "inquire server" application.

Each independent client would generally run one instance of our "client" application; however, the potential exists for a client to run more than one instance of the client application in the unlikely event that two customers with special orders approach the customer service counter at once.

The diagram in Figure 2.13 shows one example of MSMQ network topology that we canuse for our e-books application.

Figure 2.13

MSMQ network topology.

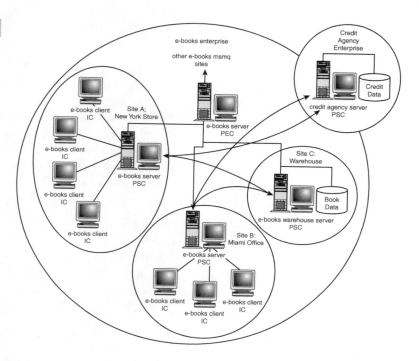

MSMQ Installation and Deployment

We have talkeda lot about PECs, PSCs, and RSs, but how do you set them up? Because this book is about programming and not administration, we've kept the installation details to a minimum.

MSMQ is included in the Option Pack CD-ROM that is available free from Microsoft's Web site. The Option Pack CD contains lots of other great applications, such as Internet Information Server, FrontPage, Microsoft Transaction Server, and Microsoft Management Console. MSMQ is also included with Windows NT Enterprise Edition. When you start to install the Enterprise Edition, a dialog box prompts you to install MSMQ. Indicate Yes or No for installation. With the release of Windows 2000, MSMQ is part of the operating system.

Before you install MSMQ from the Option Pack CD, you might want to do some planning of your enterprise. MSMQ 1.0 depends on an installation of SQL Server 6.5 or greater. We recommend that you install SQL Server before you begin installing MSMQ. MSMQ provides you with a restricted version of SQL Server.

The Option Pack Setup screen is shown in Figure 2.14. The components list represents all the applications available on the book's Web site.

 Tip

To install just MSMQ, deselect everything within the list. Then select MSMQ. This step selects all the necessary components that relate to the MSMQ installation.

Figure 2.14

Option Pack Select Components screen.

After you select MSMQ, you must choose which MSMQ server you want to install from the screen shown in Figure 2.15.

Figure 2.15

Option Pack Select MSMQ Server screen.

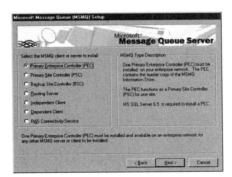

If you are installing MSMQ for the first time, which MSMQ server should you select? Right—the PEC needs to be the first machine installed in the MSMQ infrastructure. After you specify that you want the PEC installed, you would see the setup screen in Figure 2.16. The PEC setup requires you to fill in two properties: the name of the enterprise and the name of the site.

Why do we need to fill in the name of the site? Remember that the PEC is also a PSC. Therefore, we need to specify the name of the enterprise as well as the name of the site. Click Next when you complete the form.

Figure 2.16

MSMQ PEC Setup screen.

The installation procedure then asks you which directory to install MSMQ into. Specify the name of the directory and click Next.

Figure 2.17 shows a panel that provides the configuration settings for the MQIS. You can specify the location of the data and log devices and determine the size of the MQIS database (the data and log devices). Specify the desired values and click Next.

A formula is supplied for estimating the size of the MQIS:

```
computers *( 2.4K + (2K * public queues per computer)) + 2.6K *
authenticated users
```

You can use this formula to estimate the size of the data device. The log device should be 15% of the size of the data device.

Figure 2.17

PEC MQIS setup screen.

The final piece of required information is the name of the connected network (CN). The CN defines a logical group that allows machines to directly establish a session with one another. These machines are used as part of the message routing capability. The CN can be comprised of either IP or IPX machines. Again, because we are installing MSMQ server for the first time, we are responsible for setting up the CN. Figure 2.18 shows the MSMQ Connected Networks screens. After completing these setup screens, you are ready to finish your PEC setup by clicking Finish.

Figure 2.18

Option Pack PEC CN setup screens.

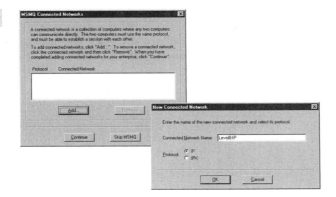

You should now see your MSMQ Explorer with the name of your enterprise followed by the name of the site. Under the site you should see the name of machine that is running the PEC instance. Within MSMQ Explorer, you can create queues on any specified computer (as long as you have proper security).

 **Tip**   If you start up MSMQ Explorer and receive the error `MQIS is not available`, make sure that the SQL services are running. To check, go to Control Panel and select Services. The list should contain an entry called SQL Executive. Make sure that the service is started.

The MSMQ infrastructure is now sufficient to continue with the example in this book. If several machines are available to you, you might want to install other MSMQ servers and build a network that looks more like that shown in our detailed design section. The strength of this design is its scalability. The program will run on one machine, or it will run on many. By hiding from the application the physical location of the queues, we can run the application on almost any network configuration.

Introducing ActiveX Programming

Microsoft uses the term *ActiveX* to cover several technologies that facilitate the development of integrated applications. Component Object Model (COM) and object linking and embedding (OLE) are two of the technologies that have been collected under the ActiveX umbrella. In the context of MSMQ, the terms *ActiveX* and *COM component* are interchangeable.

COM is more about combining than creating. Its purpose is to allow developers to create their applications at least partially from a set of prefabricated parts. Instead of having to create every program from the ground up, a developer can use objects, thus saving time and resources that she or he can later use to enhance or expand the application.

A good analogy is that of building a house. You do not start with sand, then make the bricks, and then make the house. Instead, you just get the bricks and build the house. Taking the analogy further, many components go into building the house. Each component has a specific function, associated properties, and possibly even its own method for being used. For example, bricks or concrete blocks may be used interchangeably to construct walls. Sometimes wooden frames may be used instead. Such components provide support for the roof. The methods for working with the components vary significantly. Intermingled with these interchangeable components are others that fulfill different functions, such as doors or windows. The builder must select the components to use, and if there is a choice, select the component most suited to the particular use.

Historically, programmers have been constructing the house from the raw materials. Each new project required them to start from nothing. Sometimes programs would be remodeled, stripping parts out and reusing them in a new construction. In these cases, the door never quite fit the new frame, so programs constructed this way usually required a great deal of effort and customization to get just right.

Objects are like bricks, windows, and door frames. COM has essentially simplified the programming process by providing these objects that programmers can call from within their applications. Now with the standards brought about by COM, all a developer needs is a good reference (such as this book) and a little practice, and before long he or she is writing robust, reliable applications.

Before we go on, let us cover some terminology. The first is the idea of an *ActiveX control*. Formerly known as *OLE controls*, ActiveX controls are COM objects that adhere to certain rules. For example, if a control has a user interface, it must use the ActiveX control's standards.

An ActiveX control can be very complicated or very plain. We will be using the controls provided by Microsoft for use in applications designed to use MSMQ. Also, many third-party companies sell ActiveX controls for a multitude of purposes. Fortunately, because message queuing is fairly simple, the controls we will be using are powerful enough for almost any scenario.

The other important term is an *ActiveX control container* (development environment). Any software that can load and use an ActiveX control is considered a control container. Popular control containers are VB, C++, PowerBuilder, and Internet Explorer.

We will be using VB to create our ActiveX-powered applications because of the language's popularity and simplicity.

Setting Up the Programming Environment

To build the applications used as examples in this book, you must have the following:

- Microsoft's Windows NT Server 4.0 or Windows NT Workstation 4.0 with service pack 3 installed.

 MSMQ Servers (PECs, PSCs, RSs, and BSCs) need to be installed on Windows NT Server. Windows NT Workstation supports only MSMQ's dependent or independent clients.

- Microsoft Message Queue, installed either from Microsoft's Option Pack, Windows NT Enterprise Edition, or as supplied with Windows 2000.

 If you are using a dependent client, be sure that you are connected to a MSMQ server.

- Development workspace, such as Microsoft Visual C++ or Microsoft VB. Any scripting language is also supported, such as VBScript or JavaScript.

 The examples provided in the text are for VB.

Setting Up the VB Project

 The following steps relate to Microsoft Visual Basic 6.0.

1. Start Visual Basic.
2. On the New Project window, select Standard EXE and click Open.
3. Add the MSMQ Library to the project by selecting References from the Project menu and scrolling down the list until Microsoft Message Queue Object Library is displayed. Click on the box to select the library as shown in Figure 2.19. A check mark will appear in the box. Click OK when you are done.

Figure 2.19

Visual Basic reference library.

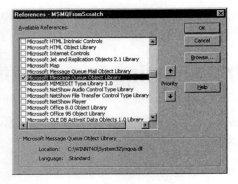

4. Select Save Project As from the File menu.

5. Provide a name for the initial form and click Save

6. Provide a name for the project and click Save.

You now have the skeleton into which you will insert your own program elements. You will need to repeat these steps each time you build a new project.

Summary

In this chapter we have outlined the design of our e-books application and the MSMQ network to support it. We have introduced some of the basic design paradigms available for programs built on message queuing technology. We have guided you through the installation of your PEC and helped you configure VB to use the ActiveX components for MSMQ.

You now have a basic MSMQ network on which to build your programs. This chapter concludes our introduction to the core concepts behind MSMQ; the following chapters introduce the details of these concepts as they relate to the e-books application.

However, before we jump in with both feet and start to build an application, we must cover two very basic procedures: sending and receiving messages. In the next two chapters, you will build two applications: one to send a message and the other to receive it. This short detour will give you the opportunity to test your MSMQ network and to use some of the features we have been talking about.

Part 2

Basics of MSMQ Application Development

Chapter 3

Sending a Message

The first and most basic step toward building our MSMQ application is being able to send a message. Even this first step, however, contains quite a few elements. Sending a message involves several objects and methods, and the same characteristics that make MSMQ a robust and powerful tool make it a complex one as well. In spite of this situation, as we develop our application you will find that the methods involved are very logical and that they fall into place and work together well.

Sending a simple message requires the use of three objects and three methods. And we must set the properties of the objects appropriately. The required objects are MSMQQueueInfo, MSMQQueue, and MSMQMessage. We will use the Open method of the MSMQQueueInfo object, the Send method of the MSMQMessage object, and the Close method of the MSMQQueue object. We will use the PathName property of the MSMQQueueInfo object and the Body property of the MSMQMessage object.

This simple application introduces two elements: the data that we want to send (the message) and the place where we want to put it (the queue). The steps to sending a message are

1. Open the queue
2. Create the message
3. Send the message
4. Close the queue

Figure 3.1 shows how our application will look when we create the Visual Basic form. The form contains entry fields into which the user provides the name of the queue and a message to be sent. Pushbuttons allow the user to create the queue by registering it in the Message Queue Information Store (MQIS) and to send a message to it. The application uses a text box to display messages relating to the results of the use of the ActiveX components.

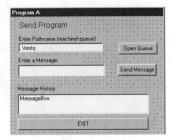

Figure 3.1

Message-sending application.

Using MSMQ Explorer to Create a Queue

Before we begin to build our program, we need a queue to send a message to. Later you will learn how to create a queue from within our application by using ActiveX components. For now, we are creating our queues through MSMQ Explorer.

Start MSMQ Explorer from the Start Programs menu. The Sites folder contains a list of all MSMQ Site Controllers in our network, and within the sites are the various computers. Go to the computer on which you want to create a queue and click the right mouse button. Figure 3.2 shows an example for our enterprise. In the picture, the queue is created on the computer ccrummer.

Figure 3.2

Using MSMQ Explorer to create a queue—right-click on the computer.

On the displayed menu, select New and Queue. The panel shown in Figure 3.3 is displayed. Provide a name for the queue and click the OK button. You can name your queue whatever you want; just remember what you called it when we run the application later in the chapter. We will name our queue myq (as shown in Figure 3.3). As soon as you click OK, the queue appears in the left panel in MSMQ Explorer.

This panel in Figure 3.3 allows us to create a transactional queue. Make sure that the box is not checked. When you use MSMQ Explorer to create a queue, you have only this one opportunity to make the queue transactional. After a queue has been created, you cannot modify this property.

→ For more information on transactional queues, see Part IV, "Advanced MSMQ Application Development: Processing an Order," page 179.

Figure 3.3

Using MSMQ Explorer to create a queue— naming the queue.

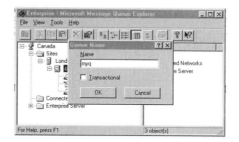

Opening a Queue

The MSMQQueue object represents a queue within a program; this object is made available to the program by first identifying which queue is to be opened (using the MSMQQueueInfo object) and invoking the Open method.

Our first step, then, is to open the queue we created by using MSMQ Explorer a moment ago.

All our form needs to open a queue is a text box in which the user enters the pathname of the queue and a command button for the execution of the Open method (see Figure 3.4 for an example).

Figure 3.4

Pathname text box and Open button.

In the example we named our text box PathNameText and our command button OpenQueueButton.

Queue pathnames consist of two parts: the machine name on which they are registered and the name of the queue. The name myq that we gave to our queue earlier was the queue name part of the queue's pathname. MSMQ automatically adds the machine name where the queue was registered when it updates the MQIS. To make our applications portable (that is, usable on different computers), we want to avoid specifying the machine name in the pathname. We can use the period character (.) to indicate the local computer. For example, to address the queue we just created in MSMQ Explorer from our application, we would specify a pathname of .\myq.

In our code (see Listing 3.1), we first declare the MSMQQueue and MSMQQueueInfo objects. We are calling our MSMQQueue object vMyQSend and our MSMQQueueInfo object vMyQSendInfo. We are also declaring a vMyQPathname object as a string, which will be the pathname we pick up from the PathNameText text box.

Next we reset the queue properties by setting a new instance of vMyQSendInfo.

We provide the PathName for the queue by setting vMyQPathName equal to PathNameText.Text, the verbatim text entered by the user in the pathname text box, and then setting the vMyQSendInfo.PathName equal to vMyQPathName. Now MSMQ knows which queue to open.

Finally, we open the queue by calling the Open method on the MSMQQueueInfo object.

Listing 3.1 Code Example to Open a Queue

```
Dim vMyQSend As MSMQQueue          '** Send Queue Object
Dim vMyQSendInfo As MSMQQueueInfo  '** Send Queue Properties
Dim vMyQPathName As String

'*********************
'**Open the Queue  ***
'*********************
Private Sub OpenQueueButton_Click()
On Error GoTo MyErrorHandler
    Set vMyQSendInfo = New MSMQQueueInfo '**Reset the queue properties
    vMyQPathName = PathNameText.Text     '**Set PathName from screen
    vMyQSendInfo.PathName = vMyQPathName '**Set PathName property
    '** Open the queue **
    Set vMyQSend = vMyQSendInfo.Open(MQ_SEND_ACCESS, MQ_DENY_NONE)
    '** Display the open message **
    MessageBox.AddItem "Queue Opened: " + vMyQSendInfo.PathName +
    " Label: " + vMyQSendInfo.Label
Exit Sub
MyErrorHandler:
    Call ErrorHandler
End Sub
```

Notice that when using the Open method of the MSMQQueueInfo object, two parameters must be specified: the access parameter and the share parameter.

The access parameter may be set to one of the following:

MQ_PEEK_ACCESS — Messages can be looked at but cannot be removed from the queue.

MQ_SEND_ACCESS — Messages can be sent to the queue but cannot be looked at or retrieved.

MQ_RECEIVE_ACCESS — Messages can be looked at or removed from the queue.

The second parameter required by the Open method, the share parameter, may be set to one of two options:

MQ_DENY_NONE — Other applications can open this queue while this application has it open. This setting is required when the access parameter is set to MQ_PEEK_ACCESS or MQ_SEND_ACCESS.

MQ_DENY_RECEIVE_SHARE — Only this application can receive messages from the queue. This option is valid only when the access parameter is set to MQ_RECEIVE_ACCESS. If another program has the queue open for MQ_RECEIVE_ACCESS, whether it is shared or not, the program attempting to open that queue for MQ_DENY_RECEIVE_SHARE will not be able to do so.

These parameters must be specified every time a queue is opened. So, for example, to send a message, we opened the queue with the parameters MQ_SEND_ACCESS and MQ_DENY_NONE.

You may also have noticed that we have an error-handler function call within our code. This call gives us a simple way to handle all errors that may occur within our application. The error-handler function is shown in Listing 3.2.

Listing 3.2   Sample Code for the Error Handler

```
'*********************************
'*** Generic Error Handler      ***
'*********************************
Public Sub ErrorHandler()
'** Error message is displayed on the screen in a list box**
MessageBox.AddItem "**Error: " + Err.Description
End Sub
```

Building and Sending a Message

Now that we have a queue opened with which to work, we can begin to write the code to send a message to that queue. First we must build a message to send.

The property of the MSMQMessage object that we must set is the Body. The body of a message can be anything from a bank transaction to a word processing document. Message queuing and MSMQ work at their best with manageable and logical packets of information. This feature explains why MSMQ is such a robust tool for e-commerce, which requires the guaranteed delivery of many transactions occurring throughout the day. At this point we simply want to send a string entered by the user in a text box. We have called our text box MessageInput and our command button SendMessageB. Figure 3.5 shows how it looks on our form.

Figure 3.5

*Message text box and
Send Message button.*

First we declare the MSMQMessage object, which we will call vMyMessageSend. We then
set the body of the message equal to the string typed by the user in the MessageInput
box (see Listing 3.3). It's that easy!

Listing 3.3   Sample Code to Create a Message Body

```
Dim vMyMessageSend As MSMQMessage          '** Message Queue Object
Dim vMyMessage As String


'***********************
'**Send Number Message**
'***********************
Private Sub SendMessageButton_Click()
On Error GoTo MyErrorHandler
Set vMyMessageSend = New MSMQMessage
vMyMessage = MessageInput.Text             '**Get number from screen
vMyMessageSend.Body = vMyMessage
```

To send our message on its way, we simply invoke the Send method of the message.

The Send Method of the MSMQMessage Component

Invoking this method takes one line of code and needs little explanation. We call
the Send method of the newly created MSMQMessage object and provide the name
of the MSMQQueue object that we opened and to which we are sending this message.
After this method executes, the message is sent to the defined queue. MSMQ takes
responsibility for the delivery of that message, and our application can officially
consider it signed, sealed, and delivered. Listing 3.4 shows what our entire Send
subroutine looks like when we've sent the message. (To be truly guaranteed, messages must be recoverable. Because our messages are express messages at this point,
if the computer holding our messages goes down, we will lose them.)

➔ For more information on recoverable messages, see Part 4, page 179.

Listing 3.4   Example of the Send Method

```
'***********************
'**Send Number Message**
'***********************
Private Sub SendMessageButton_Click()
On Error GoTo MyErrorHandler
Set vMyMessageSend = New MSMQMessage
vMyMessage = MessageInput.Text             '**Get number from screen
```

```
vMyMessageSend.Body = vMyMessage
vMyMessageSend.Send vMyQSend              '**Send the message
MessageBox.AddItem "Message sent. Message body: " + vMyMessageSend.Body

Exit Sub
MyErrorHandler:
    Call ErrorHandler
End Sub
```

Closing a Queue

Finally, it is our job as responsible MSMQ programmers to close the queue after we have done our work with it. The `Close` method of the `MSMQQueue` object handles this step.

Again, this line of code (shown in Listing 3.5) needs no elaborate exposition. It simply closes the queue, wrapping up any loose ends. We are putting this command within our Exit button.

Listing 3.5   Example of the `Close` Method

```
Private Sub ExitButton_Click()
On Error GoTo MyErrorHandler
    vMyQSend.Close          '**Close the queue
    Unload Me               '**Unload the form
Exit Sub
MyErrorHandler:
Resume Next
End Sub
```

Executing the Program

You can now test the validity of your program by running it and looking at the queue and the message from within MSMQ Explorer. You should expand the view of your computer by double-clicking its icon. Then you can click on myq to see the message displayed in the right panel. Figure 3.6 shows an example.

Figure 3.6

Using MSMQ Explorer to display the messages on a queue.

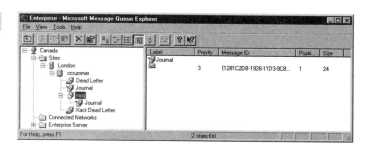

Double-click on the message to view any of its properties: General, Queues, Body, and Sender. Look at the body of the message and see how the different parts have been formatted to a fixed length. Figure 3.7 shows the body of the message that we created.

Figure 3.7

Using MSMQ Explorer to display the body of a message.

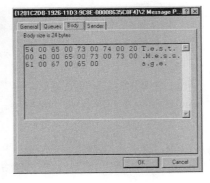

Summary

Congratulations! You have learned the fundamentals of MSMQ programming: opening a queue, constructing a message, sending a message, and closing a queue.

In this chapter you learned how to

- Create a queue by using MSMQ Explorer
- Specify in a program the properties of a queue that you would like to open by using the MSMQQueueInfo component
- Create a MSMQQueue object for your application by using the Open method of the MSMQQueueInfo component
- Create a message to send by using the MSMQMessage component
- Send a message to a queue
- Display the contents of a queue by using MSMQ Explorer

The next chapter shows you how to build a program to read from the queue the message you just created.

Receiving a Message

Now that we have successfully sent a message, we will consider the next fundamental skill in messaging, building an application to receive and display our message. After all, what good is a message without a recipient?

Figure 4.1 shows our receiving application form. You can lay out your form however you choose, but it should have at least the elements shown. The PathName box is an entry field. The other two are text boxes that display the body of the message and a trace of the steps executed by the program.

Users of the application supply the name of a queue from which messages are retrieved and press the Open Queue button to open it. They use the Receive Message button to pull messages from the open queue, one at a time.

Figure 4.1

Message receiving application.

Opening a Queue

To receive a message, we open the queue from where we wish to receive the message by using the Open method of the MSMQQueueInfo object. This step is analogous to opening a queue to send a message, as explained in Chapter 3, "Sending a Message."

Figure 4.2 shows the form element that we use to open a queue. The form contains an entry field into which the user provides a PathName (you might initialize this to a default value, such as '.\myq') and a push button to invoke the Open method on the MSMQQueueInfo object. We named the entry field 'PathNameText' as shown in Listing 4.1.

Figure 4.2

Pathname text box box and Open Queue button.

To open a queue for receipt, we first declare the MSMQQueue and MSMQQueueInfo objects and then provide the PathName for the queue. Finally, we open the queue by calling the Open method on the MSMQQueueInfo object. In contrast to our use of MSMQQueueInfo.Open in Chapter 3 when we opened the queue to send a message, this time we are opening the queue for Receive access.

In Listing 4.1 our MSMQQueue object is called vMyQReceive; our MSMQQueueInfo object is called vMyQReceiveInfo. We also have declared an intermediate String object called vMyQPathName. We will use the intermediate object to copy from the form the path name of the queue we want to open. This intermediate step is necessary in Visual Basic to manage the different data types between the form and the MSMQQueueInfo object.

Listing 4.1   Sample Code for the Open Queue Push Button

```
Dim vMyQReceive As MSMQQueue
Dim vMyQReceiveInfo As MSMQQueueInfo
Dim vMyQPathName As String

'*********************
'**Open the Queue  ***
'*********************
Private Sub OpenQueueButton_Click()
    On Error GoTo MyErrorHandler
    Set vMyQReceiveInfo = New MSMQQueueInfo
    vMyQPathName = PathNameText.Text      '**Set PathName from screen
    vMyQReceiveInfo.PathName = vMyQPathName '**Set PathName property
    '** Open the queue **
    Set vMyQReceive = vMyQReceiveInfo.Open(MQ_RECEIVE_ACCESS, MQ_DENY_NONE)
    '** Display the open message **
    MessageBox.AddItem "Queue Opened: " + vMyQReceiveInfo.PathName +
    " Label: " + vMyQReceiveInfo.Label
Exit Sub
MyErrorHandler:
    Call ErrorHandler
End Sub
```

As you learned in Chapter 3, two parameters must be specified when the queue is opened: the access parameter and the share parameter. The access parameter may be set to one of the following: MQ_PEEK_ACCESS, MQ_SEND_ACCESS, or MQ_RECEIVE_ACCESS. The second parameter required by the Open method, the share parameter, may be set to one of two options: MQ_DENY_NONE or MQ_DENY_RECEIVE_SHARE. (See Chapter 3 for an explanation of these options.)

These parameters must be set every time a queue is opened. So in this case, for example, to receive a message, we opened the queue with the parameters MQ_RECEIVE_ACCESS (instead of MQ_SEND_ACCESS) and MQ_DENY_NONE.

Receiving a Message

The most important part of this process is, of course, to actually receive the message. We use the Receive method of the MSMQQueue object to receive a message from a queue we have opened for receive access. Invoking the Receive method on the MSMQQueue object returns a MSMQMessage object to our program.

Figure 4.3 shows the form elements that we need for the receive step. Each time the push button is pressed, it invokes the Receive method on the MSMQQueue object and displays the contents of the Body property in the text box.

Figure 4.3

MessageReceiveBox and Receive Message command button.

On the form, create a command button to invoke the code segment to receive messages, an example of which is shown in Listing 4.2.

We can then receive the message by calling the Receive method on the ReplyQueue object created in Listing 4.1. The Receive method has one parameter that we need to consider at this point: ReceiveTimeout. ReceiveTimeout specifies in thousandths of seconds how long the program will wait to receive a message from the queue. We will wait 10 seconds for our message. (Because the message should be waiting on the queue for us, the time-out should not have any bearing on our application.) Finally, we display the body of the message in our MessageReceiveBox list box. Listing 4.2 shows the corresponding code.

Listing 4.2 Sample Code for the Receive Message Push Button

```
Dim vMyMessageReceive As MSMQMessage

'***********************
'**Receive the Message**
'***********************
Private Sub ReceiveMessageButton_Click()
On Error GoTo MyErrorHandler
Set vMyMessageReceive = New MSMQMessage
Set vMyMessageReceive = vMyQReceive.Receive(ReceiveTimeout:=10000)
If Not vMyMessageReceive Is Nothing Then
    MessageReceiveBox.AddItem "Message Received: " + vMyMessageReceive.Body
    Else
    MessageReceiveBox.AddItem "No Messages in queue"
End If
Exit Sub
MyErrorHandler:
    Call ErrorHandler
```

Closing the Queue

When we open a queue for receive, we are also responsible for closing it after receiving our messages. We use the same process to close the queue here as we did in Chapter 3: Call the Close method of the MSMQQueue object and associate this code with our Exit push button. Listing 4.3 provides an example of the code that might be associated with our Exit push button.

Listing 4.3 Sample Code for the Exit Push Button

```
'**************************
'**Exit button pressed ****
'**************************
Private Sub ExitButton_Click()
On Error GoTo ErrorHandler
    vMyQReceive.Close          '**Close the queue
    Unload Me                  '**Unload the form
ErrorHandler:
Resume Next
End Sub
```

Now we are a little less reliant on MSMQ Explorer to view our messages. We can receive messages through our application by using the Receive method of the MSMQQueue object.

Summary

This chapter provided the ending to the basic MSMQ applications. Chapter 3 provided the fundamentals to opening and sending message. This chapter has provided additional value by sending and receiving messages. These are the two main principles of MSMQ application construction.

In this chapter we showed you how to

> Receive a message from a queue
>
> Display the body of a message

In the following chapters, we build on these basic techniques and develop the application that we described in Chapter 2, "Introducing Our Example—Designing the Solution."

This is a good point to review both Chapters 3 and 4 and fully understand the basic principles of MSMQ. Both in terms of coding applications and infrastructure deployment (such as queue construction) of MSMQ. Making sure that you can send, receive, and view messages are very important concepts.

4

Part 3

Advanced MSMQ Application Development: Processing a Request

Inquiry Workflow: Client to Server

e-books Book Inquiry Workflow

We have already introduced the basic concepts of message queuing and presented an overview of the e-books application that we will build. In addition, the preceding two chapters, "Sending a Message" and "Receiving a Message," explained how to send and receive messages.

In this chapter we build the elements of our distributed application that service the first message flow in the Concept Web (flow 1). We work on two separate programs: the order-processing server and the order-entry client. In Chapter 6, "Inquiry Workflow: Server to Back End," we add the code for flow steps 2 and 3 in the Concept Web, and in Chapter 7, "Automating the Inquiry Workflow," we add the code for flow steps 4, 5, and 6. At the conclusion of Chapter 7 you will have built all the code to process the inquiry workflow.

Returning to the tasks ahead in this chapter, for the order-processing server we simply create a queue to which the order-entry client sends inquiries. After the queue is created, we open it, and finally, for now, we set up the program to receive an inquiry.

For the order-entry client, we build a form through which users provide their name, address, and credit card information, as well as the name of the book they want to purchase. We create a queue to which the server will send the reply, and we send an inquiry message to the server.

At the conclusion of this chapter, you will have two programs, one that builds and sends a message and another that receives it. The receiving program creates a mock reply and sends it back to the requestor.

This chapter, and those that follow it, are laid out to guide you through the construction of the applications. We begin in a moment with a detailed description of what we will build and a figure that shows the process steps we will take. As we build each step, we will show you how to add the code to your Visual Basic (VB) program and test it.

Figure 5.1 shows the inquiry workflow elements between the order-entry client and the order-processing server.

Figure 5.1

e-books book inquiry workflow.

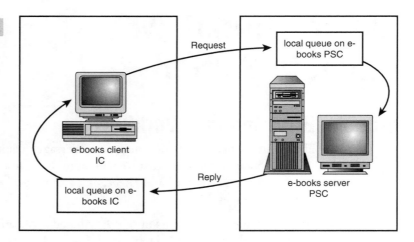

Architectural Overview

Our application begins when a bookstore customer wants to place an order for a book that is not on the shelves of the local store. In our scenario the customer approaches a customer service representative who uses our order-entry client program to capture the details of the customer and the customer's request.

The client program will be built with VB and consists of a simple entry form, as shown in Figure 5.2. The form has on it fields for the customer's name, address, and credit card information, along with the title of the book he or she wants to order. The form also has two push buttons: one to submit an inquiry concerning the book's price and availability and another to end the application.

Figure 5.2

Sample order-entry form.

In this chapter we build the order-entry client, which performs the following functions:

1. Receives from the customer the details concerning their inquiry
2. Creates a queue to which replies for this order-entry client are sent
3. Locates an order-processing queue that is expecting inquiry messages from order-entry clients
4. Opens this input queue to the order-processing server
5. Sends a message containing the customer's information and the name of the queue to which replies should be sent
6. Opens the reply queue
7. Waits for a reply
8. Receives the reply and displays the content in a pop-up message box

A program running in the store's back-office, the order-processing server, receives all such inquiries and manages the interaction between the different systems that help to process the request. Our example contains two systems: the warehouse, which maintains a list of available inventory, and the credit card agency, which authorizes the purchase and bills the customer's account. By encapsulating the business logic required to deal with these outside agencies, we are able to keep the client program small, reduce the ongoing maintenance of the client program, and, ultimately, make the same business logic available to different types of client program. (For example, in the future we might allow customers to request books themselves from a program running in a multimedia kiosk or on the World Wide Web. Either of these clients could send requests to the same order-processing server, provided that the format of the messages remains the same.)

In this chapter we build the order-processing server, which performs the following functions:

1. Creates the input queue, if it doesn't already exist
2. Opens the input queue to receive messages from it
3. Waits for a message to arrive on the input queue
4. Receives the message
5. Sends a reply to the supplied response queue
6. Repeats the previous three steps indefinitely

Before we go any further, it is worth explaining that we are using the terms *client* and *server* very loosely. People have used these terms in many different ways. Most commonly, they refer to the separation of different program elements between two different systems. Typically, a mainframe application is reengineered so that the parts that relate to presentation are hosted by an intelligent workstation instead of by a mainframe terminal. Such workstations are Windows or even DOS clients. Today this design would be known as a two-tier application architecture. The data and presentation logic are separated from one another, but the business logic resides in both layers of the application. The problem with this scenario is that to update the business logic you must update all the clients, and to add a different kind of client, such as a Web-based client, you have to build into it the business logic assumed by the server.

Our application is a three-tier application in which we break the business logic out of both the traditional client and server layers and put it into a central or middle layer all by itself. We refer to this middle tier as the server because it is the business logic server. The traditional server platforms become our back-end systems. You may also see them referred to as data-logic servers or legacy systems.

Application Architecture—Order-Processing Server

The flowchart in Figure 5.3 details the process steps in this first visit to the order-processing server. When the server process starts, it attempts to create its input queue if that queue does not already exist. The server then opens the input queue and reads a message from it. We build a default reply and send a message back to the queue name given in the message that we received. When the server is closed, its input queue is deleted. Client programs that subsequently try to start cannot find this input queue and so cannot direct messages to this server.

Figure 5.3

*Order-processing server
process steps.*

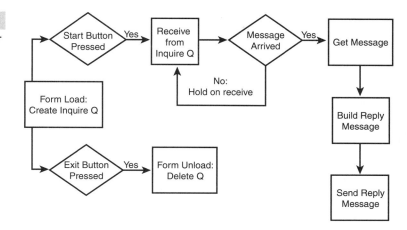

For now this application processes one message at a time as the user presses the
command buttons. In Chapter 6, however, we modify the order-processing server to
process inquiries automatically.

Listing 5.1 turns these process steps into pseudocode. In the following sections, we
examine each of these steps and start to build our program.

Listing 5.1   Pseudocode for the Order-Processing Server

```
BEGIN
        CreateQ( InquiryQ, PUBLIC )
        DO
                InquiryMsg = GetMsg( InquiryQ, WAIT = UNLIMITED,
                ➥REPLYQ = InquiryReplyQ )
                BuildReplyMsg( ReplyMsg, DefaultValues )
                SendMsg( InquiryReplyQ, ReplyMsg )
        UNTIL UserStopsProgram
        DeleteQ( InquiryQ )
END
```

This pseudocode shows five functions: `CreateQ`, `GetMsg`, `BuildReplyMsg`, `SendMsg`, and
`DeleteQ`. We will break down each of these in a moment, but first we consider the
overall flow of the program.

The server program is known as a *long-running process.* It could become an NT service application and run in the background.

To see an example of a background process, right-click on your Windows NT taskbar and select Task Manager. When the Task Manager is loaded, select the Processes tab. In the window, all the processes that are currently running on your machine are displayed. We could construct our VB application to operate in a similar fashion.

For applications that require no user interface, constructing these applications as a service greatly increases performance and stability.

We will build the server as a VB program, but it will not have a user interface to speak of. The server's role is to receive an inquiry message, process the message (we'll see what this means in the next chapter), and send a reply to the client. The server does this continually, as each message is received. The server is affording the client a level of indirection from the reality of the business transaction. That is to say, the client's only concern is getting from the user the customer's information and displaying an answer to the request. The client does not need to know how the answer is obtained. The logic required to satisfy the inquiry is encapsulated in the server. Today the business logic says that for an inquiry we must check the warehouse inventory and obtain credit approval. If tomorrow the business rules change to keep a copy of the inventory in the store or to use a different credit agency or another distributor, only the server program needs to change—the client is unaffected. This paradigm is very powerful, especially if several different kinds of clients would have to be modified to reflect the changes in the business rules.

Now, let's return to the implementation of our server. The first thing we need to do is to create a new VB project and add the MSMQ object library to it. We show you how to do this step at the end of Chapter 2, "Introducing Our Example—Designing the Solution." Follow these steps to create a new project with the name InqServ and a main form with the name Main.

On the main form, create a single list box to display a summary of the messages that we have processed. Call the list box `MessageHistory`. This item adds nothing to the function of our program, but helps you to see what is going on.

Now display the code for the form itself. This piece of code is executed when the program starts. You can access the code entry form by double-clicking on the background of our main form. The panel shown in Figure 5.4 is displayed.

Figure 5.4

Blank code entry form for main form.

We are going to enter the code that is executed when the form is loaded. Because this long-running task has no user interface, the bulk of our code goes here. The one exception is the code used to delete the input queue when the user shuts down the application.

You are now ready to start writing the program. We are going to break each process step into functions and then put the main subroutine together at the end.

CreateQ

In Chapter 3, "Sending a Message," and in Chapter 4, "Receiving a Message," we worked with statically defined queues: queues that the administrator defined using MSMQ Explorer. A very useful feature of MSMQ is that applications can create their own queues while executing. It is possible to set each of the properties of a new queue from a program, just as if the administrator created the queue from MSMQ Explorer. The capability to create a queue from a program allows the user to associate a queue with a specific purpose related to the application.

To relate this concept to our example, if several order-processing servers are available at one store, the order-entry client could look for an available queue before sending an inquiry message. If all the queues are statically defined, the order-entry program has no immediate way to tell whether the application monitoring the queue is, in fact, running. Instead, if the order-processing server creates the input queue when the server starts and destroys the queue when the server closes down, order-entry programs can easily route inquiry messages to active order-processing systems. Later in this chapter we consider the design of the client and extend this idea to reply queues, providing an easy mechanism for the client application to manage the replies to a single request.

To create a queue from a program, we must describe the properties of the queue we want to create and then create it. Both of the steps are elements of the MSMQQueueInfo component. The properties define the nature of the queue to MSMQ, and the Create method registers the queue. The MSMQQueueInfo component describes the properties of a single queue.

A queue is defined by its properties. If a property is not explicitly set when the queue is created, it assumes the default value. We will concentrate now on the properties that help us achieve our goal. We need to create a queue on the MSMQ server that hosts the order-processing server program. The queue must have a queue name of inquire_server_queue, and the client application must be able to find the queue based on the service that it offers. That is to say, a particular application function receives messages from this queue. We need a way to identify that function in the queue's properties. For a description of each of a queue's properties and what they are used for, see Appendix B, "Exploring the MSMQ Objects."

Of a queue's properties, several help to describe it, and some uniquely define it to the enterprise. These properties are the FormatName, the PathName, the ServiceTypeGUID, and the Label. Either the MSMQ administrator or the programmer can set all the properties except the FormatName.

The FormatName uniquely defines the queue, not only within this MSMQ Enterprise but also across all MSMQ Enterprises. The FormatName is, in part, a globally unique identifier (GUID) and is generated by MSMQ when the queue is created. The FormatName cannot be changed. MSMQ appends a qualifier before the GUID to indicate whether the queue is private (registered only on the local machine) or public (registered in the MSMQ Information Store [MQIS]).

The PathName is unique within the MSMQ Enterprise and is set, in part, by the programmer or the MSMQ administrator. The first part of the PathName is the name of the computer on which the physical queue exists. If the period (.) is used, MSMQ assumes the local machine is the host of the physical queue. The second part is the queue name, which must be unique on the machine hosting the queue but need not be unique within the enterprise. In this way, we can have several instances of our server program running on different MSMQ servers, all creating local queues with the name InquiryQ.

The ServiceTypeGUID property assigns a unique type to a collection of queues that offer the same service. In our example, each queue that an Order Processing server services should be created with the same ServiceTypeGUID. You can create your own GUID using the program GUIDGen.exe. This program generates several different representations of the same GUID for inclusion in your program, as shown in Figure

5.5. GUIDGen is supplied with Microsoft Visual Studio and is typically installed in ..\Microsoft Visual Studio\Common\Tools. GUIDGen places the GUIDs on the Clipboard for you to then paste into your code.

Figure 5.5

GUIDGen.exe.

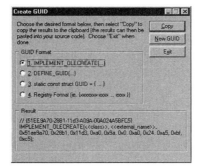

Finally, the `Label` property offers a free format for our application to use to qualify the queue further. In our example, the label might be used to name the store or the department. A program looking for an InquiryQ could use this field to select which queue to use in case several queues matched the required specification. We are going to place the computer name in this field. When the client application launches, it looks for all "inquire" queues. When the application finds more than one (a likely case when multiple servers are running throughout the enterprise), the user is given the option of which server to connect to, based on computer name (the label of the queue).

We are going to accept the default value for the other properties available for the queue.

The MSMQ ActiveX component used to contain the properties of a single queue is the `MSMQQueueInfo` component. Listing 5.2 shows how to initialize the component and set the value of the properties that we are interested in.

Listing 5.2   Creating a Queue Using the `MSMQQueueInfo` Object

```
11 ' Create Local Queue
12   Set IReceiveQInfo = New MSMQQueueInfo
13   IReceiveQInfo.PathName = ".\Inquire_Server_Queue"
14
15   ' Next is the creation of the label. We need to include the local machine
16   ' name in the label for the client to differentiate between the different
17   ' possible inquiry queues. We therefore need to get the computer name.
18      ' First we get the computer name for the local machine
19      Dim ComputerName As String
20      sBuffer = Space$(MAX_COMPUTERNAME_LENGTH + 1)
21      lSize = Len(sBuffer)
```

continues

Listing 5.2   continued

```
22        If GetComputerName(sBuffer, lSize) Then
23            ComputerName = Left(sBuffer, lSize)
24        End If
25
26    ' Then we include the computer name in the label
27    IReceiveQInfo.Label = "Inquire Queue on " & ComputerName
28
29    ' Specific ServiceType for Inquire Queues
30    IReceiveQInfo.ServiceTypeGuid = "{0BF4DBD1-254F-11d3-A091-00A024A5BFC5}"
31    IReceiveQInfo.Create
32    MessageHistory.AddItem "Inquire Queue: " + IReceiveQInfo.PathName
```

Notice how in line 30 of Listing 5.2 the output from the GUIDGen program has been placed into the ServiceTypeGuid property of the MSMQQueueInfo object. Also, we have placed the computer name in the Label property in line 27.

Getting the computer name requires the function GetComputerName to be declared within a module. To add a module, right-click anywhere on the project window and choose Add, Module. We named our module InqServModule1. The code that needs to go in that module at this point is shown in Listing 5.3.

Listing 5.3   Code to Find the Local Computer Name

```
1 Public Declare Function GetComputerName _
2    Lib "kernel32" Alias "GetComputerNameA"
    ➥(ByVal lpBuffer As String, nSize As Long) As Long
```

Having set the initial values for the properties of the MSMQQueueInfo component, you use the Create method to register the queue in the MQIS, as shown in line 31 of Listing 5.2. The result of this operation, if successful, is that the queue is registered in the MQIS. Finally, in line 32, we add a line to the message box on our form to show the user that a queue was created. At this point the queue is not yet available for the application to use. We have to open the queue first.

The Create method fails if the queue already exists. But we don't want this error to cause our program to end! Instead, we want our program to simply move on to the next step of opening the queue. Our generic error-handling subroutine has been set up to handle this case, as shown in Listing 5.4.

Listing 5.4   Sample Error Handler

```
90    ErrorHandler:
91        If Err.Number = MQ_ERROR_QUEUE_EXISTS Then
92            Resume Next
93        End If
94        MessageHistory.AddItem "Error: " + Err.Description
```

Having created the queue, or found it to already exist, we need to open it so that we can receive messages from it. Another method of the MSMQQueueInfo object is Open. Open takes two parameters, as shown in Chapter 3, and returns to the program a MSMQQueue object. We will open the queue for shared, receive access, as shown in line 34 of Listing 5.5. Line 35 is another message for the user to track the progress of the application.

Listing 5.5 Opening the Queue

```
31    IReceiveQInfo.Create
32    MessageHistory.AddItem "Inquire Queue: " + IReceiveQInfo.PathName
33    ' Open Local Inquire Queue for Receive
34    Set IReceiveQ = IReceiveQInfo.Open(MQ_RECEIVE_ACCESS, MQ_DENY_NONE)
35    MessageHistory.AddItem "Queue opened for receive"
```

Listing 5.6 shows the lines that we need to add to our generic error handler to process possible results from the Open method. We have added a case for the queue not being found. The possible cause of this temporary error is the delay in MQIS replication. We might get this error immediately after creating the queue, and so we build a loop into our program to retry the Open.

Listing 5.6 Modification to the Generic Error Handler

```
90    ErrorHandler:
91        If Err.Number = MQ_ERROR_QUEUE_EXISTS Then
92            Resume Next
93        End If
94        MessageHistory.AddItem "Error: " + Err.Description
95    If Err.Number = MQ_ERROR_QUEUE_NOT_FOUND Then
96        Err.Clear
97        DoEvents
98        Resume
99    End If
```

Finally, we need to put a few lines around our procedure to set it up. In Listing 5.7 we change the mouse pointer to an hourglass while the queue is created and opened and put the supporting lines of code around our procedure to make it a subroutine. This code is held within our Form_Load procedure and so will be executed before the form even appears to the user.

Listing 5.7 Defining the Procedure

```
1    Private Sub Form_Load()
2        On Error GoTo ErrorHandler
         ...
37    Exit Sub

101    End Sub
```

The one thing that remains is to define the global and local variables used to create and reference the open queue object. Go to the very top of the code window (General | Declarations portion of the code form) to enter the global declarations. Listing 5.8 shows the needed declarations that go at the top of the code form.

Listing 5.8   Global Declarations

```
1    Dim IReceiveQInfo As MSMQQueueInfo
2    Dim IReceiveQ As MSMQQueueInfo
3  ' Get computer Name declarations -- used to make unique queue labels
4    Dim sBuffer As String
5    Dim lSize As Long
6    Const MAX_COMPUTERNAME_LENGTH As Long = 15&
```

Locally, it is a good idea to begin a new instance of the MSMQQueueInfo object from within the subroutine as shown in Listing 5.9.

Listing 5.9   Local Variable Definition

```
1    Private Sub Form_Load()
2        On Error GoTo ErrorHandler
3
4    Set vIReceiveQInfo = New MSMQQueueInfo
```

This step concludes the development of the Form_Load subroutine.

GetMsg

Chapter 4 explains how to receive a message from a queue. We reuse that code here, making the necessary changes for our object names, of course!

Having already opened a queue to receive messages, we now have a *MSMQQueue* component. We use the Receive method of the *MSMQQueue* component to get a *MSMQMessage* component.

First add a command button called "Receive" to your form. Then double-click on the button to access the code form for that command button.

To add a control to a form, select the control from the toolbar, position your cursor on the form, and click and drag the mouse to size the control. The properties for the control, with their default settings, are displayed on the right of the screen. You can change the default settings for any control by selecting the property and assigning it a new value.

The code segment in Listing 5.10 shows the code how to receive a message from the InquiryQ. Line 7 in Listing 5.11 must be added to the global variable definitions in your project. As in Chapter 4, we use the `Receive` method of the MSMQQueue object to create a new `MSMQMessage` object.

Listing 5.10   Sample Code to Receive a Message

```
1 Private Sub Receive_Click()
2 '***** This sub is temporary: this get and reply will occur automatically
3 '***** and include queries to the back-end systems in our final product
4
5     On Error GoTo ErrorHandler
6
7     ' Get Message
8     Set Message = IReceiveQ.Receive
9     MessageHistory.AddItem "Message Arrived"
```

Listing 5.11   Global Declarations for Receive Code

```
3 ' Get computer Name declarations -- used to make unique queue labels
4    Dim sBuffer As String
5    Dim lSize As Long
6    Const MAX_COMPUTERNAME_LENGTH As Long = 15&
7    Dim Message As MSMQMessage
```

This step concludes the development of the get portion of the receive command subroutine.

BuildReplyMsg

The purpose of this code is to build the body of the message that is sent back in response to the client's inquiry. In Chapter 6 we show how the content of the response is based on replies from the credit authorization and the inventory check, but for now we are assigning default values to the response.

For the sake of our example, the book is in stock at a price of $19.95 and the credit card is authorized.

Listing 5.12 shows this code. Listing 5.13 shows the necessary global declarations of the objects.

Listing 5.12   Code to Build Default Reply Message

```
11 ' Build a mock message to send
12    Dim Body As String
13    Body = "Your book is available for $19.95. Your credit is approved."
14    Set InquireReplyMessage = New MSMQMessage
15    InquireReplyMessage.Body = Body
```

Listing 5.13   Global Declarations for Building the Reply Message

```
7    Dim Message As MSMQMessage
8    Dim InquireReplyMessge As MSMQMessage
```

This step concludes the development of the build message portion of the receive subroutine.

SendMsg

In Chapter 3 we send a message to a queue. As we did with GetMsg, for SendMsg we also reuse the code from Chapter 3, again making the necessary name changes.

To send the reply to the order-entry client, we use the queue name provided by the order-entry program when the initial request is placed on the InquiryQ. In other words, the order-processing server uses the ResponseQueueInfo property of the MSMQMessage object that the server received from the client to determine where to place the reply. This property contains the FormatName of the queue to which the requesting application wants reply messages to be sent. We will see later in this chapter how our order-entry program creates a unique reply queue for each request and passes its FormatName in the message. For now, it is enough to know that the message property contains the format name. Our program must open the response queue and send the message to it, as we show in Listing 5.14. The necessary global definitions are shown in Listing 5.15.

Listing 5.14   Code to Send Reply Message Back to Client

```
17 ' Send Reply Message
18     ' Set our QueueInfo object equal to the ResponseQueueInfo of the message
19     Set IReplyQInfo = Message.ResponseQueueInfo
20     ' Open the queue
21     Set IReplyQ = IReplyQInfo.Open(MQ_SEND_ACCESS, MQ_DENY_NONE)
22     ' Send the message
23     InquireReplyMessage.Send IReplyQ
24     MessageHistory.AddItem "Reply sent to client"
25
26     Exit Sub
```

Listing 5.15   Global Declarations for Sending the Reply Message

```
9     Dim IReplyQ As MSMQQueue
10    Dim IReplyQInfo As MSMQQueueInfo
```

In line 19 we use the ResponseQInfo property of the inquiry MSMQMessage object to initialize our new MSMQQueueInfo object, IReplyQInfo. We then perform the Open method on this object in line 21 to create a MSMQQueue object to which we can send messages. We then send the resultant message of the BuildReplyMsg code from the previous section to the queue in line 23. As with our other procedures, line 24 puts a trace line into our message box so the user can see what is going on. This line is also the end of the Receive button's code. We exit the subroutine at this point (below the exit sub code resides the ErrorHandler).

DeleteQ

The purpose of this code is to delete the input queue for the order-processing server when the server is shut down. We will see in a moment, when we discuss the development of the client, how the client looks for available order-processing servers based on the existence of their input queues. By deleting this queue when the application terminates, we prevent an order-entry client from attempting to send inquiries to a server that is not running and instead allow the client to find another server that is operational, if one exists.

`Delete` is a method of the `MSMQQueueInfo` object, and we can delete the queue with the same object that we used to create it. The code in Listing 5.16 performs this function.

Listing 5.16   Code to Delete the Queue

```
1    IReceiveQInfo.Delete
```

This step concludes the development of the DeleteQ code. We implement it in the next section when we assemble the order-processing server.

Putting It All Together

Finally, all that remains is to build our main procedure that calls the functions that we have just created.

First of all, let's make sure that we can end the server. We are going to add our `DeleteQ` function call to the window's shutdown process and then close all the MSMQ objects that we have been using. The code in Listing 5.17 should be added to the shutdown processing by creating a `Form_QueryUnload` routine. Here we give the user a confirmation box. If the user clicks No, then we do not exit the program. If the user clicks Yes, we first clean our tracks by deleting or closing the appropriate queues. In this case we have only the IReceiveQ to delete.

Listing 5.17   Shutdown Code for the Order-Processing Server

```
1    Form_QueryUnload(Cancel As Integer, UnloadMode As Integer)
2    Dim i As Integer
3    On Error GoTo ErrorHandler
4    i = MsgBox("Do you want to exit?", vbYesNo + vbQuestion, "Inquiry Server")
5    If i = vbNo Then
6        Cancel = 1
7    Else
8        IReceiveQInfo.Delete
9        End
10   End If
11   Exit Sub
```

5

Running the Order-Processing Server

After you complete the code, you can run your program. You won't see much just yet! Until the client is built to send a message to the server, the server merely starts, creates its input queue, and, when you press "Receive," waits for a message. (Be careful! If there is no message waiting in the queue, the application will hang until a message arrives!)

You might try starting the server and using MSMQ Explorer to see the queue that is created. Remember to press F5 on the MSMQ Explorer display to refresh the list of objects if MSMQ Explorer is already running when you start the server. Examine the properties of the queue and note that its ServiceTypeGUID matches that which you specified in the program. When you have seen the queue registered, close down the server and again refresh the MSMQ Explorer display. You will see that the queue has been removed from the list.

In the next section, we show you how to build the client application to send an inquiry message to the server.

Application Architecture—Order-Entry Client

Figure 5.6 shows the main panel for our order-entry client. Note the entry fields for the customer's name, address, credit card information, and so on and the name of the book the customer wants to purchase. The final product will contain two push buttons as well. The first submits the inquiry, and the second closes the program. The large text field at the bottom of the window displays a log of the MSMQ actions that the program has taken.

Figure 5.6

Sample layout of the order-entry client panel.

The flowchart in Figure 5.7 details the process steps that the order-entry client performs for the inquiry workflow. Note that when the client program starts, it attempts to find and open the input queue for the order-processing server. If the client program is not successful, it ends. If it is successful, the client waits for the user to provide the customer's information and click Submit. The bulk of the processing in this chapter is in support of the Submit button. The client program first creates a unique queue to which the replies to this inquiry are sent. The program then sends to the order-processing server a message containing the customer's information and the name of the reply queue. Finally, the client program waits for a message to arrive on the reply queue for a predetermined time and either displays a response or asks the user to try again later.

Figure 5.7

Order-entry client process steps.

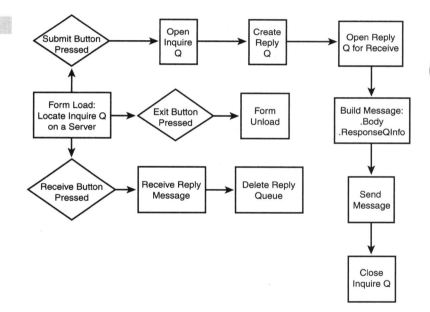

The client processes only one customer's request at a time. After the response is received, the client deletes the reply queue.

The Order-Entry Form

As with the order-processing server, we must first create a new VB project. Again, the detailed steps to do so are given at the end of Chapter 2. Name your project Client and name the main form Main. Figure 5.8 shows the sample order-entry form. At this stage, a third push button activates the receiving of the reply message. (Later we receive replies "asynchronously" through event notifications.)

Figure 5.8

*Sample order-entry
form.*

Table 5.1 gives the name and default value for each entry field shown in Figure 5.8. (We are going to assign default values to make it easier to test our program. When you have tested everything successfully, you will want to make these fields blank. For now, we can save ourselves some typing!) Create these entry fields, along with their descriptive text, in your form. We'll add the buttons and progress windows in a moment.

Table 5.1   Text Fields for the Client Application Form

Field Description	Field Name	Field Text
Customer Last Name	txtLastName	Smith
Customer First Name	txtFirstName	John
Customer Address One	txtAddressOne	100 Main Street
Customer Address Two	txtAddressTwo	
Customer City	txtCity	Anytown
Customer State Code	txtState	ST
Customer ZIP Code	txtZIP	11111
Customer Credit Card #	txtCreditCardNumber	1234123412341234
Book Title	txtBookTitle	MSMQ From Scratch
Book Author Last Name	txtBookAuthorLast	
Book Author First Name	txtBookAuthorFirst	

Table 5.2 gives the name and description of the various push buttons on our form. Create these buttons on your form.

Table 5.2   Command Buttons for the Client Application Form

Button Text	Button Name
Submit	cmdInquiry
Receive	cmdReceive
Clear	cmdClear
Exit	cmdExit

Finally, our form has two list boxes that we will use to write summary progress messages while our client is running. These are to help you see what is going on and add no function to the application or value to the user in the store. The fields are named MessageHistory and QueueList, respectively.

Five events of interest to us may occur on this form. The first occurs when the form is loaded; the others occur when the Submit, Receive, Clear, or Exit button is clicked. We are allowing the default Windows event handler to process all the other window events.

Form Load Event

Earlier in this chapter we showed you that the order-processing server creates its input queue when it is started and that it deletes this queue when it is shut down. This step ensures that messages are sent only to servers that are available to process inquiries. We showed you how to uniquely identify this group of queues by using the ServiceTypeGUID property of the queue and how to identify each machine by using the Label property of the queue. We will use these two properties now as we locate a queue to send our inquiry messages to.

When the entry form is first loaded, and before it is displayed, we will search the input queue for the order-processing server. One of three things results from this search:

- No queues are found, in which case we end the client program with a message to the user.
- Only one queue is found, in which case we open the queue and display the order form.
- More than one queue is found, in which case we display a list of the queues found and allow the user to choose which one to open. We then open the queue and display the entry form.

Before we look at the code that we must add to our program, let's take a minute to introduce a couple of new MSMQ ActiveX objects, MSMQQuery and MSMQQueueInfos (yes, that's right—MSMQQueueInfos, not to be confused with MSMQQueueInfo, the properties of a queue).

The MSMQQuery object allows your program to interrogate the MQIS for existing public queues, based on their properties. MSMQQuery has one method, LookupQueue, which takes as parameters a list of properties on which the search is based. The LookupQueue method returns to the program a MSMQQueueInfos object.

The MSMQQueueInfos object may be thought of as an index into the MQIS. MSMQQueueInfos is a dynamic list of queues that match the search argument provided when the LookupQueue method is called. The list has no given length (because it is dynamic), but instead the end-of-list condition is supported. The MSMQQueueInfos object offers two methods: Reset and Next. Reset restores the index pointer to the beginning of the list, and Next, as you might expect, moves the index pointer to the next queue that matches the search argument.

Let's begin to build the locate logic into our program to illustrate these objects. Start by double-clicking on the background on our entry form to display the code for the Form Load condition.

The first thing we need to do is to initialize the query of the MQIS. To do so, we use the MSMQQuery object, as shown in Listing 5.18

Listing 5.18 Initialize the Search for the Input Queue

```
1 Private Sub Form_Load()
2
3 On Error GoTo ErrorHandler
4
5   ' Do a lookupqueue to find the inquire queue
6
7   ' Declare objects local
8   Set IQList = New MSMQQueueInfos
9   Set IQListQuery = New MSMQQuery
10  Set ISendQInfoFirst = New MSMQQueueInfo
11  Set ISendQInfo = New MSMQQueueInfo
12
13  ' Do LookupQueue on the Query object based on ServiceTypeGuid
14  Set IQList = IQListQuery.LookupQueue _
      (ServiceTypeGuid:="{0BF4DBD1-254F-11d3-A091-00A024A5BFC5}")
15
16  ' Move cursor to beginning of Infos index
17  IQList.Reset
```

In lines 8–11, we initialize local variables for use in our search of the MQIS and also for the MSMQQueueInfo objects to be used later. The only search argument that we need to supply is the ServiceTypeGUID, as we see in line 14. This search returns a pointer into a list of all the registered queues that can process inquiries pertaining to new special book orders. The GUID we use here is identical to the one we used when creating the queue in the server. Finally, for this segment we reset the search index to the beginning of the list of queues that match the search argument.

The next step is to decide which of the available queues we will use to process our inquiries. If no queues match the search argument, then our application cannot proceed. We prompt the user to try again later and end the program. If only one queue matches, then we open it and proceed to the entry form automatically. If more than one queue matches, then we display a list of the available queues and let the user decide which one to use.

We already know that the MSMQQueueInfo object represents the properties of an individual queue. (Notice we've returned to the singular!) Our search index actually points to a single MSMQQueueInfo object. In the code segment shown in Listing 5.19, we declare two MSMQQueueInfo objects to help with our processing of the search index.

Listing 5.19   Processing the Returns of a MSMQQuery

```
19      ' Get first queue object from Infos index
20      Set ISendQInfoFirst = IQList.Next
21  ' If there were no returns, no server running at this time
22      If ISendQInfoFirst Is Nothing Then
23          intPress = MsgBox("e-books server unavailable at this time.",
             ➥ vbInformation, "Client")
24          End
25      End If
26
27      ' Get next queue object from the Infos index
28      Set ISendQInfo = IQList.Next
29
30      ' If there are no more returns, then we have our one QueueInfo object
31      If ISendQInfo Is Nothing Then
32          Set ISendQ = ISendQInfoFirst.Open(2, 0)
33          QueueList.AddItem "Inquire queue: " & ISendQInfoFirst.PathName
34
35      ' Otherwise, continue through list until we have all returned queues
36      ' We will add every available queue to our listbox
37
38      Else
39          Dialog.lbAvailableServers.AddItem ISendQInfoFirst.Label
40              While Not ISendQInfo Is Nothing
41
42                  ' We will add the queue to a listbox
43                  Dialog.lbAvailableServers.AddItem ISendQInfo.Label
44
45                  ' and get the next one
46                  Set ISendQInfo = IQList.Next
47              Wend
```

In line 20 we set the MSMQQueueInfo object ISendQInfoFirst to contain the first queue that matches our search argument. Because the search does not return a count of the number of queues that match the argument, we must use the end-of-list condition to determine how to proceed. Therefore, in line 22 our first test is that the first item is not blank. If it is, no order-processing servers are running and we must end the client program. Otherwise, we skip ahead to line 28. Here we set a second MSMQQueueInfo object, ISendQInfo, to point to the second item in the search list. If it is blank (line 31), then we know that only one queue was found (its properties are still held in ISendQInfoFirst) and so we proceed to open it in line 32. Otherwise, we have at least two queues to choose from and, hence, at least two active order-processing servers. Line 39 puts into a list box called lbAvailableServers the label of the first queue found, and line 28 adds the label of the second and subsequent queues that match the search argument until all are displayed.

In Figure 5.9 the window contains the list of servers to choose from.

Figure 5.9

Form allowing user to select from list of available servers.

To build this list, then, we need first to add a new form to our project. Select Add Form   from the Project Menu and then select Open a New Dialog. Add one control to the form, a list box called lbAvailableServers. Change the text of the OK button to **Connect**. Delete the Cancel button by selecting it and pressing the delete key.

Associated with the Connect button is the code to hide the dialog box as we use the list box entry that the user selected. This value is the label of the queue that we want to use. To the user, the value is the name of the machine on which the order-processing server resides.

Double-click on the Connect button to display its code form. Add the code shown is Listing 5.20 to hide the dialog and return to the Form Load processing of our main window.

Listing 5.20   Dialog Box Code

```
1 Public Sub OKButton_Click()
2    Dialog.Hide
3 End Sub
```

Returning to the code for the Form Load of our main window, we need to add the code to display and pass control to the dialog. Listing 5.21 shows this code (line 50) in the context of that which we built earlier.

Listing 5.21   Code to Display List of Servers

```
38 Else
39         Dialog.lbAvailableServers.AddItem ISendQInfoFirst.Label
40            While Not ISendQInfo Is Nothing
41
42                ' We will add the queue to a listbox
43                Dialog.lbAvailableServers.AddItem ISendQInfo.Label
44
45                ' and get the next one
46                Set ISendQInfo = IQList.Next
47            Wend
48
49            ' The user chooses a server off the list
50            Dialog.Show vbModal
```

The final step is to open the queue that we have selected and to load the entry form. We initiate another query and specify both the ServiceTypeGUID we had before and the Label we just retrieved from the dialog. We then open the one queue that matches the search. Listing 5.22 shows this code in context.

Listing 5.22   Locate and Open Inquire Queue Based on User's Selection from the lbAvailableServers List Box

```
38 Else
39         Dialog.lbAvailableServers.AddItem ISendQInfoFirst.Label
40            While Not ISendQInfo Is Nothing
41
42                ' We will add the queue to a listbox
43                Dialog.lbAvailableServers.AddItem ISendQInfo.Label
44
45                ' and get the next one
46                Set ISendQInfo = IQList.Next
47            Wend
48
49            ' The user chooses a server off the list
50            Dialog.Show vbModal
51
52            ' We re-obtain that QueueInfo object by now doing a lookup on the
53            ' unique label instance
54            Dim QLabel As String
55            QLabel = Dialog.lbAvailableServers.Text
56            Set IQList = IQListQuery.LookupQueue(,
              ➥"{0BF4DBD1-254F-11d3-A091-00A024A5BFC5}", QLabel)
57            IQList.Reset
58            Set ISendQInfo = IQList.Next
```

continues

5

Listing 5.22   continued

```
59              Set ISendQ = ISendQInfo.Open(2, 0)
60              QueueList.AddItem "Inquire queue: " & ISendQInfo.PathName
61              Unload Dialog
62      End If
63
64      cmdReceive.Enabled = False
65      Exit Sub
66
67 ErrorHandler:
68      MessageHistory.AddItem Err.Description
69
70 End Sub
```

This step is also the end of this command's code, so we exit the subroutine at the end of this code and include our ErrorHandler. Note on line 61 that we unload our dialog box when we are done with it (after we've retrieved the necessary information from lbAvailableServers).

We now have an open queue through which we can send messages to the order-processing server, and the entry form is displayed for the user.

Submit Button Event

The function of the Submit button is to extract from the form the details of the inquiry, build a message, and send it to the input queue of the order-processing server that we opened when the application started. Because this message is a request, we expect a reply! To make pairing of requests and replies simple, we will create a unique private reply queue for each request that is submitted. The reply queue is created as part of the processing of this button event, and its name is sent with the message.

The flowchart in Figure 5.10 shows the process steps associated with the Submit button being clicked.

When the Submit button is pushed, the first task is to gather the information from the entry fields on the form. The next step is to create a private reply queue, followed by steps to build and send the message. The pseudocode in Listing 5.23 breaks out the process steps, and we explore each step in detail in a moment. For usability, we have added steps to disable the Submit button and enable the Receive button while a request is outstanding. Also, because we are keeping the state of the request on the entry form, we must disable the form to prevent the user from changing any of its content. In fact, after submitting the request, the controls the user has access to are the Receive and Exit buttons.

Figure 5.10

Process steps in the
Submit Button event.

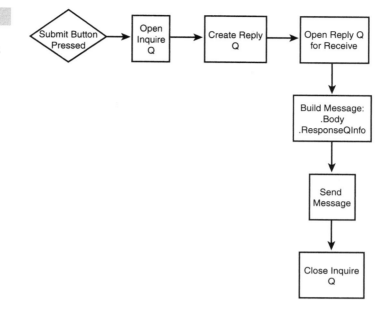

5

Listing 5.23   Pseudocode for Submit Button

```
BEGIN
    DiableButton( Submit )
    DisableEntryField( all of them )
    CreateQ( ReplyQ )
    BuildInquiryMsg( )
    SendMsg( )
    EnableButton( Receive )
END
```

On the main form, double-click on the Submit button to display its code form. Add the code shown in Listing 5.24 to process the enabling and disabling of various form controls. We'll add our MSMQ logic in a moment.

Listing 5.24   Submit Command Button Code

```
1 Private Sub cmdSubmit_Click()
2 'Submit an book inquiry
3
4 On Error GoTo ErrorHandler
5     cmdInquiry.Enabled = False
6     txtLastName.Enabled = False
7     txtFirstName.Enabled = False
8     txtAddressOne.Enabled = False
9     txtAddressTwo.Enabled = False
10    txtCity.Enabled = False
```

continues

Listing 5.24   continued

```
11    txtState.Enabled = False
12    txtZIP.Enabled = False
13    txtCreditCardNumber.Enabled = False
14    txtBookTitle.Enabled = False
15    txtBookAuthorLast.Enabled = False
16    txtBookAuthorFirst.Enabled = False
17    cmdClear.Enabled = False
```

> **Tip**
>
> To ease the enabling and disabling of the different fields throughout the client workflow, you can hold these commands in a function that can be called whenever the fields need to be enabled or disabled. You can even create an object to hold all the fields and then also create "enable" and "disable" methods on that object.

CreateQ

We introduced the Create method earlier in this chapter when we created the input queue for the order-processing server. At that time we created a queue that we wanted other programs to be able to find while they were executing.

Now we want to create a queue that will be used by a single program to receive its replies. We do not want this queue registered in the MQIS and will instead pass around its address in the inquiry message that we send.

To this end, we will create what is known as a Private queue. It is created in the same manner as a Public queue, its pathname being set differently to indicate that it should not be registered in the MQIS.

The code in Listing 5.25 should be inserted into the main code for our Submit button. Line 36 shows the syntax to create the private queue. The pathname is made up of the machine name (the local machine is represented by the '.'), PRIVATE$, and the name given to the queue.

To create an instance of this reply queue specific to the message we are sending, our pathname uses the machine name and the date/time. It will be impossible for our users to submit two inquiries within one second. We already learned how to get the name of the local machine programmatically. Getting the time is as simple as using the built-in VB function, format. The syntax for this function to retrieve the date and time (in seconds) is in line 36.

Listing 5.25   Code to Create the Private Reply Queue

```
17     '********************
18     'Create reply queue
19     '********************
20
21     Set IReplyQInfo = New MSMQQueueInfo
22     IReplyQInfo.Label = "Book Inquire Reply Queue"
23
24     ' We want to create unique reply queue instances.
25     ' We will accomplish this by incorporating the machine name
26     ' and the date/time in the queue name
27     Dim PathName As String
28     Dim ComputerName As String
29     ' First we get the computer name for the local machine
30     sBuffer = Space$(MAX_COMPUTERNAME_LENGTH + 1)
31     lSize = Len(sBuffer)
32     If GetComputerName(sBuffer, lSize) Then
33         ComputerName = Left(sBuffer, lSize)
34     End If
35     ' Now we make a private queue with the computer name and time in it
36     PathName = ".\private$\Client_Inquire_Reply_Queue_" &
       ➥ComputerName & "_" & (Format(Now, "ddddd ttttt"))
37     IReplyQInfo.PathName = PathName
38
39     IReplyQInfo.Create
40     MessageHistory.AddItem "Reply Queue Created"
```

Finally, we must open the reply queue we just created. Listing 5.26 shows this code.

Listing 5.26   Opening the Reply Queue for Receive

```
39     IReplyQInfo.Create
40     MessageHistory.AddItem "Reply Queue Created"
41
42     ' Open reply queue for receive
43     Set IReplyQ = IReplyQInfo.Open(MQ_RECEIVE_ACCESS, MQ_DENY_RECEIVE_SHARE)
44     MessageHistory.AddItem "Reply Queue Opened for Receive"
```

Now we have created our specific reply queue and opened it for receive. Later in the chapter, we build the Receive button to receive the reply message off that queue. We will also be populating the ResponseQueueInfo property of our message with the MSMQQueueInfo object of our reply queue (IReplyQInfo). Now let's build that message.

BuildInquiryMsg

Building our message this time around requires a bit more than just assigning the value of one text box to a string and then assigning that string to the body of our message. Although we will still be using a string value as the body of our message, we need to create a fixed-format message by controlling exactly how long each element of that string is. The back-end systems are going to be expecting a string formatted a certain way no matter what, so as the client, we must deliver. Table 5.3 gives the number of bytes in each portion of the message.

Table 5.3　Message Portions in Bytes

Field	Bytes
Last Name	25
First Name	25
Address 1	25
Address 2	25
City	25
State	2
ZIP	9
CC Number	16
Book Title	25
Book Author Last Name	25
Book Author First Name	25

To create this string, we are going to create an object within VB called `OrderInfo`. We do so by creating a class module. Here's how: Right-click on the project window and choose Add, Class Module. Call the class module **OrderInfo**. The first code to go into our OrderInfo class module is the declaration of strings we are using to populate the `OrderInfo` object. Listing 5.27 shows these declarations.

Listing 5.27　Declarations in the OrderInfo Class Module

```
1  Option Explicit
2  Public LastName As String
3  Public FirstName As String
4  Public Address As String
5  Public Address2 As String
6  Public City As String
7  Public State As String
8  Public ZIP As String
9  Public CCNumber As String
10 Public BookTitle As String
11 Public AuthorFirst As String
12 Public AuthorLast As String
```

Moving back to the code window for our main form, we need to populate these strings of the OrderInfo module. Listing 5.28 creates a new `Order` instance of the `OrderInfo` object and populates it.

Listing 5.28   Code to Declare and Populate the `Order` Object

```
42 ' Open reply queue for receive
43    Set IReplyQ = IReplyQInfo.Open(MQ_RECEIVE_ACCESS, MQ_DENY_RECEIVE_SHARE)
44    MessageHistory.AddItem "Reply Queue Opened for Receive"
45
46    '******************************
47    'Build and send inquire message
48    '******************************
49
50    ' Create data structure
51    Dim Order As New OrderInfo
52    With Order
53      .LastName = txtLastName.Text
54      .FirstName = txtFirstName.Text
55      .Address = txtAddressOne.Text
56      .Address2 = txtAddressTwo.Text
57      .City = txtCity.Text
58      .State = txtState.Text
59      .ZIP = txtZIP.Text
60      .CCNumber = txtCreditCardNumber.Text
61      .BookTitle = txtBookTitle.Text
62      .AuthorLast = txtBookAuthorLast.Text
63      .AuthorFirst = txtBookAuthorFirst.Text
64    End With
```

Over in the OrderInfo module, we are going to create two functions: `Serialize`, which we call from the Main code, and `FixedString`, which we call from within `Serialize`. `Serialize` combines all the separate strings (LastName, FirstName, on down the line) into one string and then converts it from Unicode. The `FixedString` function is actually responsible for making each element conform to the lengths specified in Table 5.3.

 All VB strings are Unicode strings. The normal ASCII character set requires only 1 byte (8 bits) of storage per character. Unicode, on the other hand, requires 2 bytes (16 bits) of storage per character. The extra byte allows Unicode to represent all characters used in every language (English, Japanese, Hebrew, and so on). We do not need 16-bit characters, so we will convert from Unicode to ASCII.

Listing 5.29 shows the remaining code for the OrderInfo module.

Listing 5.29 `Serialize` and `FixedString` Functions in the OrderInfo Module

```
13 Public Function Serialize() As Variant
14    Dim Buffer As Variant
15    Buffer = FixedString(LastName, 25) & FixedString(FirstName, 25) & _
         FixedString(Address, 25) & _
         FixedString(Address2, 25) & FixedString(City, 25) & _
         FixedString(State, 2) & _
         FixedString(ZIP, 9) & FixedString(CCNumber, 16) & _
         FixedString(BookTitle, 25) & _
         FixedString(AuthorLast, 25) & FixedString(AuthorFirst, 25)
16    Serialize = StrConv(Buffer, vbFromUnicode)
17 End Function
18
19 Private Function FixedString(InputString As String, length As Long) As String
20    Dim n As Integer
21    If Len(InputString) = length Then
22        FixedString = InputString
23    ElseIf Len(InputString) > length Then
24        FixedString = Left(InputString, length)
25    Else
26        FixedString = InputString
27        For n = 1 To (length - Len(FixedString))
28            FixedString = FixedString & " "
29        Next
30    End If
31 End Function
```

We are now ready to go back into our main form code and build the message. Listing 5.30 shows this code. You need to be aware of two things in this code. First, in line 68, we create the message body by calling the `Serialize` function on our `Order` object. This step executes the functions we just coded into our module on the data with which we just populated our `OrderInfo` object (remember `Order` is the instance of the `OrderInfo` object we created with the class module). Second, in line 71, we populate the `ResponseQueueInfo` of our message with the `MSMQQueueInfo` of the reply queue we created in the preceding section.

Listing 5.30   Building the Inquire Message

```
60    Order.CCNumber = txtCreditCardNumber.Text
61    Order.BookTitle = txtBookTitle.Text
62    Order.AuthorLast = txtBookAuthorLast.Text
63    Order.AuthorFirst = txtBookAuthorFirst.Text
64
65 ' Build message
66    Set Message = New MSMQMessage
67    Message.Label = "Book Inquire Message"
68    Message.Body = Order.Serialize
69
```

```
70     ' Set responsequeueinfo of message equal to the reply queue we just
created
71     Set Message.ResponseQueueInfo = IReplyQInfo
72     MessageHistory.AddItem "Message created"
```

We have now built our inquire message and are ready to send it on its way to the server application.

SendMsg

As we have seen before, we use the `Send` method of the `MSMQMessage` object to put a message on queue. For a detailed explanation of this procedure, please refer to Chapter 3. Listing 5.31 shows the code that we add to our client. This segment is also the end of this subroutine, so we need to code Exit Sub before our ErrorHandler code. In the ErrorHandler, we need to reset everything to the default.

Listing 5.31   Code to Send the Inquiry Message

```
72     MessageHistory.AddItem "Message created"
73 ' Send message
74     Message.Send ISendQ
75     MessageHistory.AddItem "Message sent"
76
77     cmdReceive.Enabled = True
78
79 Exit Sub
80
81 ErrorHandler:
82     MessageHistory.AddItem "Error: " & Err.Description
83     cmdSubmit.Enabled = True
84     txtLastName.Enabled = True
85     txtFirstName.Enabled = True
86     txtAddressOne.Enabled = True
87     txtAddressTwo.Enabled = True
88     txtCity.Enabled = True
89     txtState.Enabled = True
90     txtZIP.Enabled = True
91     txtCreditCardNumber.Enabled = True
92     txtBookTitle.Enabled = True
93     txtBookAuthorLast.Enabled = True
94     txtBookAuthorFirst.Enabled = True
95     Screen.MousePointer = vbDefault
96 End Sub
```

Receive Button Event

The function of the Receive button is to get and display the response to our inquiry. For now we are going to process replies manually to aid the development and testing of our program. It will be easier for you to see how the application fits together if we break down the flow when we test it later in this chapter. We automate the reply processing in Chapter 7.

The flowchart in Figure 5.11 shows the process steps associated with the Receive button being clicked.

Figure 5.11

Process steps in the
`Receive Button` *event.*

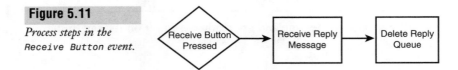

When the Receive button is clicked we attempt to get a message from the reply queue. If the queue is empty, the user is prompted to try again or abort. If a message is waiting, we display its content in a message box with the user options to confirm or cancel.

A message box is a VB function that allows you to programmatically display information to a user in a window. The message box has nothing to do with a MSMQ message.

The Cancel step returns the user to the entry form. At this point the Receive button is disabled, and the Submit button, along with the entry fields on the form, is enabled. No message flow occurs. The Confirm step also returns the user to the entry form. The entry fields are cleared to accommodate a new order. In Chapter 8, "Confirm Order—Client Application," we add to the Confirm step to send a message completing the order.

Whether the order is confirmed or cancelled, the reply queue is deleted. The pseudocode in Listing 5.32 shows these steps. We break out the detail of each step in a moment.

Listing 5.32   Pseudocode for the Reply Button

```
BEGIN
    ReplyMsg = GetMsg( ReplyQ )
    If ReplyMsg is not Empty
        MsgBox( ReplyMsg.Body, Confirm¦Cancel )
        If Confirm selected
            ResetEntryFields( all of them )
        DisableButton( Receive )
        EnableButton( Submit )
        EnableEntryFields( all of them )
END
```

Double-click on the Receive button on our main form to access its code form. The first thing we must do is to attempt to read a message from the reply queue. We already opened the queue in our Submit code, so we have a `MSMQQueue` object instantiated. We will just call the receive method of that queue object (line 8 of Listing 5.33). We have a receive time-out so that our program will not hang if there is no

message, but we control for the fact that a message may be on its way, and we just
did not wait long enough (lines 9–20). If the user decides to stop trying to receive
the message, we need to delete the reply queue by calling the `Delete` method of the
`MSMQQueueInfo` object. When we get a message, we display just the body of the message (we're expecting something descriptive in the body, which is the server's job) in
lines 26–28. Lines 30–37, submit the order?, do not do much right now, but this is
where we will be expanding the code later to send a transactional order message.

Listing 5.33   Receive Button Code

```
1 Private Sub cmdReceive_Click()
2
3     Screen.MousePointer = vbHourglass
4
5 Start:
6     'Get the message
7     Set Message = New MSMQMessage
8     Set Message = IReplyQ.Receive(ReceiveTimeout:=1000)
9     If Message Is Nothing Then
10        intPress = MsgBox("Unable to receive inquire reply message",
          ➥ vbInformation, "e-books Client")
11        intPress = MsgBox("Try again?", vbYesNo, "e-books Client")
12            If intPress = vbNo Then
13                cmdSubmit.Enabled = True
14                Screen.MousePointer = vbDefault
15                IReplyQInfo.Delete
16                Exit Sub
17            Else
18                GoTo Start
19            End If
20    End If
21
22    ' The back end systems are sending set reply messages like
23    ' "Your book is in stock for 19.95" and "Your credit approved."
24    ' In real life we would need to do some work based on the reply
25    ' we received....
26    Dim ReplyMessage As String
27    ReplyMessage = Message.Body
28    intPress = MsgBox("Message arrived from e-books server:" & Chr(13) & _
      ReplyMessage, vbInformation, "Client")
29
30    'Submit the order?
31    intPress = MsgBox("Submit order?", vbOKCancel, "Client")
32    If intPress = 1 Then
33        intPress = MsgBox("Order submitted", vbOKOnly, "Client")
34    Else
35        'They changed their mind
36        intPress = MsgBox("Order not submitted at this time.",
          ➥ vbInformation, "Client")
37    End If
```

After this, we need to delete the reply queue. We have received the only message it will ever get, and we need to clean up! Listing 5.34 shows this code. We simply call the Delete method of the MSMQQueueInfo object (line 46), and the queue is gone! This step also ends the Receive code, so we need to reset our form (line 49) and include an ErrorHandler (lines 41 and 42). You will notice that we are simply calling the Clear command. This command contains all the code for resetting the form. As a command button, the user can reset the form whenever they need to, and we can also call the routine whenever we need to clear the form! The code for this button is shown in Listing 5.35.

Listing 5.34   **Deleting the Reply Queue and Completing the Receive Subroutine**

```
34 Else
35        'They changed their mind
36        intPress = MsgBox("Order not submitted at this time.",
         ➥ vbInformation, "Client")
37    End If
38
39    GoTo Reset
40
41 ErrorHandler:
42    MessageHistory.AddItem "Error: " & Err.Description
43
44 Reset:
45    ' Destroy the reply queue
46    IReplyQInfo.Delete
47
48    ' Clear the form
49    Call cmdClear_Click
50
51 End Sub
```

Listing 5.35   **The cmdClear_Click Subroutine**

```
Private Sub cmdClear_Click()
    txtLastName.Enabled = True
    txtLastName.Text = ""
    txtFirstName.Enabled = True
    txtFirstName.Text = ""
    txtAddressOne.Enabled = True
    txtAddressOne.Text = ""
    txtAddressTwo.Enabled = True
    txtAddressTwo.Text = ""
    txtCity.Enabled = True
    txtCity.Text = ""
    txtState.Enabled = True
    txtState.Text = ""
    txtZIP.Enabled = True
    txtZIP.Text = ""
    txtCreditCardNumber.Enabled = True
```

```
txtCreditCardNumber.Text = ""
txtBookTitle.Enabled = True
txtBookTitle.Text = ""
txtBookAuthorLast.Enabled = True
txtBookAuthorLast.Text = ""
txtBookAuthorFirst.Enabled = True
txtBookAuthorFirst.Text = ""
Screen.MousePointer =vbDefault

End Sub
```

Exit Button Event

The function of the Exit button is to clean up the temporary objects in use by the client application and close the window. We'll associate this code with the `Form_QueryUnload` procedure. As with the server, we confirm the user's exit wish, and then upon said confirmation we exit. Our Exit button, then, simply unloads the form. The Exit button code is displayed in Listing 5.36; the `Form_QueryUnload` code is displayed in Listing 5.37.

Listing 5.36   Exit Button Code

```
1 Private Sub cmdExit_Click()
2     Unload Me
3 End Sub
```

Listing 5.37   Form_QueryUnload Code

```
1 Private Sub Form_QueryUnload(Cancel As Integer, UnloadMode As Integer)
2     Dim i As Integer
3     On Error GoTo ErrorHandler
4     i = MsgBox("Do you want to exit?", vbYesNo + vbQuestion, "e-books Client")
5     If i = vbNo Then
6         Cancel = 1
7     Else
8         End
9     End If
10    Exit Sub
11
12 ErrorHandler:
13     Resume Next
14 End Sub
```

Global Declarations

We have made use of many objects in the development of this client application. Do not forget to add global declarations of these objects to the top of your code form. Listing 5.38 shows all of the necessary global declarations.

Listing 5.38   Global Declarations of Objects

```
'******** Global declaration of objects

1  Dim Message As MSMQMessage                          'any and all messages
2  Dim intPress As Integer
3
4  Dim lSendQInfo As MSMQQueueInfo
5  Dim lSendQInfoFirst As MSMQQueueInfo
6  Dim lSendQ As MSMQQueue                             'queue to which inquire
                                                       'messages will be sent
7  Dim IQList As MSMQQueueInfos                        'QueueInfos object for
                                                       'inquire queue
8  Dim IQListQuery As MSMQQuery                        'Query for inquire queue
9  Dim lReplyQInfo As MSMQQueueInfo
10 Dim lReplyQ As MSMQQueue                            'inquire reply queue
11
12 Dim WithEvents lReplyQEvent As MSMQEvent            'wait event on the inquire
                                                       'reply queue
13
14 ' Get computer Name declarations -- used to make unique queue instances
15 Dim sBuffer As String
16 Dim lSize As Long
17 Const MAX_COMPUTERNAME_LENGTH As Long = 15&
```

Testing the Client and Server

Now that we have completed the development of the code to support workflows 1 and 6 from our Concept Web, all that remains in this chapter is to run the programs and test them. We will run them in stages to show you things as they occur. If any stage does not complete successfully, you need to debug it before proceeding to the next.

1. Start the server. Look in MSMQ Explorer to see that the inquiry queue was created. Check that the ServiceTypeGUID is what you expect.

2. Start the client.

3. Submit the default inquiry.

4. Using MSMQ Explorer, look at the inquiry queue and see the new message on it. Look at the properties of the message, particularly the Body.

5. Click the Receive button on the server to trigger message processing. In MSMQ Explorer note that the message has gone from the inquiry queue.

6. Click the Receive button on the client to display the results of the inquiry.

And there you have it—your first MSMQ application is complete! You have used the request/reply programming paradigm between two distributed programs.

Summary

In this chapter you built the order-entry client and the order-processing server programs to perform flows 1 and 6 in the Concept Web diagram. The client receives from the user a customer's name, address and credit card information, along with the name of the book he or she wants to purchase. This information is sent in a message to the server, which then builds a default reply. The reply is sent to the reply queue the client named when it sent the message. You have seen the request/reply programming paradigm in action!

We introduced the MSMQQueueInfo object, showed you the properties that identify a queue, and explained the methods to create, open and delete a queue.

We recapped the MSMQQueue object and used the receive method to get a message from the queue.

We reviewed the MSMQMessage object and the method to send a message to a queue. We introduced the ResponseQInfo property and showed how a request can use that property to specify a reply queue.

As we built the client application, we introduced the objects required to find a queue from the definitions stored in the MQIS. These were the MSMQQuery and the MSMQQueueInfos objects.

In the next chapter, we modify the server program to process the message it receives, sending out to the credit agency and the warehouse for the necessary information to build a response.

5

Inquiry Workflow: Server to Back End

Client Architectural Overview

In Chapter 5, "Inquiry Workflow: Client to Server," we build the piece of our e-books application that receives from a user an inquiry concerning the purchase of a book. That inquiry is sent to the order-processing server where a standard response is prepared and sent back for the client to display.

The actual response sent to the order-entry client depends on responses from two back-end systems: the warehouse and the credit card company. In this chapter we build programs to handle the inquiry for the warehouse and the credit card company, and we modify the order-processing server to ask for the information from these back-end applications. Again, all of the communication between the applications use message queuing.

Relating this to our Concept Web, this chapter completes the code to service communication flows 2 and 4 and 3 and 5. Because the order-entry client is one step removed from how the answer is obtained, it is not necessary to modify that program in this chapter.

Returning to the tasks ahead in this chapter, we will build back-end server type processes that receive on an input queue a request for information. In the case of the credit card company, the request pertains to authorization of the customer's credit card. In the case of the warehouse, the request is to verify stock of the item requested and its price. Each back-end system replies to a queue named in the inquiry message that it receives and that is monitored by the order-processing server.

We continue to keep the programs as simple as possible and continue the approach that allows you to step through the messages flows. In the next chapter, we modify the programs to improve their performance and to automate the processing of the entire inquiry flow.

At the conclusion of this chapter, you will have two more programs and you will have modified the server. The response displayed by the client is based on responses from the credit card company and the warehouse, although the client does not change.

Architectural Overview

We pick up this chapter where we left off in the previous one. Our order-processing server, having been sent a request, made up a standard response that it sent to the client. In this chapter we use two back-end systems to build a response and have business logic in the server formulate the reply for the client.

The request that the server receives contains a customer's name, address, and credit card information, along with the name of the book the customer wants to purchase. The server must verify that the book's availability and price with the warehouse, that the customer's credit card is valid, and that the charge amount requested is available.

The warehouse is sent title and author information for the requested book and replies with an estimated delivery time and a price. The credit card company is sent the customer's credit card number, name, and address and a default amount; the company replies with an authorization code.

In this chapter the order-processing server

1. Receives from its input queue an inquiry message
2. Creates a queue to which the replies for this inquiry are sent
3. Locates input queues for the credit card company and the warehouse programs
4. Opens these input queues to the back-end systems
5. Strips out from its own input message the pertinent information to send to each back-end system (decomposes the message)
6. Sends messages to each back-end system
7. Opens the reply queue
8. Waits for the two replies
9. Compiles a response to the client from the replies (recomposes)
10. Sends a response to the client's reply queue

The program running in the warehouse receives a message containing the book title and/or author that the customer wants to purchase. At this stage the warehouse does not receive any personal information concerning the customer. The warehouse program interrogates the inventory to find out whether the title is in stock and at what price. This step normally involves a database lookup, but because we are teaching MSMQ programming and not SQL, we will make up the answer. All books will be available at a price of $19.95.

In this chapter the warehouse program

1. Creates its input queue
2. Opens its input queue to receive messages from it
3. Waits for a message to arrive on its input queue
4. Receives the message
5. Sends a default reply containing price and availability information
6. Repeats the preceding three steps indefinitely

The program running in the credit card company receives a message containing the customer's credit card number, name, and address. The message also contains the amount of the transaction for which the store wants to obtain approval.

We can now make several design choices concerning the overall flow. The first is that we can make the credit check follow the inventory check. We can then send the cost of the book to the credit card company. The downside of this approach is that the two steps must occur one after the other, and therefore the time to process the customer's order is lengthened. A second approach is to send both messages in parallel and have the warehouse send a follow-up message to the credit card company when the price of the book is known. This approach introduces some parallel processing (assuming that some part of the credit check can occur without the specific amount) but still requires serial processing for every order. A third approach is to obtain credit approval for a fixed amount that covers the cost of most books, say $50. The two requests could then be processed in parallel with the need to serialize only if the book's price exceeds the limit. This alternative ensures that most requests are processed in parallel, and it is this approach that we will take.

Whatever approach is taken, the credit card company uses the information provided to assess the customer's creditworthiness. Assessing creditworthiness may require a complex algorithm based on many factors, or it may be as simple as a lookup of a person's existing account and payment history. Whatever the case, it is beyond the scope of our topic! For our example, all requests will be approved.

In this chapter the credit card approval program

1. Creates its input queue
2. Opens its input queue to receive messages from it
3. Waits for a message to arrive on its input queue
4. Receives the message
5. Sends a default reply indicating approval of the request
6. Repeats the preceding three steps indefinitely

In the balance of this chapter, we build the back-end programs and modify the order-processing server that we created in Chapter 5. We start with the back-end systems, taking the warehouse as our example. You will have to repeat this section for the credit card company, making the necessary changes where we highlight them.

Application Architecture—Back-End System

Figure 6.1 shows a flowchart detailing the process steps in our back-end program. You will note that the processing is almost identical to that of the order-processing server in Chapter 5. When the program starts, it creates its own input queue, reads a message from it, builds a reply, and sends the reply to the response queue provided in the original message. When the back-end process is closed down, its queue is deleted. This step prevents the order-processing server from sending messages to a system that is not active. We consider what this action means to the server if it cannot find any queues of this type later in the chapter.

Figure 6.1

Back-end system process steps.

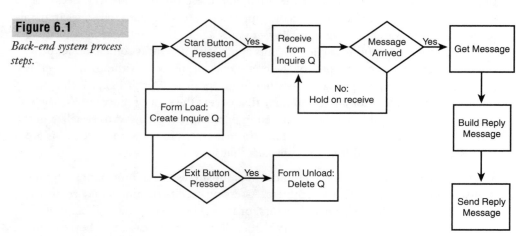

The back-end system processes one message at a time.

Listing 6.1 turns this flowchart into pseudocode for the warehouse. In the following sections, we examine each step in turn and build our program.

Listing 6.1   Pseudocode for the Back-End Systems

```
BEGIN
    CreateQ( InventoryQ, PUBLIC )
    DO
        InventoryMsg = GetMsg( InventoryQ, WAIT=UNLIMITED, ReplyQ =
        ➡ServerReplyQ )
        BuildReplyMsg( ReplyMsg, InventoryMsg )
        SendMsg( ServerReplyQ, ReplyMsg )
    UNTIL UserStopsProgram
    DeleteQ( InventoryQ )
END
```

This pseudocode should look familiar—it is almost identical to that of the order-processing server in Chapter 5. Like that program, this program is a long-running process.

We start by creating a new VB project. Refer to the end of Chapter 2, "Introducing Our Example: Designing the Solution," for the details. Call the project Inventory and the main form Main.

On the main form, create a list box to display a history of the activity of the program. Call the list box MessageHistory. Add a button to the form called cmdReceive and set its text to Receive. This widely used button controls when messages are received so that we can break down the processing of our complete, distributed application. In the next chapter, we remove this button and automate the workflow. Finally, add a button to the form to end the program. Call it cmdExit and set its text to Exit. You should now have a form that looks something like that shown in Figure 6.2.

Figure 6.2

Warehouse Inventory Check program window.

Repeat the steps to create a project and main window for the credit card company. Use the same names we used for the warehouse for each form element.

The following sections detail the code for the process steps identified in the pseudocode shown in Figure 6.1. In this application we need to be concerned with three window events. First is the loading of the form, during which we create and open the input queue. The second is the clicking of the Receive button, during which we will collect a message from the input queue, build a reply, and send it. Finally is the clicking of the Exit button, or the closing of the window. In this event we must close any open objects and delete the input queue to prevent order-processing servers from sending messages to a system that is not available.

Form Load Event

Double-click on the background of the main form to display its code form. The steps that we must execute at this time are to create and open the input queue. These steps are the same as those we detail in Chapter 5, and you should refer to the CreateQ section under the order-processing server for a more complete explanation if one is required.

Listing 6.2 gives the complete code to be executed under the Form Load event.

Notice that we have used a new globally unique identifier GUID for the ServiceTypeGUID property of the queue. All inventory queues for the warehouse use this GUID, and another one is used for the credit check queues. You can use GUIDGen.exe to create your own, or you can copy ours.

Listing 6.2 Code for Form Load Event

```
1 Private Sub Form_Load()
2
3 On Error GoTo ErrorHandler
4
5    '**********************
6    '* Create inquire queue
7    '**********************
8
9    Set IReceiveQ = New MSMQQueue
10   Set IReceiveQInfo = New MSMQQueueInfo
11
12   IReceiveQInfo.PathName = ".\Inquire_Warehouse_Queue"
13   IReceiveQInfo.Label = "Warehouse Inquire Queue"
14   IReceiveQInfo.ServiceTypeGuid = "{32188510-2883-11d3-A098-7A1CD3000000}"
15   IReceiveQInfo.Create
16   MessageHistory.AddItem "Inquire Queue: " & IReceiveQInfo.PathName
17
18   'Open the queue for receive
19   Set IReceiveQ = IReceiveQInfo.Open(MQ_RECEIVE_ACCESS, MQ_DENY_NONE)
20   MessageHistory.AddItem "Queue opened for receive"
21
22   Exit Sub
23
24 ErrorHandler:
25 ' If we are trying to create the queue and the queue already exists,
26   ' then we can continue on with opening the queue.
27   ' This code will be in every ErrorHandler that creates a queue.
```

```
28    If Err.Number = MQ_ERROR_QUEUE_EXISTS Then
29        Resume Next
30    End If
31    'This error will occur if we just created the queue and it
32    'has not been replicated throughout the MQIS yet. We will
33    'just wait until it is (we just created it so we know it exists).
34    If Err.Number = MQ_ERROR_QUEUE_NOT_FOUND Then
35        Err.Clear
36        DoEvents
37        Resume
38    Else
39        MessageHistory.AddItem Err.Description
40    End If
41
42 End Sub
```

As before, we have built in a retry loop in case we cannot open the queue immediately after we create it. Remember, this condition could occur because of MQIS (Message Queue Information Store) replication delays. We also have a loop in the unlikely event that the queue already exists when we call the `Create` method.

EXCURSION
Sharing Data Across Enterprises

Although we are building all our programs to run in the same MSMQ network, in a production system the credit card check would probably be performed by a different company, one with its own primary enterprise controller (PEC). The MQIS cannot be shared across different MSMQ Enterprises. Our server application would not be able to locate the queue for the credit check, however carefully we might set its properties. Later in this chapter, we consider how such a queue might be addressed. A good practice is to associate a particular service type with these queues.

Receive Button Event

The `Receive Button` event sets in motion most of this program's functionality. When the Receive button is clicked, we attempt to read a message from the input queue, and if one is available, we process the request and send a reply to the given response queue.

To receive a message from a queue, we must first have it open for receive access. We do so during our processing of the `Form Load` event. This event gives us a `MSMQQueue` object against which we can invoke the `Receive` method to get a `MSMQMessage` object. We are going to use the same receive logic as we did in Chapter 4, "Receiving a Message." You can refer back for further details.

Double-click on the Receive button to display its code form and then add the code shown in Listing 6.3 to receive the message.

Listing 6.3   Receive Button Code

```
1 Private Sub cmdReceive_Click()
2
3 On Error GoTo MyErrorHandler
4
5     '*************
6     '* Get Message
7     '*************
8
9     warehouse.SetFocus
10    Set IReceiveMessage = New MSMQMessage
11    Set IReceiveMessage = IReceiveQ.Receive(ReceiveTimeout:=10000)
12    ' This should not timeout, but if it does...
13    If IReceiveMessage Is Nothing Then
14        MessageHistory.AddItem "Unable to get message off queue"
15        Exit Sub
16    End If
17    MessageHistory.AddItem "Message Arrived"
18
19    '*********************
20    '* Query on database...
21    '*********************
22
23    Dim Body As String
24    Body = IReceiveMessage.Body
25    MessageHistory.AddItem Body
```

Having obtained a request, we need to process it and build a response.

EXCURSION

What's In a Response

Let's take a moment to consider the nature of this response. MSMQ does not impose any format restrictions on the body of the message. In fact, MSMQ makes no assumptions whatsoever on the format of the body, treating it simply as a blob of data, a stream of bytes. Therefore, the response can be anything we like, as long as the sender and the receiver agree on the format of what will be sent.

Taking the credit check as an example, our response can be as simple as True or False, 1 or 0, indicating that the credit is approved or not. The response can also be more complex, indicating not only whether credit has been approved but also for what amount. The response might also contain an approval code that can be used later to cross-reference the approval decision. That code might be a text string that anyone who views the message body can read.

In the case of the warehouse inventory check, we need to extract from the input message the name of the book and the author. We need to verify availability and send back the delivery time and the price of the book. We return the two values as binary data in case the server wants to process the response. (For example, if the request is being sent to several suppliers, we might want to show the user only the response with the shortest delivery time or the lowest price.) Listing 6.4 shows the code for the warehouse to process the inventory check. In line 46 we have assumed that the book is in stock, at a price of $19.95. We are not, after all, trying to teach you database programming! The first two numbers of our reply indicate the number of days necessary to ship the book to the requesting store, and the last five numbers indicate the price (assuming that no book costs more than $999.99) as three dollar digits and two cents digits.

We are also using the `AppSpecific` message property. This property allows our order-processing server to distinguish between messages coming from the warehouse and messages coming from the credit agency. The server is expecting messages of certain (different) formats from both the warehouse and the credit agency (more on that in just a minute). Both replies, however, land in the same reply queue. When the server picks a message off its reply queue, the `AppSpecific` property of the message tells the server whether that message came from the warehouse or the credit agency. Warehouse messages have an `AppSpecific` value of 2; credit agency messages will have an `AppSpecific` value of 1.

Listing 6.4   Code to Build the Inventory Response

```
40     '**************
41     'Send the reply
42     '**************
43
44     Set ISendMessage = New MSMQMessage
45     ' For the sake of testing, we will send the same reply every time
46     Body = "0301995"
47     ISendMessage.Body = Body
48     ISendMessage.AppSpecific = 2
```

In the case of the credit card approval, we need to extract from the input message the details of the customer's account and the amount of the transaction. We then send back a response to the server. We send back a 1 if the credit is approved and a 0 if it is not. These values are common codes for true and false. Listing 6.5 shows the code to process the credit approval. As with the inventory check, you will notice from lines 9 and 28 that we are making the assumption that all credit requests are approved.

Listing 6.5   Code to Build the Credit Approval

```
1      '**********************
2      'Query on database.....
3      '**********************
```

continues

Listing 6.5　continued

```
4    Dim body As String
5    body = IReceiveMessage.body
6    MessageHistory.AddItem Left$(body, 50)
7    ' For our purposes, everyone's credit is approved. What a world!
8    Dim result As String
9    result = 1
10
. . .
22
23       '***********
24       'Send the reply
25       '***********
26
27       Set ISendMessage = New MSMQMessage
28       ISendMessage.body = result
29       ISendMessage.AppSpecific = 1
```

Finally, we need to send the reply to the response queue that was named in the original inquiry message. As we show in Chapter 5, the ResponseQInfo property of the MSMQMessage object contains a MSMQQueueInfo object that describes exactly the queue to which we need to send the message. Listing 6.6 shows the code that we need to add to send the message.

Listing 6.6　Code to Send the Response

```
11       '************
12       'Open reply queue for send
13       '************
14
15       Set ISendQInfo = New MSMQQueueInfo
16       Set ISendQ = New MSMQQueue
17       'We get the information about what queue to open from the message
18       'we just received; the MSMQMessage.ResponseQueueInfo property.
19       Set ISendQInfo = IReceiveMessage.ResponseQueueInfo
20       Set ISendQ = ISendQInfo.Open(MQ_SEND_ACCESS, MQ_DENY_NONE)
21       MessageHistory.AddItem "Reply queue opened for send"
. . .
48       ISendMessage.AppSpecific = 2
49
50       ' Send the Message
51       ISendMessage.Send ISendQ
52       MessageHistory.AddItem "Reply message sent"
53
54       Exit Sub
55
56 MyErrorHandler:
57       MessageHistory.AddItem "Error: " & Err.Description
58
59 End Sub
```

In line 20 we invoke the Open method with the send access parameter against the MSMQQueueInfo object described in the response queue property of the inquiry message (line 19) to create a new MSMQQueue object. In line 51, we invoke the Send method against the current MSMQMessage object (ISendMessage), using the newly opened MSMQQueue object as a parameter.

This step concludes our processing of the Receive Button click event. Remember to repeat the steps for the credit check also.

Form Unload Event

Form Unload button processing is also much the same as it is for the order-processing server. The only MSMQ object that we have open is our own input queue, which we must delete. As before, the Delete method is associated with the MSMQQueueInfo object that we have used to describe our queue.

The code shown in Listing 6.7 should be associated with the unloading of the form, which can be triggered from the Window Close icon or the Exit push button.

Listing 6.7 Sample Shutdown Code for the Warehouse Inventory System

```
1 Private Sub Form_QueryUnload(Cancel As Integer, UnloadMode As Integer)
2     Dim i As Integer
3     On Error GoTo ErrorHandler
4     i = MsgBox("Do you want to exit?", vbYesNo + vbQuestion,
➥ "e-books Warehouse")
5     If i = vbNo Then
6         Cancel = 1
7     Else
8         IReceiveQInfo.Delete
9         Unload Me
10        End
11    End If
12    Exit Sub
13
14 ErrorHandler:
15     Resume Next
16
17 End Sub
```

Add similar code to the credit check program.

Application Architecture—Order-Processing Server

In Chapter 5 the order-processing server is not performing any more of a service for the client than the back-end systems we have just built. The server is asked a question, and it gives a response. Now we are going to add to the server the capability to hide from the client the complexities of the network of applications required to process the request and the capability to make decisions about the response that is given based on business rules.

EXCURSION

Message Brokers

We are not about to build a general-purpose message broker, although the logical extension of what we are describing is to use one in place of our customized server. Message brokers are part of an emerging technology that helps to integrate multiple applications. In simple terms, message brokers take data or requests from one application and apply business rules to pass the data on to other applications and, if necessary, assemble a response. Message brokers may reformat data, and they certainly deal with the issue of decomposing a large input message into elements that are required for the different applications with which it must communicate. Several commercial products offer this and other application integration functions; one such product is the Geneva Integrator from Level 8.

First of all, then, let's consider the complexity of the request. In this request we have a customer's name and address and some credit card information, along with the description of the item the customer wants to purchase. To the customer the request is very simple, and as a bookstore, isn't it better that we keep it that way for the customer? The last thing we would expect the customer to do would be to ask one person to check the inventory and another to complete the order form. (Let's look at the ideal world and forget the last time we went to the store and actually tried this!) What if there were several inventories to check: the local store, the regional and national warehouses, the different wholesale suppliers of the bookstore, and so on? Would the customer or even the associate want to know or care about all these? By providing a single place to go for the information, we can make a much larger inventory available to our customers with no more complexity than if they were dealing with only one source.

To extend our example, instead of sending a message to only one warehouse to check on stock, we could send to several in parallel and answer the customer based on the first favorable answer that we received. Of course, our example has the additional complexity of a second information type, that of the credit approval. This time we not only have a second entity to deal with, but this new entity expects to receive a different view of the data, the billing information. We might also have management information systems that want to help our store managers track details about the types of books that are being ordered in different regions, or we might have marketing systems that want to track a particular customer's preferences for targeted campaigns. Get the point? Having a centralized process managing the flow of the information greatly enhances our ability to leverage the information and gain competitive advantage.

Second, let's consider some business rules concerning how the response is generated. Consider what would happen if one of the back-end systems is not available or is not responding in a timely manner? We could hold up the business transaction or lose the customer altogether.

The use of the order-processing server between the client and the back-ends allows us to build some business rules that surround the workflow and support the manner in which the response is generated. What would happen if the warehouse stopped responding? We could just tell the customer we're sorry and that he or she should try again later (right!), or we could take a business risk and take the order based on a worst-case-availability survey for special-order books, say four to six weeks. In the latter case, we will probably retain the business, and when the system comes back online and completes the order, we may be able to significantly exceed the customer's expectation by delivering the book in four to six days instead! We could apply similar business rules to credit card approvals if the connection to the credit agency is unavailable. We would set a floor limit, below which all transactions would be approved. The risk to the store is low and is offset against the business that would be lost by turning away legitimate customers.

The flowchart in Figure 6.3 details the steps that our server performs from the moment it receives the message to the moment it sends the reply. This flow replaces the step BuildReplyMessage in Chapter 5.

6

Figure 6.3

Order-processing server process steps.

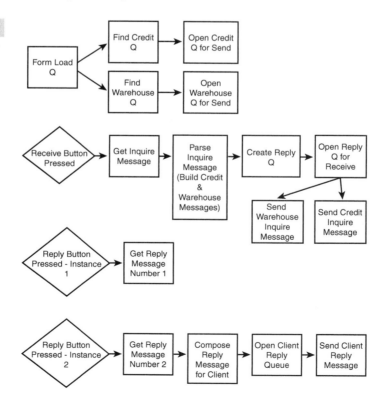

The first step is to break up the inquiry message into the different elements required by each of the workflow steps. The step to check the inventory requires only the book title and/or author. The step to gain credit card approval requires the customer's personal details and an amount. Here's the first of our business rules. We are making a standard request of the credit agency to approve an amount of $50 to halve the processing time of most requests. The second step is to build a queue to which the replies are sent, and the next step is to send the requests to the back-end systems. The server then waits for the replies. In this chapter, receipt of the replies is a manual step triggered by a button on the server window, but in the next chapter the process will be automatic and will discuss how time-outs can be used. If the request for information from one of the back ends is not received in a timely manner, another business rule can prepare a default response for the customer. Finally, the response is sent to the customer.

Listing 6.8 shows pseudocode for the steps following the receipt of the inquiry message through sending of the response to the client. In the following sections, we examine each step and build our program.

Listing 6.8   Pseudocode for Processing the Inquiry

```
1    BEGIN
2        Find&Open( InventoryQ )
3        Find&Open( CreditCheckQ)
4        BuildInventoryMsg( InputMsg, InventoryMsg )
5        BuildCreditCheckMsg( InputMsg, CreditMsg )
6        CreateQ( ReplyQ, PRIVATE )
7        SendMsg( InventoryMsg, InventoryQ )
8        SendMsg( CreditMsg, CreditCheckQ )
9        ReplyMsg1 = GetMsg( ReplyQ )
10        ReplyMsg2 = GetMsg( ReplyQ )
11        DeleteQ( ReplyQ )
12        BuildResponseMsg( ResponseMsg, ReplyMsg1, ReplyMsg2 )
13    END
```

In lines 2–3, we locate the input queues for the warehouse and the credit agency. In real life, to do this step every time a message is received is extremely inefficient, and we actually open these queues when the order-processing server starts. Because we have already stated that these queues are deleted when the program reading them stops, we may get a condition that the send step in either line 7 or 8 fails. We address this situation in a moment, when we consider those steps in detail.

While we're on the subject of locating the input queue for the credit agency, we hope you remember our comment earlier in this chapter to the effect that a real credit agency would run on a different MSMQ network with its own PEC. Bad news! The queue will not be registered in our MQIS, and so we cannot locate or even open it by any method we have described so far. In a moment we describe how you can open such queues by using their direct format name.

In lines 4–5, we build the bodies of the two messages that we send, and in line 6 we create a unique reply queue for the responses to these inquiries. For every message that we receive and process, we create a unique, private reply queue. This approach helps us match responses with requests and avoid the need to maintain state tables in the server to track the progress of our inquiries.

In lines 7–8, we send the messages, and in lines 9–10 we receive the replies. For now we assume that we will get both replies, and we wait for both before proceeding. In Chapter 7, "Automating the Inquiry Workflow," we add some of the business rules that we talked about earlier to intelligently handle the case that one or both replies are not received in a timely manner.

In line 11 we delete the queue that was created for the back-end replies.

Finally, in line 12 we build the response for the client. We take the cryptic responses received from the back-end systems and format a text string that can be displayed for the client's user.

As we said earlier, most of this code replaces the BuildReplyMsg step of the order-processing server in Chapter 5. In addition, we must add the opening of the back-end input queues to the Form Load event, and we will tackle this task first. Start by reloading the order-processing server project from Chapter 5. (You may want to save what you already have under a different name first.)

Form Load Event

Double-click on the background of the form to display the code executed when the form is loaded. You should see the steps that we added in Chapter 5 to create the server's input queue. We are going to add the code to locate the input queues of the warehouse and credit agency.

Let's consider the warehouse first. When we created the client application in Chapter 5, we introduced the MSMQQuery and MSMQQueueInfos objects and showed how they can be used to set up an index into the MQIS that points to the definitions of queues that match a set a search criteria. Listing 6.9 shows the code that we must add to our Form Load event to locate the warehouse inventory check input queue.

Listing 6.9   Code to Locate a Warehouse Inventory Queue

```
1    '********************
2    'Find warehouse queue
3    '********************
```

continues

Listing 6.9   continued

```
4
5     Set SendQList = New MSMQQueueInfos
6     Set SendQListQuery = New MSMQQuery
7     Set IWarehouseSendQInfo = New MSMQQueueInfo
8     Set SendQList = SendQListQuery.LookupQueue_
          (ServiceTypeGuid:="{32188510-2883-11d3-A098-7A1CD3000000}")
9
10    '***There will be only one queue with this ServiceTypeGuid, so we do not
11    '***loop the List.Next....The Infos object has only one queue in it
12    SendQList.Reset
13    Set IWarehouseSendQInfo = SendQList.Next
14
15    If IWarehouseSendQInfo Is Nothing Then
16        MessageHistory.AddItem "No warehouse queue was found"
17        Exit Sub
18    End If
```

We are going to locate the warehouse queues based on the ServiceTypeGUID that we used to indicate the class of inventory queues. We create a MSMQQuery object and invoke the LookupQueue method against it, specifying the value of the ServiceTypeGUID that we are searching on. This step gives us an index into the MQIS in the form of a MSMQQueueInfos object. We reset the index cursor to the first queue found and set up a MSMQQueueInfo object to contain the properties of the first queue that matches the search argument. We open the first queue found to match our search argument. If no queue is found, for now we issue a warning message and shut down the server. In the next chapter we consider how we can continue without the warehouse being available.

Now let's turn our attention to the credit card company. If the program runs on the same MSMQ network then we can locate the input queue in exactly the same manner that we just used for the inventory check (that is, with the MSMQQuery object). Of course, we need to change the value of the ServiceTypeGUID that we search for. However, as we have already said, the credit agency is likely to be running an entirely separate MSMQ network with its own PEC and, therefore, its own MQIS. We cannot use the LookupQueue method on a foreign enterprise. The only way we can address such a queue is by using its direct format name.

Listing 6.10 shows the code that must be added to our Form Load event to open a credit check input queue by its direct format name. The local MSMQ Enterprise accepts messages addressed to this queue and forwards them to the appropriate server. If the queue does not exist, the messages are written to the dead-letter queue of the foreign computer. The implication of this approach is that the input queue for the credit check must be statically defined and its format name published to stores that want to use it. If you choose to implement the credit check queue this way, you should remove from your credit agency program the code to create and delete the queue.

To see an example of a format name, view the properties of any message in a queue. In the Queues tab (see Figure 6.4), the format name of the destination queue is shown. The format to use a direct format name, however, is a little different. The format for direct format names is as follows: DIRECT=TCP:machine IP address\queue name. An example of using a direct format name is shown in Listing 6.10 (line 1).

Figure 6.4

The Queues tab of the message properties, as displayed in MSMQ Explorer.

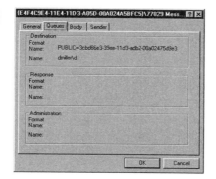

Listing 6.10   Using Direct Format Name to Open a Queue

```
1   CreditQInfo.FormatName = "{DIRECT=TCP:207.124.41.184/credit_inquire_queue"
2      ' Make sure to use the actual protocol, address, and queue name
3   CreditQ = CreditQInfo.Open(ACCESS, SHARE)
```

If, on the other hand, you prefer to keep the credit agency as part of your enterprise (and we do for the remainder of the discussion in this book), insert the code shown in Listing 6.11 into your Form Load event processing code. This code is almost identical to that which we added a moment ago for the inventory check. We have changed only the variable names and the ServiceTypeGUID to search against.

Listing 6.11   Accessing the Credit Agency Queues from Within the Same Enterprise

```
1   '**************
2   'Same for Credit Message
3   '**************
4
5   Set SendQList = New MSMQQueueInfos
6   Set SendQListQuery = New MSMQQuery
7   Set ICreditSendQInfo = New MSMQQueueInfo
8   Set SendQList = SendQListQuery.LookupQueue_
        (ServiceTypeGuid:="{32188511-2883-11d3-A098-7A1CD3000000}")
```

continues

Listing 6.11   continued

```
9    SendQList.Reset
10   Set ICreditSendQInfo = SendQList.Next
11   If ICreditSendQInfo Is Nothing Then
12       MessageHistory.AddItem "No credit queue was found"
13       Exit Sub
14   End If
```

This action concludes the steps surrounding the Form Load event.

BuildReplyMsg

Double-click on the Receive button on the form to display its code form. You should see the code that you created in Chapter 5 to simply receive a message, build a standard reply, and send the response.

Remove the code to create the standard response so that you are left only with the instructions to receive a message and send a reply.

The first step is to build the bodies of the messages that are sent to the back-end systems. Strip out from the message that we have received the information concerning the book title and author and put this information into a message for the warehouse, as shown in Listing 6.12. We are putting this code into a function, called Parse, that we call from within our Receive button code, as shown in Listing 6.13. (Remember that we are adding this code to our already existing Receive code. This code appears in lines 1–3 of Listing 6.13.)

Listing 6.12   Code to Build the Inventory Inquiry Message

```
1 Public Function Parse()
2
3 On Error GoTo ErrorHandler
4
5    Set WarehouseMessage = New MSMQMessage
6    Set CreditMessage = New MSMQMessage
7
8    'Message Parse
9    Dim MessageBody As String
10   MessageBody = Message.Body
11   Dim CreditMessageBody As String
12   Dim WarehouseMessageBody As String
13
14   'We know exactly which part of the message body pertains to which
15   'back-end process, so we simply pull out those parts of the
16   'string and assign them to new string objects.
17   WarehouseMessageBody = Right(StrConv(MessageBody, vbUnicode), 75)
18   WarehouseMessage.Body = WarehouseMessageBody
```

Listing 6.13   Code to Call the `Parse` Function

```
1 ' Get Message
2   Set Message = IReceiveQ.Receive
3   MessageHistory.AddItem "Message Arrived"
4
5   '*************
6   'Parse Message
7   '*************
8
9   Call Parse
```

The `Parse` function is really straightforward. We know exactly which portion of the message corresponds to what information because the client has formatted the message body in a predetermined way. We know that for the warehouse, we need the last 75 characters of the string (25 characters each for book title, author last name, and author first name). So we simply use the VB function `Right`, which pulls x number of bytes from the right of the string.

Next we must strip out the personal information about the customer, including his or her credit card number, and put this information into a message for the credit agency, as shown in Listing 6.14. You can see that this code is simply the remainder of the `Parse` function. For the credit check, we need all the customer's personal information (the left 152 characters of the string) and our default dollar amount for the credit check, $50.00 (or in the lowest possible unit of measure, 5000 cents).

Listing 6.14   Code to Build the Credit Check Message

```
17    WarehouseMessage.Body = WarehouseMessageBody
18    CreditMessageBody = Left(StrConv(MessageBody, vbUnicode), 152) & "5000"
19    CreditMessage.Body = CreditMessageBody
20
21 Exit Function
22
23 ErrorHandler:
24    MessageHistory.AddItem "Error: " & Err.Description
25
26 End Function
```

Before we can send out the inquiries to the back-end systems, we need to provide a queue to which the replies are sent. We created a reply queue in Chapter 5 when we built the response queue for the client. The code in Listing 6.15 shows what we must add to our Receive button processing to create the reply queue for the back-end workflows.

Listing 6.15   Creating the Reply Queue in the Order-Processing Server

```
1     '*******************
2     'Create Reply Queue
3     '*******************
4
5     Set IReplyQInfo = New MSMQQueueInfo
6
7     '******Creating the reply queue
8     ' We want to create unique reply queue instances.
9     ' We will accomplish this by incorporating the machine name
10    ' and the date/time (to mil secs) in the queue name
11    Dim PathName As String
12    Dim ComputerName As String
13    ' First we get the computer name for the local machine
14    sBuffer = Space$(MAX_COMPUTERNAME_LENGTH + 1)
15    lSize = Len(sBuffer)
16    If GetComputerName(sBuffer, lSize) Then
17        ComputerName = Left(sBuffer, lSize)
18    End If
19    ' Now we make a private queue with these unique strings
20    PathName = ".\private$\Server_Inquire_Reply_Queue_" _
        & ComputerName & "_" & Format(Now, "ddddd ttttt")
21    IReplyQInfo.PathName = PathName
22    IReplyQInfo.Label = "Inquire Warehouse Reply Queue"
23    IReplyQInfo.Create
24    Set IReplyQ = IReplyQInfo.Open(MQ_RECEIVE_ACCESS, MQ_DENY_NONE)
25
26    MessageHistory.AddItem "Reply queue created and opened for receive"
```

Again, as with the client, we are creating a specific and unique reply queue for this thread by placing a date and time stamp into the pathname of the queue.

The next step is to send to the back-end input queues the messages that we prepared earlier in this code segment, as shown in Listing 6.16. We set the ResponseQueueInfo of the message (lines 6 and 21), open the queue for send access (lines 13 and 23), and then send the message (lines 17 and 26).

Listing 6.16   Sending the Requests to the Back-End Systems

```
1     '****
2     'Send
3     '****
4
5     ' Set the ResponseQueueInfo
6     Set WarehouseMessage.ResponseQueueInfo = IReplyQInfo
7
8     ' Send the message
9
10
11
```

```
12 ' Open queue
13   Set IWarehouseSendQ = IWarehouseSendQInfo.Open(MQ_SEND_ACCESS,
   ➥ MQ_DENY_NONE)
14   MessageHistory.AddItem "Warehouse queue opened for send"
15
16
17   WarehouseMessage.Send IWarehouseSendQ
18   MessageHistory.AddItem "Warehouse inquire sent"
19
20   ' Ditto for the credit message
21   Set CreditMessage.ResponseQueueInfo = IReplyQInfo
22   ' Open queue
23   Set ICreditSendQ = ICreditSendQInfo.Open(MQ_SEND_ACCESS, MQ_DENY_NONE)
24   MessageHistory.AddItem "Credit queue opened for send"
25
26   CreditMessage.Send ICreditSendQ
27   MessageHistory.AddItem "Credit inquire sent"
28
29   Exit Sub
```

Because we opened these queues when the program started and it is a long-running process, one or both of the queues may no longer be available. In this case the Open method generates an error that the queue was not found. In our error handler, we must code for this condition by locating an alternative queue of the appropriate type and sending the message again. Listing 6.17 shows the code necessary for this condition. Within our ErrorHandler for this subroutine, we first need to know which queue we failed on (determined by the WYesNo variable set in line 11 and tested for in line 33); then we can find another queue of the same type. This code is simply cut and pasted from the Form_Load code. (A better coding practice is to make the locate code a function, but we do not want to be distracted at this point; you can do so on your own.)

Listing 6.17   Test to Control in ErrorHandler for Warehouse or Credit Queue

```
8 ' Send the message
9    ' Test for ErrorHandler
10   Dim WYesNo As Integer
11   WYesNo = 1  'Test for ErrorHandler to know if we failed on warehouse
12   ' Open queue
13   Set IWarehouseSendQ = IWarehouseSendQInfo.Open(MQ_SEND_ACCESS,
   ➥ MQ_DENY_NONE)
14   MessageHistory.AddItem "Warehouse queue opened for send"
15   WYesNo = 0
16
17   WarehouseMessage.Send IWarehouseSendQ
18   MessageHistory.AddItem "Warehouse inquire sent"
19
20   ' Ditto for the credit message
```

continues

Listing 6.17   continued

```
21    Set CreditMessage.ResponseQueueInfo = IReplyQInfo
22    ' Open queue
23    Set ICreditSendQ = ICreditSendQInfo.Open(MQ_SEND_ACCESS, MQ_DENY_NONE)
24    MessageHistory.AddItem "Credit queue opened for send"
25
26    CreditMessage.Send ICreditSendQ
27    MessageHistory.AddItem "Credit inquire sent"
28
29    Exit Sub
30
31 ErrorHandler:
32    If Err.Number = MQ_ERROR_QUEUE_NOT_FOUND Then
33        If WYesNo = 1 Then
34            '*********************
35            'Find warehouse queue
36            '*********************
37
38            Set SendQList = New MSMQQueueInfos
39            Set SendQListQuery = New MSMQQuery
40            Set IWarehouseSendQInfo = New MSMQQueueInfo
41            Set SendQList = SendQListQuery.LookupQueue(ServiceTypeGuid:= _
                  "{32188510-2883-11d3-A098-7A1CD3000000}")
42            '*** There will be only one queue with this ServiceTypeGuid,
              '*** so we do not loop the List.Next....The Infos object
43            '*** has only one queue in it
44            SendQList.Reset
45            Set IWarehouseSendQInfo = SendQList.Next
46
47            If IWarehouseSendQInfo Is Nothing Then
48                intPress = MsgBox("No warehouse queue was found", _
                      vbOKOnly, "e-books inquire server")
49            End
50        End If
51
52        Resume
53        Else
54            '***********************
55            'Same for Credit Message
56            '***********************
57
58            Set SendQList = New MSMQQueueInfos
59            Set SendQListQuery = New MSMQQuery
60            Set ICreditSendQInfo = New MSMQQueueInfo
61            Set SendQList = SendQListQuery.LookupQueue(ServiceTypeGuid:= _
                  "{32188511-2883-11d3-A098-7A1CD3000000}")
62            SendQList.Reset
63            Set ICreditSendQInfo = SendQList.Next
64            If ICreditSendQInfo Is Nothing Then
65                intPress = MsgBox("No credit queue was found", _
                      vbOKOnly, "e-books inquire server")
```

```
66              End
67          End If
68
69          Resume
70        End If
71    End If
72    intPress = MsgBox("Error: " & Err.Description & Err.Number, _
          vbOKOnly, "MSMQ From Scratch Iquire Server")
73
74 End Sub
```

This step concludes the processing of the Receive Button event except to disable the Receive button itself and enable a new button that initiates the processing of the replies. The code in Listing 6.18 shows these form events and concludes the code for our Receive Button event.

Listing 6.18   Disabling the Receive Button and Enabling the Reply Button

```
1    cmdReceive.Enabled = False
2    cmdReply.Enabled = True
```

Process Back-End Replies

First we need to add a new push button to the server form. The button has the name cmdReply (see Listing 6.18) and displays the caption Process Replies. By default the button is disabled. When the button is clicked, we attempt to receive a message from the server's response queue and add it to the reply for the client. When both replies have been received, we delete the response queue and send the reply to the client. We then re-enable the Receive button and disable the Reply button so that we are ready to process another inquiry from the store.

The first time the button is clicked, we simply read a message off the reply queue and save the resulting MSMQMessage object for later processing.

The second time the button is clicked, we read the message and combine the response with that of the first to build the reply that is sent to the client.

Double-click on the Process Replies button to display its code form. Add the code shown in Listing 6.19 to receive and process the replies. Finally, we delete the reply queue (line 54). Our processing works as follows:

1. We receive the first reply message off the queue (line 7).
2. We check to see whether the message is from the credit agency (line 13). We know the credit agency set the AppSpecific property of the message to 1. We also are expecting either a 1 (credit approved) or 0 (credit denied) from the credit agency. We create the credit portion of our final reply (the string CBody) based on this information (lines 16–24).

3. We are going to use a tester (AllEvents) to determine whether we have received both reply messages yet. AllEvents starts at 1 (you can set it at the form load). Each time we pick up a message, we add 1 to AllEvents. When AllEvents is 3, we know we have received both replies and can create our final reply for the client. We modify AllEvents in lines 25, 37, and 52. We test for it in line 39.

4. If the AppSpecific of the message is 2 (line 26) then we know the message is from the warehouse. We also know the format of messages from the warehouse (seven numbers, the first two representing the shipping time in days and the last five representing the price in cents). We do the appropriate work on this type of message (lines 27–36).

5. When we have received both reply messages, we create our final reply for the client and send it, resetting our variables, deleting our local reply queue, and resetting our form buttons (lines 40–56).

Listing 6.19 Reply Button Code

```
1 Private Sub cmdReply_Click()
2 ' This button is a temporary way to get our messages back from
3 ' the back end systems and process a reply for the client
4 On Error GoTo ErrorHandler
5
6    ' Get the message in the reply queue
7    Set ReplyMessage = IReplyQ.Receive(ReceiveTimeout:=10000)
8        If ReplyMessage Is Nothing Then
9            ' A message has not arrived from the warehouse or credit agency yet
10           intPress = MsgBox("Problem getting reply message off queue.", _
                     vbOKOnly, "Inquire server")
11           Exit Sub
12       End If
13    If ReplyMessage.AppSpecific = 1 Then
14        ' A message arrived from the credit agency
15        MessageHistory.AddItem "Reply from credit agency received"
16        CReplyBody = ReplyMessage.Body
17        If CReplyBody = 1 Then
18            CBody = "Credit has been approved."
19        ElseIf CReplyBody = 0 Then
20            CBody = "Credit has been denied."
21        Else
22            MessageHistory.AddItem "Invalid reply from credit agency"
23            CBody = ""
24        End If
25        AllEvents = AllEvents + 1
26    ElseIf ReplyMessage.AppSpecific = 2 Then
27        ' A message from the warehouse
28        MessageHistory.AddItem "Reply from warehouse received"
29        WReplyBody = ReplyMessage.Body
30        If Len(WReplyBody) = 7 Then
31            WBody = "Your book can be delivered in " & Left$(WReplyBody, 2) _
```

```
                          " & days.  Price: $" & _32 Mid$(WReplyBody, 3, 3) & "." &
                          ➡ Right$(WReplyBody, 2)
33          Else
34              MessageHistory.AddItem "Invalid reply from warehouse"
35              WBody = ""
36          End If
37          AllEvents = AllEvents + 1
38      End If
39      If AllEvents = 3 Then
40          ' Send Reply Message
41          ' Set our QueueInfo object equal to the ResponseQueueInfo _
            ' of the original client message
42          Set IClientReplyQInfo = Message.ResponseQueueInfo
43          ' Open the queue
44          Set IClientReplyQ = IClientReplyQInfo.Open(MQ_SEND_ACCESS,
            ➡ MQ_DENY_NONE)
45          ' Send the message
46          Set CreditReplyMessage = New MSMQMessage
47          Dim Body As String
48          Body = WBody & "  " & CBody
49          CreditReplyMessage.Body = Body
50          CreditReplyMessage.Send IClientReplyQ
51          MessageHistory.AddItem "Reply sent to client"
52          AllEvents = 1
53          IReplyQInfo.Delete
54          cmdReceive.Enabled = True
55          cmdReply.Enabled = False
56      End If
57
58      Exit Sub
59
60  ErrorHandler:
61      MessageHistory.AddItem "Error:  " & Err.Description
62
63  End Sub
```

Adding to the Global Variables

A few more objects have been added to our inquiry processing server. Our global declarations section should now look something like Listing 6.20. IReplyQ now represents our local reply queue, and IClientReplyQ represents the client's local reply queue.

Listing 6.20   Global Declaration of Objects

```
1 Option Explicit
2
3 '****Global declaration of objects
4 ' ** Local inquire q
5 Dim IReceiveQ As MSMQQueue
```

continues

Listing 6.20   continued

```
6 Dim IReceiveQInfo As MSMQQueueInfo
7 ' ** Warehouse and Credit inquire q's
8 Dim IWarehouseSendQInfo As MSMQQueueInfo
9 Dim IWarehouseSendQ As MSMQQueue
10 Dim ICreditSendQInfo As MSMQQueueInfo
11 Dim ICreditSendQ As MSMQQueue
12 ' ** Local reply q
13 Dim IReplyQ As MSMQQueue
14 Dim IReplyQInfo As MSMQQueueInfo
15 ' ** Outgoing to client reply q
16 Dim IClientReplyQInfo As MSMQQueueInfo
17 Dim IClientReplyQ As MSMQQueue
18 ' ** Messages
19 Dim Message As MSMQMessage              ' Incoming message from client
20 Dim CreditReplyMessage As MSMQMessage   ' Outgoing reply message to client
21 Dim WarehouseMessage As MSMQMessage     ' Outgoing message to warehouse
22 Dim CreditMessage As MSMQMessage        ' Outgoing message to credit
23 Dim ReplyMessage As MSMQMessage         ' Incoming reply from either
                                           ' warehouse or credit
24
25 ' ** Queries and Infos objects
26 Dim SendQListQuery As MSMQQuery
27 Dim SendQList As MSMQQueueInfos
28
29 ' ** Strings to get from or assign to message bodies
30 Dim WReplyBody As String     ' Message body from warehouse
31 Dim CReplyBody As Integer    ' Message body from credit
32 Dim WBody As String          ' Piece of final client reply message created
                                ' from warehouse message
33 Dim CBody As String          ' Piece of final client reply message created
                                ' from credit message
34 Dim ReplyToClient As String  ' Body of final client reply message created
                                ' from above 2 strings
35
36 ' ** Tests, messageboxes, and other variables
37 Dim AllEvents As Integer
38 Dim intPress As Integer
39 ' Get computer Name declarations -- used to make unique queue labels
40 Dim sBuffer As String
41 Dim lSize As Long
42 Const MAX_COMPUTERNAME_LENGTH As Long = 15&
```

This step concludes the development of the programs required to complete this chapter. In the next section, we run and test the programs from this and the preceding chapter.

Testing the e-books Application

In this chapter we have completed the code to support workflows 2 and 4 as well as 3 and 5. Coupled with the code in Chapter 5, we have all the programs to support our inquiry workflow. All that remains is to test them. As we did in Chapter 5, we will execute each step in turn and show you things as they occur. If any step does not complete as described, you need to debug the application before proceeding to the next step.

1. Start the credit check program. Use MSMQ Explorer to see that the input queue was created. Check the properties to see that the `ServiceTypeGUID` is what you expect.

2. Start the warehouse inventory check programs. Again use MSMQ Explorer to check the properties of the queue.

3. Start the order-processing server. Check that the input queue is registered.

4. Start the order-processing client.

5. Submit the default inquiry from the client.

6. Check the input queue for the server and see that one message is waiting on the queue. Examine the properties of the message and check the body. (You may need to press F5 to refresh the display.)

7. Click the Receive button on the server.

8. Check the input queue for the server. See that the message has been removed. (Remember to press F5 first!)

9. Check the input queues for the credit and inventory checks. Each should have a message on it. Display the properties for each message and look at the body. It should appear as you expect.

10. On each back-end system, click the Receive buttons and then check the input queues to see that the inquiries have been removed from them.

11. The reply queues for this application are all created as private queues and, as such, are not automatically displayed by MSMQ Explorer. To display the private queues for a computer, select the computer's icon in the MSMQ Explorer display and right-click to display the menu. Select Show Private Queues from the menu. The server's reply queue should have two messages on it. Examine the properties of these messages.

12. On the server, double-click the Processor Reply button to pick up these messages and send a response to the client. Check the queues and messages to ensure that this step is successful.

13. On the client, click the Receive button to get the response. A message box should be displayed with the response to your inquiry.

Well done! You now have built and tested a three-tier MSMQ application.

Summary

In this chapter we built the back-end programs for our inquiry workflow and added the function to our middle-tier to manage the interaction between the different back-end systems.

This chapter did not require any new MSMQ objects. In the next chapter, we revisit the `Receive` method, and we consider further the properties of a message.

In the next chapter, we also remove the Receive buttons from our programs and automate the entire workflow. In addition, we allow the server to process more inquiries while it is handling the first. We also introduce the concepts of message expiry and receive time-outs.

Chapter 7

Automating the Inquiry Workflow

e-Books Inquiry Workflow Automation

In the last two chapters, we have built the programs to support our inquiry workflow. We have completed this process manually to this point so that we could keep the concepts as simple as possible and make it easy for you to step through the flow while you test your application.

In this chapter, we're going to modify each of the programs that we've built. We're going to automate the processing of the replies.

A question you may be asking yourself is "what's the big deal?" So far we haven't done anything that you couldn't have achieved using a more traditional programming paradigm. Our client, server, and back-end systems have been dependent upon one another and we haven't used any of the store-and-forward features of message queuing to full effect. In the next chapter, we will be addressing that very issue by making use of message queuing's ability to store-and-forward. In the second half of this chapter, we will look at the features of expiry and timeout. These characteristics of message queuing allow us to build some business rules into our program to deal with the situation that arises when one or more of the systems do not respond in a timely manner.

But first, we will remove the need for user intervention on each of the long running processes. We're going to take away each of the "Receive" buttons, starting with the back-ends.

Receiving Messages Automatically

In this section, we're going to modify each use of the Receive method in each of our programs, in turn, so that they automatically wait for a message while at the same time allow normal processing to continue.

Receive is a method of the MSMQQueue object. It has associated with it several parameters, the most commonly used being ReceiveTimeout. This optional parameter, whose default is INFINITE, specifies, in milliseconds, how long MSMQ will wait for a message to arrive on the queue if there is not one available when the call is made. Using Receive as we have shown you so far will result in your program waiting as long as it takes for a message to arrive on the queue. The good news is that you will receive the next message to arrive on the queue. The bad news is your application will hang until that message arrives.

In this section, we are going to introduce another method of the MSMQQueue object, EnableNotification. This method issues a receive call on the queue, but immediately returns control to the program. When a message arrives on the queue the event handler will start a new process to handle the receipt of the message (or any other work done within the event code). EnableNotification is called with three parameters: Event, Cursor position, and ReceiveTimeout. ReceiveTimeout is, again, optional and indicates in milliseconds how long MSMQ will monitor the event. The Event parameter is not optional and is used to reference an MSMQEvent object. The Cursor parameter indicates at which cursor position MSMQ will wait for a message.

The MSMQEvent object has two events: Arrived and ArrivedError. The Arrived event is triggered when a message arrives on the queue. It does not return the message from the queue and you should note that if the queue permits shared access, it is possible that another program could receive the message before yours does. The Arrived event does not hold the message for your application in any way. The ArrivedError event is triggered when the ReceiveTimeout is exceeded on the queue without a message being delivered to the queue that was being monitored.

EnableNotification triggers only once for each invocation. Once it has triggered and you have processed the message, you need to reissue the EnableNotification, if you want to process other messages as they arrive on the queue.

Receiving Inquiries at the Back-End

We will start with our warehouse inventory check program. We'll work on one program at a time and test our results as we go. Reload the warehouse project that you created in Chapter 6, "Inquiry Workflow: Server to Back-End."

In Chapter 6, we built this program to create an input queue when it was started and to display a form. We had on the form a pushbutton that was used to attempt to receive a message from the input queue that we created. The user controlled when the receipt of the message occurred, provided that a message was on the queue.

We really want this program to receive messages automatically as they arrive, process them and send a reply, then wait for the next message. We're going to change how we receive messages using EnableNotification and the MSMQEvent object, instead of the Receive pushbutton. We've actually built most of the code already; the task in this chapter will be to move it around and kick it off.

When the form is first loaded we will enable notification on the input queue that we create.

Listing 7.1 shows the code that you have already for the form_load event as we built it in Chapter 6. We have added lines 23-24 (shown in bold type) to enable notification of a message arriving on the queue.

Listing 7.1   Warehouse Form Load

```
1 Private Sub Form_Load()
2
3 On Error GoTo ErrorHandler
4
5     '***********************
6     '* Create inquire queue
7     '***********************
8
9     Set IReceiveQ = New MSMQQueue
10    Set IReceiveQInfo = New MSMQQueueInfo
11
12    IReceiveQInfo.PathName = ".\Inquire_Warehouse_Queue"
13    IReceiveQInfo.Label = "Warehouse Inquire Queue"
14    IReceiveQInfo.ServiceTypeGuid = "{32188510-2883-11d3-A098-7A1CD3000000}"
15    IReceiveQInfo.Create
16    MessageHistory.AddItem "Inquire Queue: " & IReceiveQInfo.PathName
17
18    ' Open the queue for receive
19    Set IReceiveQ = IReceiveQInfo.Open(MQ_RECEIVE_ACCESS, MQ_DENY_NONE)
20    MessageHistory.AddItem "Queue opened for receive"
21
22    ' Enable event notification on the queue
23    Set IEvent = New MSMQEvent
24    IReceiveQ.EnableNotification IEvent
25    MessageHistory.AddItem "Waiting on queue"
26
27    Exit Sub
28
```

continues

Listing 7.1   continued

```
29 ErrorHandler:
30     ' If we are trying to create the queue and the queue already exists,
31     ' then we can continue on with opening the queue.
32     ' This code will be in every ErrorHandler that creates a queue.
33     If Err.Number = MQ_ERROR_QUEUE_EXISTS Then
34         Resume Next
35     End If
36
37     ' This error will occur if we just created the queue and it
38     ' has not been replicated throughout the MQIS yet. We will
39     ' just wait until it is (we just created it so we know it exists).
40     If Err.Number = MQ_ERROR_QUEUE_NOT_FOUND Then
41         Err.Clear
42         DoEvents
43         Resume
44     Else
45         MessageHistory.AddItem "Error: " & Err.Description
46     End If
47
48 End Sub
```

We have used the EnableNotification method of the MSMQQueue object to set up the condition that, when a message arrives on the queue defined by the Queue object, the event handler IEvent gets kicked off.

The next step is to create the event handler. Double-click on the Receive button that is still displayed on your main form to display its code form. You should see Listing 7.2, which we created in Chapter 6.

Listing 7.2   Warehouse Receive Command Button Code

```
1 Private Sub cmdReceive_Click()
2
3 On Error GoTo MyErrorHandler
4
5     '*************
6     '* Get Message
7     '*************
8
9     warehouse.SetFocus
10    Set IReceiveMessage = New MSMQMessage
11    Set IReceiveMessage = IReceiveQ.Receive(ReceiveTimeout:=10000)
12    ' This should not timeout, but if it does...
13    If IReceiveMessage Is Nothing Then
14        MessageHistory.AddItem "Unable to get message off queue"
15        Exit Sub
16    End If
17    MessageHistory.AddItem "Message Arrived"
18
```

```
19    '**********************
20    '* Query on database...
21    '**********************
22
23    Dim Body As String
24    Body = IReceiveMessage.Body
25    MessageHistory.AddItem Body
26.. .. .. .. ..
```

Cut this entire subroutine to the Windows clipboard. Create a subroutine into which you can paste the code that is in the clipboard from the receive button. The syntax is as follows:

 The Windows clipboard is a holding area for you to maintain application data, whether it is a picture, sound, or text from a document. The keystroke to copy data is Ctrl+Insert (or Ctrl+C), to paste data, use Shift+Insert (or Ctrl+V), to cut data, use Shift+Delete (or Ctrl+X).

Listing 7.3   Syntax for an Event Arrived Handler

```
1 Private Sub MSMQEvent_Arrived(ByVal MSMQQueue As Object, ByVal Cursor As Long)
```

Listing 7.4 shows our example.

 To add a new subroutine to the main form, position the cursor below the last subroutine and start typing. VB will do the rest!

Listing 7.4   Sample Event Handler for the Warehouse

```
1 Private Sub IEvent_Arrived(ByVal IReceiveQ As Object, ByVal Cursor As Long)
2     ' This is our event handler for our inquire receive queue
      ' (requests from client)
3
4     On Error GoTo ErrorHandler
5
6     '*************
7     '* Get Message
8     '*************
9
10    warehouse.SetFocus
11    Set IReceiveMessage = New MSMQMessage
12    Set IReceiveMessage = IReceiveQ.Receive(ReceiveTimeout:=10000)
13    ' This should not timeout, but if it does...
14    If IReceiveMessage Is Nothing Then
15        MessageHistory.AddItem "Unable to get message off queue"
16        GoTo Wait
```

continues

Listing 7.4   continued

```
17    End If
18
19    MessageHistory.AddItem "Message Arrived"
20
21    '****************
22    '*  Open reply
23    '*  queue for send
24    '****************
25
26    Set ISendQInfo = New MSMQQueueInfo
27    Set ISendQ = New MSMQQueue
28    ' We get the information about what queue to open from the message
29    ' we just received; the MSMQMessage.ResponseQueueInfo property.
30    Set ISendQInfo = IReceiveMessage.ResponseQueueInfo
31    Set ISendQ = ISendQInfo.Open(MQ_SEND_ACCESS, MQ_DENY_NONE)
32    MessageHistory.AddItem "Reply queue opened for send"
33
34    '**********************
35    '* Query on database...
36    '**********************
37
38    Dim Body As String
39    Body = IReceiveMessage.Body
40    MessageHistory.AddItem Body
41
42    '**************
43    'Send the reply
44    '**************
45
46    Set ISendMessage = New MSMQMessage
47    ' For the sake of testing, we will send the same reply every time
48    Body = "0301995"
49    ISendMessage.Body = Body
50    ISendMessage.AppSpecific = 2
51
52    ' Send the Message
53    ISendMessage.Send ISendQ
54    MessageHistory.AddItem "Reply message sent"
55
56    GoTo Wait
57
58 ErrorHandler:
59    If Err.Number = MQ_ERROR_QUEUE_NOT_FOUND Then
60        Err.Clear
61        DoEvents
62        Resume
63    End If
64
65    MessageHistory.AddItem "Error: " & Err.Description
```

```
66
67 Wait:
68    ' Wait on Q -- reset the event handler
69    Set IEvent = New MSMQEvent
70    IReceiveQ.EnableNotification IEvent
71
72 End Sub
```

When we set up this event we set an infinite timeout on it. Therefore we should never get the event 'ArrivedError'. We'll save discussion of this for when we discuss time-outs and message expiry in the second half of this chapter. We reset the event notification before any exit from the sub (lines 16, 56, and 67–70).

Finally, delete the Receive pushbutton and the code associated with it (see Figure 7.1). We won't need this anymore!

Figure 7.1

Warehouse application without Receive command button.

Before we go any further, we'll test what we have so far. Rerun the tests from the end of Chapter 6, in the same order. The only step you will not have to make is the pressing of the receive button on the inventory check program.

Once you have the inventory check program working correctly make these same changes to the credit check program and run the tests again. Make sure both of these programs function correctly before moving on to the next stage.

Receiving Inquiries at the Server

We will return next to the order-processing server that we built in Chapter 6 and write the code to remove the need for the button used to process the inquiries coming in from the client. Reload the project that you built in Chapter 6 for the order-processing server.

The changes that we will make to the server at this stage are identical to those we just made for each of the back-end systems. When the server's main form is first loaded we will enable event notification on the input queue and we will move the code associated with the Receive pushbutton to the Arrived event handler.

Double-click on the main form to display its code form. You will see the Form_load subroutine that we created in Chapter 5 and shown in Listing 7.5. Add, as before, the lines to set up event notification.

Listing 7.5   Form Load for Server Program

```
1 Private Sub Form_Load()
2
3 On Error GoTo ErrorHandler
4
5    ' Set back end reply tester
6    AllEvents = 1
7
8    ' Create Local Queue
9    Set IReceiveQInfo = New MSMQQueueInfo
10   IReceiveQInfo.PathName = ".\Inquire_Server_Queue"
11
12   ' Creation of the label.
13   ' First we get the computer name for the local machine
14   Dim ComputerName As String
15   sBuffer = Space$(MAX_COMPUTERNAME_LENGTH + 1)
16   lSize = Len(sBuffer)
17   If GetComputerName(sBuffer, lSize) Then
18       ComputerName = Left(sBuffer, lSize)
19   End If
20
21   ' Then we include the computer name in the label
22   IReceiveQInfo.Label = "Inquire Queue on " & ComputerName
23
24   ' Specific ServiceType for Inquire Queues
25   IReceiveQInfo.ServiceTypeGuid = "{0BF4DBD1-254F-11d3-A091-00A024A5BFC5}"
26   IReceiveQInfo.Create
27   MessageHistory.AddItem "Inquire Queue: " + IReceiveQInfo.PathName
28
29   ' Open Q
30   Set IReceiveQ = IReceiveQInfo.Open(1, 0)
31
32   ' Wait on Q
33   Set IQEvent = New MSMQEvent
34   IReceiveQ.EnableNotification IQEvent
35
36   ' ********************
37   ' Find warehouse queue
38
39   Set SendQList = New MSMQQueueInfos
40   Set SendQListQuery = New MSMQQuery
41   Set IWarehouseSendQInfo = New MSMQQueueInfo
42   Set SendQList = SendQListQuery.LookupQueue(ServiceTypeGuid:=
     ➥"{32188510-2883-11d3-A098-7A1CD3000000}")
43
44   ' Only need one available queue; no need to go through entire index
45   SendQList.Reset
46   Set IWarehouseSendQInfo = SendQList.Next
47
48   If IWarehouseSendQInfo Is Nothing Then
49       intPress = MsgBox("No warehouse queue was found", vbOKOnly,
         ➥ "e-books inquire server")
```

```
50        End
51    End If
52
53    ' *********************
54    ' Same for credit queue
55
56    Set SendQList = New MSMQQueueInfos
57    Set SendQListQuery = New MSMQQuery
58    Set ICreditSendQInfo = New MSMQQueueInfo
59    Set SendQList = SendQListQuery.LookupQueue(ServiceTypeGuid:=
      ➥ "{32188511-2883-11d3-A098-7A1CD3000000}")
60    SendQList.Reset
61    Set ICreditSendQInfo = SendQList.Next
62    If ICreditSendQInfo Is Nothing Then
63        intPress = MsgBox("No credit queue was found", vbOKOnly,
          ➥ "e-books inquire server")
64        End
65    End If
66
67    Exit Sub
68
69 ErrorHandler:
70 .. .. .. ..
```

Now, the first time a message arrives on the input queue the event handler will be triggered. However, we need to build the event handler! First, we'll get the bulk of the code we need from our existing Receive pushbutton. Double-click on the Receive pushbutton to display its code form and cut the code to the clipboard. Create a new subroutine for the Arrived event handler into which this code can be pasted, as shown in Listing 7.6.

Listing 7.6   Code for the Event Handler in the Inquire Server

```
1 Private Sub IQEvent_Arrived(ByVal IReceiveQ As Object, ByVal Cursor As Long)
2
3     On Error GoTo ErrorHandler
4     Main.SetFocus
5
6     ' Get Message
7     Set Message = IReceiveQ.Receive
8     ' This should not timeout, but if it does...
9     If Message Is Nothing Then
10        MessageHistory.AddItem "Unable to get message off queue"
11        Set IQEvent = New MSMQEvent
12        IReceiveQ.EnableNotification IQEvent
13        Exit Sub
14    End If
15
16    '*************
```

continues

Listing 7.6   continued

```
17      'Parse Message
18
19      Call Parse
20
21      '*******************
22      'Create Reply Queue
23
24      Set IReplyQInfo = New MSMQQueueInfo
25
26      ' We want to create unique reply queue instances.
27      '          We will incorporate the machine name
28      '          and a date/time stamp in the pathname.
29      Dim PathName As String
30      Dim ComputerName As String
31
32      ' First we get the computer name for the local machine
33      sBuffer = Space$(MAX_COMPUTERNAME_LENGTH + 1)
34      lSize = Len(sBuffer)
35      If GetComputerName(sBuffer, lSize) Then
36          ComputerName = Left(sBuffer, lSize)
37      End If
38
39      ' Now we make a private queue with these unique strings in the pathname
40      PathName = ".\private$\Server_Inquire_Reply_Queue_" & ComputerName & "_"
        ➥ & Format(Now, "ddddd ttttt")
41      IReplyQInfo.PathName = PathName
42      IReplyQInfo.Label = "Inquire Warehouse Reply Queue"
43      IReplyQInfo.Create
44
45      ' Open
46      Set IReplyQ = IReplyQInfo.Open(MQ_RECEIVE_ACCESS, MQ_DENY_NONE)
47      MessageHistory.AddItem "Reply queue created and opened for receive"
48
49      '*******************************************
50      'Send the requests to the back-end systems
51
52      ' Set the ResponseQueueInfo
53      Set WarehouseMessage.ResponseQueueInfo = IReplyQInfo
54
55      ' Send the message
56
57      ' Test for ErrorHandler
58      Dim WYesNo As Integer
59      WYesNo = 1   'Test for ErrorHandler to know if we failed on warehouse
60
61      ' Open queue
62      Set IWarehouseSendQ = IWarehouseSendQInfo.Open(MQ_SEND_ACCESS,
        ➥ MQ_DENY_NONE)
63      MessageHistory.AddItem "Warehouse queue opened for send"
```

```
64    WYesNo = 0
65
66    WarehouseMessage.Send IWarehouseSendQ
67    MessageHistory.AddItem "Warehouse inquire sent"
68
69    ' Ditto for the credit message
70    Set CreditMessage.ResponseQueueInfo = IReplyQInfo
71
72    ' Open queue
73    Set ICreditSendQ = ICreditSendQInfo.Open(MQ_SEND_ACCESS, MQ_DENY_NONE)
74    MessageHistory.AddItem "Credit queue opened for send"
75
76 ' Send
77    CreditMessage.Send ICreditSendQ
78    MessageHistory.AddItem "Credit inquire sent"
79
80
81    Exit Sub
82
83 ErrorHandler:
84    If Err.Number = MQ_ERROR_QUEUE_NOT_FOUND Then
.. .. .. ..' Code to check for new queue at either the warehouse or
          ' credit agency
85    End If
86
87    Set IQEvent = New MSMQEvent
88    IReceiveQ.EnableNotification IQEvent
89
90 End Sub
```

We must be careful to re-enable the event notification in the case where we do not get the message off the queue or some other error (lines 11-12 and in the ErrorHandler [not shown]).

Finally, and again as before, delete the Receive button and the code associated with it.

Rerun the tests from the end of Chapter 6. Make sure that each of the programs works properly before proceeding to the next section. We are about to start looking at the replies!

Receiving Replies at the Client

In Chapter 5, we built the client program to receive the reply message when a button was pressed. We are now going to automate this operation. As with the server and backend processes, we will wait an infinite period for the response to arrive, for now. We will start waiting for an event on our reply queue when the inquiry message is sent to the server.

Reload the client project from Chapter 5. Double-click on the Submit button to display the button's code form. At the end of the code block add the line to enable notification on the reply queue. Listing 7.7 shows the code for the Submit button from Chapter 5 with the lines (48 and 49) to enable event notification.

Listing 7.7   Enable Event Notification on the Reply Queue in the Client

```
1 Private Sub cmdSubmit_Click()
2 'Submit an book inquiry
3
4 On Error GoTo ErrorHandler
5     cmdSubmit.Enabled = False
6     txtLastName.Enabled = False
7     txtFirstName.Enabled = False
8     txtAddressOne.Enabled = False
9     txtAddressTwo.Enabled = False
10    txtCity.Enabled = False
11    txtState.Enabled = False
12    txtZIP.Enabled = False
13    txtCreditCardNumber.Enabled = False
14    txtBookTitle.Enabled = False
15    txtBookAuthorLast.Enabled = False
16    txtBookAuthorFirst.Enabled = False
17
18    '*******************
19    'Create reply queue
20    '*******************
21
22    Set IReplyQInfo = New MSMQQueueInfo
23    IReplyQInfo.Label = "Book Inquire Reply Queue"
24
25    ' We want to create unique reply queue instances.
26    ' We will accomplish this by incorporating the machine name
27    ' and the date/time in the queue name
28    Dim PathName As String
29    Dim ComputerName As String
30    ' First we get the computer name for the local machine
31    sBuffer = Space$(MAX_COMPUTERNAME_LENGTH + 1)
32    lSize = Len(sBuffer)
33    If GetComputerName(sBuffer, lSize) Then
34        ComputerName = Left(sBuffer, lSize)
35    End If
36    ' Now we make a private queue with the computer name and time in it
37    PathName = ".\private$\Client_Inquire_Reply_Queue_" & ComputerName & "_"
➥ & (Format(Now, "ddddd ttttt"))
38    IReplyQInfo.PathName = PathName
39
40    IReplyQInfo.Create
41    MessageHistory.AddItem "Reply Queue Created"
42
43    ' Open reply queue for receive
```

```
44   Set IReplyQ = IReplyQInfo.Open(MQ_RECEIVE_ACCESS, MQ_DENY_RECEIVE_SHARE)
45   MessageHistory.AddItem "Reply Queue Opened for Receive"
46
47   ' Wait on reply queue
48   Set IReplyQEvent = New MSMQEvent
49   IReplyQ.EnableNotification IReplyQEvent
50
51   '*****************************
52   'Build and send inquire message
53   '*****************************
54
55   .. .. .. ..
```

As before, the next step is to build the event handler. Double-click on the existing receive button and cut the code into the clipboard. Add a new subroutine to be the Arrived event handler, as shown in Listing 7.8 (line 1). Simply copy the code from the receive button into the event handler. There is no difference in what will happen, only that now we will receive and process the reply automatically. It will not be necessary to re-enable event notification on the queue since this queue will only receive the one message.

Listing 7.8   Client Event Handler for Response Message

```
1 Private Sub IReplyQEvent_Arrived(ByVal IReplyQ As Object, ByVal Cursor As Long)
2
3    Screen.MousePointer = vbHourglass
4    Main.SetFocus
5
6 Start:
7    ' Get the message
8    Set Message = New MSMQMessage
9    Set Message = IReplyQ.Receive(ReceiveTimeout:=10000)
10   If Message Is Nothing Then
11       intPress = MsgBox("Unable to receive inquire reply message",
         ➥ vbInformation, "e-books Client")
12       intPress = MsgBox("Try again?", vbYesNo, "e-books Client")
13           If intPress = vbNo Then
14               cmdSubmit.Enabled = True
15               Screen.MousePointer = vbDefault
16               IReplyQInfo.Delete
17               Exit Sub
18           Else
19               GoTo Start
20           End If
21   End If
22
23   ' Display reply message
24   Dim ReplyMessage As String
25   ReplyMessage = Message.Body
```

continues

Listing 7.8   continued

```
26    intPress = MsgBox("Message arrived from e-books server" _
      & Chr(13) & ReplyMessage, vbInformation, "Client")
27
28    ' Submit the order?
29    intPress = MsgBox("Submit order?", vbOKCancel, "Client")
30    If intPress = 1 Then
31        intPress = MsgBox("Order submitted", vbOKOnly, "Client")
32    Else
33        'They changed their mind
34        intPress = MsgBox("Order not submitted at this time.",
          ➡ vbInformation, "Client")
35    End If
36
37    ' Destroy the reply queue
38    IReplyQInfo.Delete
39 GoTo Reset
40
41    Exit Sub
42
43 MyErrorHandler:
44    intPress = MsgBox("Error #" & Err.Number & ": " & Err.Description,
      ➡ vbInformation, "Client")
45
46 Reset:
47    Call cmdClear_Click
48    IReplyQInfo.Delete
49    MessageHistory.AddItem "Inquire reply queue deleted"
50
51 End Sub
```

Delete the Receive pushbutton and the code associated with it, and rerun the tests of the complete application, as shown in Figure 7.2. Again, make sure the tests complete successfully before continuing to the next step.

Receiving Replies at the Server

The final pushbutton to be removed from our application is the server's Process Replies button. In Chapter 6 it was necessary to push this button twice in succession to receive and process the replies from the back-end. Now we will enable event notification on the reply queue when the inquiries are sent to the back-end systems.

In Chapter 6, the code associated with the Process Replies button was run twice. The first time, it simply received the message on the queue, and the second, it received the message and built a response for the client from the two replies that it held. The automated operation will behave in the same way for now. In the second half of this chapter, we will modify this behavior as we consider time-outs and expiry.

Figure 7.2

Client application with-
out Receive command
button.

We need to enable event notification on the reply queue when the inquiry messages
are sent to the back-end systems. The code to send the messages is contained within
the event handler for the inquiry queue. Double-click on the main form and scroll
down to the subroutine handling the Arrived event. At the end of the code add the
lines to enable event notification on the reply queue, as shown in Listing 7.9 (lines
37 and 38). (This listing is a continuation from Listing 7.6.)

Listing 7.9   Code to Enable Event Notification on the Reply Queue in the Inquire Server

```
1  ' Open
2    Set IReplyQ = IReplyQInfo.Open(MQ_RECEIVE_ACCESS, MQ_DENY_NONE)
3    MessageHistory.AddItem "Reply queue created and opened for receive"
4
5    '*****************************************
6    'Send the requests to the back-end systems
7
8    ' Set the ResponseQueueInfo
9    Set WarehouseMessage.ResponseQueueInfo = IReplyQInfo
10
11   ' Send the message
12
13   ' Test for ErrorHandler
14   Dim WYesNo As Integer
15   WYesNo = 1  'Test for ErrorHandler to know if we failed on warehouse
16
17   ' Open queue
```

continues

Listing 7.9 continued

```
18    Set IWarehouseSendQ = IWarehouseSendQInfo.Open(MQ_SEND_ACCESS,
    ➥ MQ_DENY_NONE)
19    MessageHistory.AddItem "Warehouse queue opened for send"
20    WYesNo = 0
21
22    WarehouseMessage.Send IWarehouseSendQ
23    MessageHistory.AddItem "Warehouse inquire sent"
24
25    ' Ditto for the credit message
26    Set CreditMessage.ResponseQueueInfo = IReplyQInfo
27
28    ' Open queue
29    Set ICreditSendQ = ICreditSendQInfo.Open(MQ_SEND_ACCESS, MQ_DENY_NONE)
30    MessageHistory.AddItem "Credit queue opened for send"
31
32    ' Send
33    CreditMessage.Send ICreditSendQ
34    MessageHistory.AddItem "Credit inquire sent"
35
36    ' Wait on ReplyQ
37    Set IReplyQEvent = New MSMQEvent
38    IReplyQ.EnableNotification IReplyQEvent
39    Exit Sub
```

The next step is to build the subroutine to handle an event. Cut the code from the process reply pushbutton into a new subroutine in the main form, just as you did for each of the other programs. Create a new Arrived event handler and place the code from the Process Reply button into it, as shown in Listing 7.10.

Listing 7.10 Code for the Reply Queue Event Handler

```
1 Private Sub IReplyQEvent_Arrived(ByVal IReplyQ As Object, ByVal Cursor As Long)
2
3 On Error GoTo ErrorHandler
4 Main.SetFocus
5
6    ' Get the message in the reply queue
7    Set ReplyMessage = IReplyQ.Receive(ReceiveTimeout:=10000)
8        If ReplyMessage Is Nothing Then
9            ' A message has not arrived from the warehouse or credit agency yet
10           intPress = MsgBox("Problem getting reply message off queue.",
                ➥ vbOKOnly, "Inquire server")
11           Set IReplyQEvent = New MSMQEvent
12           IReplyQ.EnableNotification IReplyQEvent
13           Exit Sub
14       End If
15
16   If ReplyMessage.AppSpecific = 1 Then
17       ' A message arrived from the credit agency
```

```
18          MessageHistory.AddItem "Reply from credit agency received"
19          CReplyBody = ReplyMessage.Body
20          If CReplyBody = 1 Then
21              CBody = "Credit has been approved."
22          ElseIf CReplyBody = 0 Then
23              CBody = "Credit has been denied."
24          Else
25              MessageHistory.AddItem "Invalid reply from credit agency"
26              CBody = ""
27          End If
28
29          ' Set tester
30          AllEvents = AllEvents + 1
31
32      ElseIf ReplyMessage.AppSpecific = 2 Then
33          ' A message from the warehouse
34          MessageHistory.AddItem "Reply from warehouse received"
35          MessageHistory.AddItem "Message Arrived"
36          WReplyBody = ReplyMessage.Body
37          If Len(WReplyBody) = 7 Then
38              WBody = "Your book can be delivered in " & Left$(WReplyBody, 2)
            ➥ & " days.  Price:  $" & _
39                  Mid$(WReplyBody, 3, 3) & "." & Right$(WReplyBody, 2)
40          Else
41              MessageHistory.AddItem "Invalid reply from warehouse"
42              WBody = ""
43          End If
44
45          ' Set tester
46          AllEvents = AllEvents + 1
47
48      End If
49
50      If AllEvents = 3 Then
51          ' Send Reply Message
52          ' Set our QueueInfo object equal to the ResponseQueueInfo of the
            ' original client message
53          Set IClientReplyQInfo = Message.ResponseQueueInfo
54          ' Open the queue
55          Set IClientReplyQ = IClientReplyQInfo.Open(MQ_SEND_ACCESS,
            ➥ MQ_DENY_NONE)
56          ' Create the message
57          Set ClientReplyMessage = New MSMQMessage
58          Dim Body As String
59          Body = WBody & "  " & CBody
60          ClientReplyMessage.Body = Body
61          ' Send the message
62          ClientReplyMessage.Send IClientReplyQ
63          MessageHistory.AddItem "Reply sent to client"
64          AllEvents = 1
65          ' Delete our local reply queue
```

continues

Listing 7.10   continued

```
66          IReplyQInfo.Delete
67          ' Reset body values
68          CBody = " "
69          WBody = " "
70          Exit Sub
71      End If
72
73      ' Wait on Q (for next reply message)
74      Set IReplyQEvent = New MSMQEvent
75      IReplyQ.EnableNotification IReplyQEvent,
76
77      Exit Sub
78
79  ErrorHandler:
80      MessageHistory.AddItem "Error:   " & Err.Description
81
82  End Sub
```

Finally, delete the Process Reply button and the code associated with it (see Figure 7.3). Test the application as you did before. This time you will not have to interact with any of the programs after the submit button is pressed.

Figure 7.3

Server application without Reply or Receive command button.

Once you have tested this successfully you will be ready to proceed to the next section. So far, we have assumed that all the programs are available and responding. In the next section, we will consider receive time-outs and message expiry, and look at how these features may be used to further automate our processing of the inquiry.

Discarding Obsolete Messages Automatically

We now have our inquiry workflow working to automatically receive and forward the messages required to process the user's request. So far, we have assumed that all of the elements required to process our workflow are available. That is, each of the programs is running and a connection is available between the different machines on which the programs run. If this were assumed to be the case, we need not be using message queuing to provide the infrastructure for our application. (That is not to say that it still would not be the best choice. However, if the network and programs are 100% available there are other paradigms that would work also.)

Of course, it is not the case that the network and programs are always available. In this case, we will modify our programs to handle the case where some part of the inquiry cannot be processed. We are going to introduce timeouts on the receive method and expiry as a message property. These are the tools that help us break out of an automatic receive if nothing arrives, and then prevent something from arriving late. Having determined that a response is not forthcoming in a timely manner, we will then introduce business logic to our application to make a judgement about the value of the information that is missing.

For the purposes of this application, we are going to set some ground rules about time-outs and business rules. The values that we select are somewhat arbitrary and could be given realism by performance study and usage patterns. Everyone needs to start somewhere, and so we will set a baseline and show you where our assumptions could be modified to suit your own business needs.

The rules that we will use:

- A customer will not wait more than 30 seconds for a response to his or her inquiry. (This is one of the rules that can be modified based on your own business experience. If it is found that your customers are, on average, more or less patient, you can change this rule.)

- In the event that the credit agency does not respond, we will automatically accept transactions of up to $50 in value. This comes down to a business risk assessment, and is purely arbitrary.

- In the event that the inventory cannot be checked, we will notify the customer that delivery will be within six weeks, a period within which we have determined we can satisfy 95% of all special orders.

Let's consider first the timeouts. In our inquiry workflow we have a total of five places where we perform the receive method. (It may help you to refer to the concept web for this discussion.)

1. In the server to support message flow 1, client to server.
2. In each of the back-end systems to support message flows 2 and 4, server to back-end systems.
3. In the server to support message flows 3 and 5, back-end replies to server.
4. In the client to support message flow 6, server reply to client.

The first two of these four cases relate to receipt of the inquiry by the long-running processes of the server and the back-ends. We do not want to associate any time-out value with these requests. Rather, we want each of these to occur every time and as soon as a message arrives.

The latter two of these four cases relate to the processing of a single reply. It is these that we wish to set time-out values for.

Setting the Server Response Time-Out in the Client

We stated in our rules that the maximum time a customer would wait for an answer was 30 seconds from when he or she submits the request. We will, therefore, set a time-out on the receipt of the reply of 30 seconds. This also means that the request is valid for only 30 seconds, so we will set an expiry on the request message of 30 seconds.

In the case where the reply is received before the time-out interval expires we will receive an Arrived event. If a message does not arrive within the time-out period, we will receive an ArrivedError event, something which we will have to add code to our application for.

In the following paragraphs of this section we will illustrate these design steps as we modify the programs we have built up to this point.

The first step is to set the expiry time on the request message that we send to the server. Open, again, the project for the client application. Double-click on the Submit pushbutton to display its code form. Immediately before the message is sent to the server's input queue set the expiry property to the time-out interval.

The MSMQMessage object has two fields that describe the expiry properties of a message. They are MaxTimeToReachQueue and MaxTimeToReceive.

The MaxTimeToReachQueue property specifies a period, in seconds, during which the message must be written to the target queue. After the timer is exceeded, the message will be discarded, according to the value of the Journal property (more on this in Chapter 11). The default value of this property is LONG_LIVED, a value specified by the MSMQ Administrator and, by default, 90 days (no message should ever come close to 90 days).

The MaxTimeToReceive property specifies a period, in seconds, during which the message must be read from the target queue by an application. It includes the time taken to reach the target queue. The default value of this property is INFINITE.

When both MaxTimeToReachQueue and MaxTimeToReceive are used together, MaxTimeToReceive takes precedence over MaxTimeToReachQueue, except if the MaxTimeToReachQueue is exceeded before the message is written to the target queue and before the MaxTimeToReceive is exceeded.

For our example, we are interested in the maximum length of time that the message is valid, regardless of where it is. We will, therefore, use the MaxTimeToReceive property. Listing 7.11 shows the code built earlier to build and send the message from our client with our message expiry code added to it.

Listing 7.11   Sending the Message from the Client

```
1  ' Build message
2    Set Message = New MSMQMessage
3    Message.Label = "Book Inquire Message"
4    Message.Body = Order.Serialize
5
6    ' Set responsequeueinfo of message equal to the reply queue we just created
7    Set Message.ResponseQueueInfo = IReplyQInfo
8
9    ' Set MaxTimeToReceive
10   Message.MaxTimeToReceive = 30
11
12   MessageHistory.AddItem "Message created"
```

The second step is to set the receive time-out interval on our reply queue for the client. Continuing with the modification of the code associated with the Submit button, change the line in which the EnableNotification method is called as shown in Listing 7.12. Unlike the message expiry, the value of the ReceiveTimeout parameter is given in milliseconds.

Listing 7.12   Further Modification of the EnableNotification Method

```
1  ' Wait on reply queue
2    Set IReplyQEvent = New MSMQEvent
3    IReplyQ.EnableNotification IReplyQEvent, , 30000
```

The third and final step is to build the event handler for the ArrivedError event. This code will be executed in the event that the server does not give a response within the assigned period. We could put some business logic in here to apply the rules we introduced earlier, or we could display a default message asking the customer to try again later. We'll do the latter to differentiate this from the processing that the server will perform in its event handler. Listing 7.13 shows the code for our ArrivedError event handler. It should be associated with the code in the main form.

Listing 7.13   The code for the ArrivedError Event Handler

```
1 Private Sub IReplyQEvent_ArrivedError(ByVal IReplyQ As Object, ByVal
  ➥ ErrorCode As Long, ByVal Cursor As Long)
2 'Our wait on the inquire reply queue timed out.
3
4 On Error GoTo ErrorHandler
5
6    Main.SetFocus
```

continues

Listing 7.13   The code for the ArrivedError Event Handler

```
 7     intPress = MsgBox("Your request cannot be processed at this time. "
    ➥ & Chr(13) & _
         "Please try again later.", vbInformation, "Client")
 8
 9     ' Destroy the reply queue
10     IReplyQInfo.Delete
11
12     Call cmdClear_Click
13     Exit Sub
14
15 ErrorHandler:
16     MessageHistory.AddItem "Error: " & Err.Description
17     Call cmdClear_Click
18 End Sub
```

Setting the Back-End Response Time-Out in the Server

The second time-out that we must set is on the messages going from the server to the back-end systems. We need to allow for the time taken to get the message to the server and the time taken within the server to build the messages for the back-end. When the server receives the inquire message, we can read the MaxTimeToReceive property of that message. The good news is that this property will be adjusted for the time it took for the message to get to us. For example, our inquire message's MaxTimeToReceive is 30 seconds. If it takes 1 second for that message to get to our server and our server to pick the message up off the queue, when the server gets the message its MaxTimeToReceive will be 29 seconds. We can take this value and pass it on to our requests to the back-end. We simply take the client's inquire message's MaxTimeToReceive, subtract our application latency from that value, take our new value, and pass it to our back-end inquire messages' MaxTimeToReceive properties.

Consider the following example:

- A message is sent from the client to the server at exactly 11:30 a.m. The message from the client will continue to be valid until 11:30.30, at which time the client will time-out the pending receive.
- The message is received and processed by the server, and just before it is sent to the back-end system the time is 11:30.02.
- The difference between the time now and the time the message was sent is 2 seconds. This will be deducted from the expiry time when the message is forwarded to the back-end.

Continuing this process, we then need to set the time-out for which we will wait to receive the message from the reply queue. Remember, however, that we are expecting to receive two replies to our request. The first time we post the receive notice we will set the time-out equal to the value of the expiry that we sent in the message (remember to adjust for the fact that the value of the message expiry is in seconds and the value of the event time-out is in milliseconds). Since the first reply can be received at any time during this period, we must decrement the second receive time-out by the actual time taken by the first reply. Because we are also going to pass the expiry value through the back end applications, we can read the reply message's expiry value and apply it to our second wait. For example, the warehouse passes the inquire message expiry to its reply. The server's event fires and it picks up the message. The remaining expiry value on that reply message, minus application latency, then becomes the event notification time-out for the second wait (for the credit message, in this case). In the case where either of the receive intervals expires before a message is received, we will get an ArrivedError event.

Finally, so far we have run the time allowed for receipt and processing of the back-end replies right up to the client time-out. This makes the assumption that it would take no time whatsoever for us to build and send a response to the client. Clearly, this is not realistic. We must make an assessment of what is realistic and deduct this value from the expiry interval that we receive on the incoming message. We will set an arbitrary interval of 3 seconds to build and send a default response to the client in the event we receive an ArrivedError event for the servers reply queue (we do not receive a reply from one of the back-end systems).

In the following paragraphs of this section, we will illustrate these design steps as we modify the programs we have built up to this point.

First, we must take a look at our event handler for receiving the requests from the client. We have to pass the message expiry value to our new inquire messages sent to the back-end systems, while also accounting for our application latency. Listing 7.14 shows the IQEvent_Arrived code with the additional code needed to pass the expiry value in bold.

1. First, as soon as we receive the message, we must pick up the current machine time so that we can later calculate the application latency. This is shown in line 16. You will notice that we are calling a function, "GetDateTimeEx." The code for this function is shown in Listing 7.15. Our current time variable is called strTime.

2. Next, we pick up the MaxTimeToReceive value from the message we just received. This MaxTimeToReceive value is essentially the lifetime of the message, and is the key feature allowing us to manage the lifetime of our entire workflow. The MaxTimeToReceive value was set by the client to be 30 seconds. If it took one second for the server to pick it up, then its current value would be 29 seconds. We assign whatever the value is to a variable "MsgExp" in line 17.

3. When we are ready to send our request out to the back-ends, we must again get the current time; this time is assigned to the variable "strTimei" (line 80).

4. We then calculate the application latency (strTimei - strTime) in line 81.

5. For calculation purposes, we convert our strTimei (application latency from line 81) to a long (line 82).

6. We can then calculate our outgoing message's expiry. We take the incoming message expiry, subtract our application latency, and also subtract at this time our (arbitrary) 3 seconds to allow us to process the final reply back to the client (line 83).

7. We can then pass this value to our Message.MaxTimeToReceive (line 85) and display the value in our listbox for our tracking purposes during testing (line 86).

This procedure is repeated for the credit message (our second outgoing message) in lines 102-108.

Listing 7.14   IQEvent_Arrived: Passing the Expiry Value of the Received Inquire Message to the Sent Inquire Message, Accounting for Application Latency

```
1  Private Sub IQEvent_Arrived(ByVal IReceiveQ As Object, ByVal Cursor As Long)
2     On Error GoTo ErrorHandler
3     Main.SetFocus
4
5     ' Get Message
6     Set Message = IReceiveQ.Receive
7     ' This should not timeout, but if it does...
8     If Message Is Nothing Then
9        MessageHistory.AddItem "Unable to get message off queue"
10       Set IQEvent = New MSMQEvent
11       IReceiveQ.EnableNotification IQEvent
12       Exit Sub
13    End If
14
15    ' Get the current time and message expiry time left
16    strTime = GetDateTimeEx
17    MsgExp = Message.MaxTimeToReceive
18
19    ' Wait on Q -- reset the event handler to enable multiple treads
20    Set IQEvent = New MSMQEvent
21    IReceiveQ.EnableNotification IQEvent
22
23    ' Display the expiry from the message
24    MessageHistory.AddItem "Message Arrived"
25    MessageHistory.AddItem "Message Life: " & MsgExp
26
27    '*************
28    'Parse Message
```

```
29    '*************
30
31    Call Parse
32
33    '******************
34    'Create Reply Queue
35    '******************
36
37    Set IReplyQInfo = New MSMQQueueInfo
38
39    '******Creating the reply queue for the warehouse to reply to
40    ' We want to create unique reply queue instances.
41    ' We will accomplish this by incorporating the machine name
42    ' and the date/time (to mil secs) in the queue name
43    Dim PathName As String
44    Dim ComputerName As String
45    ' First we get the computer name for the local machine
46    sBuffer = Space$(MAX_COMPUTERNAME_LENGTH + 1)
47    lSize = Len(sBuffer)
48    If GetComputerName(sBuffer, lSize) Then
49        ComputerName = Left(sBuffer, lSize)
50    End If
51    ' Now we make a private queue with these unique strings
52    PathName = ".\private$\Server_Inquire_Reply_Queue_" & ComputerName &
       ➥ "_" & Format(Now, "ddddd ttttt")
53    IReplyQInfo.PathName = PathName
54    IReplyQInfo.Label = "Inquire Warehouse Reply Queue"
55    IReplyQInfo.Create
56    Set IReplyQ = IReplyQInfo.Open(MQ_RECEIVE_ACCESS, MQ_DENY_NONE)
57
58    MessageHistory.AddItem "Reply queue created and opened for receive"
59
60
61    '****
62    'Send
63    '****
64
65    ' Set the ResponseQueueInfo
66    Set WarehouseMessage.ResponseQueueInfo = IReplyQInfo
67
68    ' Send the message
69
70    ' Test for ErrorHandler
71    Dim WYesNo As Integer
72    WYesNo = 1   'Test for ErrorHandler to know if we failed on warehouse
73
74    ' Open queue
75    Set IWarehouseSendQ = IWarehouseSendQInfo.Open(MQ_SEND_ACCESS,
       ➥ MQ_DENY_NONE)
76    MessageHistory.AddItem "Warehouse queue opened for send"
77    WYesNo = 0
```

continues

Listing 7.14 continued

```
78
79    ' Make new MaxTimeToReceive
80    strTimei = GetDateTimeEx
81    strTimei = strTimei - strTime
82    MsgExpi = CLng(strTimei)
83    MsgExpi = MsgExp - MsgExpi - 3
84        '(We take the extra three seconds off at this time to account for
          'our reply processing latency)
85    WarehouseMessage.MaxTimeToReceive = MsgExpi
86    MessageHistory.AddItem "WarehouseMessage.MaxTimeToReceive : " & _
          WarehouseMessage.MaxTimeToReceive
87
88    WarehouseMessage.Send IWarehouseSendQ
89    MessageHistory.AddItem "Warehouse inquire sent"
90
91    ' Wait on ReplyQ
92    Set IReplyQEvent = New MSMQEvent
93    IReplyQ.EnableNotification IReplyQEvent, , (MsgExpi * 1000)
94
95    ' Ditto for the credit message
96    Set CreditMessage.ResponseQueueInfo = IReplyQInfo
97
98    ' Open queue
99    Set ICreditSendQ = ICreditSendQInfo.Open(MQ_SEND_ACCESS, MQ_DENY_NONE)
100   MessageHistory.AddItem "Credit queue opened for send"
101
102   ' Make new MaxTimeToReceive
103   strTimei = GetDateTimeEx
104   strTimei = strTimei - strTime
105   MsgExpi = CLng(strTimei)
106   MsgExpi = MsgExp - MsgExpi - 3
107   CreditMessage.MaxTimeToReceive = MsgExpi
108   MessageHistory.AddItem "CreditMessage.MaxTimeToReceive : " & _
          CreditMessage.MaxTimeToReceive
109
110   ' Send
111   CreditMessage.Send ICreditSendQ
112   MessageHistory.AddItem "Credit inquire sent"
113
114   Exit Sub
```

Our "GetDateTimeEx" function resides in our module for this project. We first assign values to the type "SYSTEMTIME" (year all the way down to millisecond) in lines 4-13. We declare the function as well in the declarations of our module (lines 15 and 16). Within the function (lines 22-36), we get the local machine time and then create the "GetDateTimeEx" string from that value. (Because MaxTimeToReceive is only in seconds, we assign only seconds to our GetDateTimeEx.)

Listing 7.15   Inquire Server Module, Including Code to Retrieve Current Local System Time

```
1 Option Explicit
2
3 ' NT Kernel API Declares
4 Private Type SYSTEMTIME
5         wYear As Integer
6         wMonth As Integer
7         wDayOfWeek As Integer
8         wDay As Integer
9         wHour As Integer
10        wMinute As Integer
11        wSecond As Integer
12        wMillisecond As Integer
13 End Type
14
15 Private Declare Sub GetLocalTime _
16    Lib "Kernel32.dll" (lpSystemTime As SYSTEMTIME)
17
18 Public Declare Function GetComputerName _
19    Lib "kernel32" Alias "GetComputerNameA" (ByVal lpBuffer As String,
   ➥ nSize As Long) As Long
20
21
22 Public Function GetDateTimeEx() As String
23 ' Gets the Date and Time with extended time (including milliseconds)
24    Dim udtSystemTime As SYSTEMTIME
25
26    GetLocalTime udtSystemTime
27    With udtSystemTime
28       GetDateTimeEx = Right$("0000" & CStr(.wYear), 4) & _
29           Right$("00" & CStr(.wMonth), 2) & _
30           Right$("00" & CStr(.wDay), 2) & _
31           Right$("00" & CStr(.wHour), 2) & _
32           Right$("00" & CStr(.wMinute), 2) & _
33           Right$("00" & CStr(.wSecond), 2)
34    End With
35
36 End Function
```

7

The second step is to set the time-out interval for the receipt of the first and second replies and to set the expiry for the final client reply message. The first receive time-out interval will be the same as the message expiry interval that was just used to send the inquiries (line 93 of Listing 7.14). The second will be set to the value of the first incoming reply message's expiry (remember that we are about to enable this same expiry passing feature in our back-end systems) minus application latency (in the same manner as before, except this time we are passing the value to the ReceiveTimeout of the enable notification instead of the MaxTimeToReceive of the message). The final reply to the client will have an expiry built the same way as the other inquire messages, that is the last message's MaxTimeToReceive minus application latency. The code in Listing 7.16 shows, in context, what we have added to the Arrived event handler to account for the receive time-outs for the reply waits (lines 16-17 and 104-111) and also for the final expiry of the credit reply message (lines 80-85).

Listing 7.16   Adding to the Arrived Event Handler

```
1  Private Sub IReplyQEvent_Arrived(ByVal IReplyQ As Object, ByVal Cursor As Long)
2
3      On Error GoTo ErrorHandler
4      Main.SetFocus
5
6      ' Get the message in the reply queue
7      Set ReplyMessage = IReplyQ.Receive(ReceiveTimeout:=10000)
8          If ReplyMessage Is Nothing Then
9              ' A problem occured receiving the message
10             intPress = MsgBox("Problem getting reply message off queue.",
                 ➥ vbOKOnly, "Inquire server")
11             GoTo Wait
12             Exit Sub
13         End If
14
15     ' Get the current time and message expiry time left
16     strTime = GetDateTimeEx
17     MsgExp = ReplyMessage.MaxTimeToReceive
18
19     If ReplyMessage.AppSpecific = 1 Then
20         ' A message arrived from the credit agency
21         MessageHistory.AddItem "Reply from credit agency received"
22         ' Display the expiry from the message
23         MessageHistory.AddItem "Message Life: " & MsgExp
24         CReplyBody = ReplyMessage.Body
25         If CReplyBody = 1 Then
26             CBody = "Credit has been approved. "
27         ElseIf CReplyBody = 0 Then
28             CBody = "Credit has been denied. "
29         Else
30             MessageHistory.AddItem "Invalid reply from credit agency"
31             CBody = ""
32         End If
33
34         ' Set tester
35         AllEvents = AllEvents + 1
36
37     ElseIf ReplyMessage.AppSpecific = 2 Then
38         ' A message from the warehouse
39         MessageHistory.AddItem "Reply from warehouse received"
40         ' Display the expiry from the message
41         MessageHistory.AddItem "Message Life: " & _MsgExp
42         WReplyBody = ReplyMessage.Body
```

```
43        If Len(WReplyBody) = 7 Then
44            Dim Cents As Long
45            Cents = Right$(WReplyBody, 2)
46            Dim Dollar As Long
47            If Mid$(WReplyBody, 3, 1) = "0" Then
48                Dollar = Mid$(WReplyBody, 4, 2)
49            Else
50                Dollar = Mid$(WReplyBody, 3, 3)
51            End If
52            Dim Days As Long
53            If Left$(WReplyBody, 1) = "0" Then
54                Days = Mid$(WReplyBody, 2, 1)
55            Else
56                Days = Left$(WReplyBody, 2)
57            End If
58            WBody = "Your book can be delivered in " & Days &
          ➥ " days.  Price:  $" & _
              Dollar & "." & Cents & ". "
59        Else
60            MessageHistory.AddItem "Invalid reply from warehouse"
61            WBody = ""
62        End If
63
64        ' Set tester
65        AllEvents = AllEvents + 1
66    End If
67
68    If AllEvents = 3 Then
69        ' Send Reply Message
70        ' Set our QueueInfo object equal to the ResponseQueueInfo of the
          ' original client message
71        Set IClientReplyQInfo = Message.ResponseQueueInfo
72        ' Open the queue
73        Set IClientReplyQ = IClientReplyQInfo.Open(MQ_SEND_ACCESS,
          ➥ MQ_DENY_NONE)
74        ' Create the message
75        Set ClientReplyMessage = New MSMQMessage
76        Dim Body As String
77        Body = CBody & WBody
78        ClientReplyMessage.Body = Body
79        ' Make new MaxTimeToReceive
80        strTimei = GetDateTimeEx
81        strTimei = strTimei - strTime
82        MsgExpi = CLng(strTimei)
83        MsgExpi = MsgExp - MsgExpi
84        ClientReplyMessage.MaxTimeToReceive = MsgExpi
85        MessageHistory.AddItem "ClientReplyMessage.MaxTimeToReceive : " & _
              ClientReplyMessage.MaxTimeToReceive
86        ' Send the message
87        ClientReplyMessage.Send IClientReplyQ
88        MessageHistory.AddItem "Reply sent to client"
```

continues

Listing 7.16   continued

```
 89          ' Reset tester
 90          AllEvents = 1
 91          ' Delete our local reply queue
 92          IReplyQInfo.Delete
 93          ' Reset body values
 94          CBody = ""
 95          WBody = ""
 96          Exit Sub
 97      End If
 98
 99      GoTo Wait
100
101  ErrorHandler:
102      intPress = MsgBox("Error #" & Err.Number & ": " & Err.Description,
         ➥ vbOKOnly, _
          "MSMQ From Scratch Inquire Server")
103
104  Wait:
105      ' Wait on Q (for next reply message)
106      Set IReplyQEvent = New MSMQEvent
107      strTimei = GetDateTimeEx
108      strTimei = strTimei - strTime
109      MsgExpi = CLng(strTimei)
110      MsgExpi = MsgExp - MsgExpi
111      IReplyQ.EnableNotification IReplyQEvent, , (MsgExpi * 1000)
112
113  End Sub
```

The last step is to build an event handler for the ArrivedError event. This event will occur if either of the replies do not arrive on the server's response queue before the time-out interval expires. Under such a circumstance, the server will reply with the information it has, using the business rules to provide default responses for the information not available.

For example, if the credit agency or the warehouse does not respond, we will apply the business rules to give a standard answer. If neither respond in time, we will give a complete, default response to the client.

The code in Listing 7.17 shows the complete ArrivedError event handler for the server's back-end reply queue. It should be inserted into the code for the main form immediately following the Arrived event handler for the server's back-end reply queue.

You can see that in the case we have no reply from the credit agency (line 6), we create the default response, "Your credit has been approved" (line 7). If we have no reply from the warehouse, we create the default response, "Book can be shipped in no later than six weeks" (line 10). In this way we get a reply back to the client no matter what, based on the business logic we set in place beforehand.

Listing 7.17   The Complete ArrivedError Event Handler

```
1 Private Sub IReplyQEvent_ArrivedError(ByVal IReplyQ As Object, ByVal
  ➥ ErrorCode As Long, ByVal Cursor As Long)
2
3    On Error GoTo ErrorHandler
4    Main.SetFocus
5
6    If CBody = "" Then
7        CBody = "Your credit has been approved. "
8        Exit Sub
9    If WBody = "" Then
10        WBody = "Book can be shipped in no later than six weeks. "
11        Exit Sub
12    End If
13
14    ' Set our QueueInfo object equal to the ResponseQueueInfo of the
       ' original client message
15    Set IClientReplyQInfo = Message.ResponseQueueInfo
16    ' Open the queue
17    Set IClientReplyQ = IClientReplyQInfo.Open(MQ_SEND_ACCESS, MQ_DENY_NONE)
18    ' Create the message
19    Set ClientReplyMessage = New MSMQMessage
20    ClientReplyMessage.Body = CBody & WBody
21    ' Make new MaxTimeToReceive
22    strTimei = GetDateTimeEx
23    strTimei = strTimei - strTime
24    MsgExpi = CLng(strTimei)
25    MsgExpi = MsgExp - MsgExpi
26    ClientReplyMessage.MaxTimeToReceive = MsgExpi
27    MessageHistory.AddItem "ClientReplyMessage.MaxTimeToReceive : " & _
28    ClientReplyMessage.MaxTimeToReceive
29    ' Send the message
30    ClientReplyMessage.Send IClientReplyQ
31    MessageHistory.AddItem "Reply sent to client"
32    AllEvents = 1
33    ' Delete our local reply queue
34    IReplyQInfo.Delete
35    ' Reset body values
36
37    Exit Sub
38
39 ErrorHandler:
40    intPress = MsgBox("Error #" & Err.Number & ": " & _
       Err.Description, vbOKOnly, "MSMQ From Scratch Inquire Server")
41
42 End Sub
```

Setting the Back-End Response Time-Out in the Back-End

Finally, we need to arrange for the responses sent by the back-end to expire correctly. We will use the same processing steps as we did with the server.

Double-click on the main form of the back-end program. (You will need to repeat these steps for each of the two back-end programs, warehouse inventory and credit verification.) The code shown in Listing 7.18 is that for the main form of the back-end program. Set the MaxTimeToReceive equal to that of the request, less the difference between the time the message was received and the current time (application latency).

Listing 7.18   The Back-End Program's Main Form

```
1 Private Sub IEvent_Arrived(ByVal IReceiveQ As Object, ByVal Cursor As Long)
2    ' This is our event handler for our inquire receive queue
     ' (requests from client)
3
4    On Error GoTo ErrorHandler
5
6    '*************
7    '* Get Message
8    '*************
9
10   warehouse.SetFocus
11   Set IReceiveMessage = New MSMQMessage
12   Set IReceiveMessage = IReceiveQ.Receive(ReceiveTimeout:=10000)
13   ' This should not timeout, but if it does...
14   If IReceiveMessage Is Nothing Then
15      MessageHistory.AddItem "Unable to get message off queue"
16      Set IEvent = New MSMQEvent
17      IReceiveQ.EnableNotification IEvent
18      Exit Sub
19   End If
20
21   ' Get the current time and message expiry time left
22   strTime = GetDateTimeEx
23   MsgExp = IReceiveMessage.MaxTimeToReceive
25
26   ' Display the expiry from the message
27   MessageHistory.AddItem "Message Arrived"
28   MessageHistory.AddItem "Message Life: " & MsgExp
29
30   '****************
31   '*  Open reply
32   '* queue for send
33   '****************
34
35   Set ISendQInfo = New MSMQQueueInfo
36   Set ISendQ = New MSMQQueue
37   ' We get the information about what queue to open from the message
38   ' we just received; the MSMQMessage.ResponseQueueInfo property.
```

```
39    Set ISendQInfo = IReceiveMessage.ResponseQueueInfo
40    Set ISendQ = ISendQInfo.Open(MQ_SEND_ACCESS, MQ_DENY_NONE)
41    MessageHistory.AddItem "Reply queue opened for send"
42
43    '**********************
44    '* Query on database...
45    '**********************
46
47    Dim Body As String
48    Body = IReceiveMessage.Body
49    MessageHistory.AddItem Body
50
51    '**************
52    'Send the reply
53    '**************
54
55    Set ISendMessage = New MSMQMessage
56    ' For the sake of testing, we will send the same reply every time
57    Body = "0301995"
58    ISendMessage.Body = Body
59    ISendMessage.AppSpecific = 2
60
61    ' Make new MaxTimeToReceive
62    strTimei = GetDateTimeEx
63    strTimei = strTimei - strTime
64    MsgExpi = CLng(strTimei)
65    MsgExpi = MsgExp - MsgExpi
66    ISendMessage.MaxTimeToReceive = MsgExpi
67    MessageHistory.AddItem "ISendMessage.MaxTimeToReceive : " & _
          ISendMessage.MaxTimeToReceive
68
69
70    ' Send the Message
71    ISendMessage.Send ISendQ
72    MessageHistory.AddItem "Reply message sent"
73
74
75    Exit Sub
76
77 ErrorHandler:
78    If Err.Number = MQ_ERROR_QUEUE_NOT_FOUND Then
79        Err.Clear
80        DoEvents
81        Resume
82    End If
83
84    MessageHistory.AddItem "Error: " & Err.Description
85
86    ' Wait on Q -- reset the event handler
87    Set IEvent = New MSMQEvent
88    IReceiveQ.EnableNotification IEvent
89
90 End Sub
```

Summary

You can see that this chapter starts to make the distinction between messaging and home-grown applications. We took our existing applications that we built in previous chapters and expanded their ability to provide more logical processing. By allowing for asynchronous processing, we don't require a long-running application to constantly poll for messages. Instead, our application will "sleep" until a message arrives, at which point an event will be generated. In this case, the event is a Receive process.

We introduced additional properties to messages such as Timeout, MaxTimeToReachQueue and MaxTimeToReceive. These properties allowed us to specify business rules that are associated with how the message should be processed. As detailed in the chapters, the rules that apply to the application are purely arbitrary and would need to be modified for a specific application's role.

In the next chapter, we will confirm an order, completing the code that executes when the user clicks Confirm at the end of the inquire process. In this, we will examine transactional processing and messaging's guaranteed one-time delivery.

Part 4

Advanced MSMQ Application Development: Processing an Order

Chapter 8

Order-Confirmation Workflow: Client to Server

e-books Book Order Workflow

In the last three chapters, we have built the programs to complete the inquiry workflow in the book purchase process. These were steps 1 through 6 in the Concept Web. We left the client application asking the user to confirm or cancel the order, as shown in Figure 8.1.

Figure 8.1

Closing display of the client after the inquiry workflow completes.

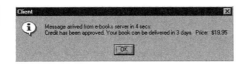

In this and the next chapter, we add the programs to support workflow steps 7 through 9, those that complete the customer's order.

The inquiry workflow demonstrates the message queuing paradigm of request/reply. The customer's inquiry causes a request for information to be sent to a server. A reply is formulated in response to the request and sent to the client. The inquiry workflow is purely an information-gathering process: We need to verify the books availability and price and the customer's ability to pay for the book. No change is made to the state of any of our business data. If the transaction fails to complete because a message is lost or a machine fails, we may lose the customer but not the integrity of our business data.

The order workflow, on the other hand, causes a change in state of our business data. As a result of the user confirming the order, we issue a billing request to the credit card company and a dispatch order to the warehouse. After the customer confirms the order, we cannot lose any piece of the data associated with the order. We must bill for a book we dispatch, or we lose money; and we must dispatch a book that we bill for, or we lose a customer. This chapter introduces the concepts of data persistence and workflow management.

By the end of this chapter, you will have modified and built the programs to support workflow 7 in the Concept Web. You will have learned about data persistence as it relates to MSMQ and about unit-of-work management.

Data Persistence

MSMQ has three different types of messages when it comes to data persistence: express, recoverable, and transactional. Up until this point, you have sent only express messages.

An express message resides in memory. If the machine that is holding the message stops for any reason, the message is lost with no chance of recovery.

In terms of memory, we are referring to *random access memory* (RAM). All information that relates to an application is stored in RAM for use with the operating system. If the system is restarted, for example, the RAM is erased. Therefore, when the system is restarted, the information that was in RAM is no longer available.

A recoverable message is logged to disk and can be recovered in the event of a machine failure. Delivery of a recoverable message is guaranteed, but it may be delivered more than once. For instance, consider the event of a receiving machine failing after receiving the message but before sending a receipt confirmation to the sender. When the receiving machine is restored, the sender detects that it is holding a message for which it does not have receipt confirmation and forwards the message again. (This receipt confirmation is a MSMQ internal processing step and has nothing whatsoever to do with the acknowledgment and journal messages that we introduce in Chapter 10, "Delivery Confirmation and Audit.")

A transactional message is logged to disk and can be recovered in the event of a system failure. Its delivery is also guaranteed. It differs from the recoverable message in two important ways. First, a transactional message is guaranteed to be delivered only once. Second, transactional messages can be part of a managed unit of work, whereas express and recoverable messages cannot.

Transactional messages can be written only to queues for which the transactional property is set. Express and recoverable messages cannot be written to such queues.

Our order workflow uses transactional messages only.

While we're talking about message types, it's worth comparing their performance features. Express messages are by far the fastest of the three. MSMQ can process thousands of express messages a second. Transactional messages are the slowest because more communication must occur between the MSMQ servers to guarantee the once-only delivery of the message. Even then, though, MSMQ can process tens of transactional messages every second. If performance is critical to your application, you need to take benchmarks of message throughput given the hardware that you have available.

Units of Work

A business unit of work is a number of steps that must occur all together, or not at all, to preserve the integrity of the operation. Using our example, when the customer confirms the order for a book, we want to receive the order, ship the book, and bill the credit card all together or not at all. To ship the book and not bill the credit card would be disastrous for us, and we certainly would not satisfy our customers if we lost their orders, or worse, billed their credit cards without shipping the books.

 Incidentally, a unit of work is often referred to as a *transaction*, and you will see this term used in MSMQ.

MSMQ makes a distinction between two types of units of work. The first is simpler to use and is known as an internal transaction. The steps of an internal transaction relate only to MSMQ operations. The second is set up a little differently but is then used in the same way. It is known as an external transaction, and the steps contained in it affect not only the update of MSMQ resources but also resources managed by other resource managers, such as SQL database tables. Microsoft Transaction Server (MTS) is required to manage an internal transaction, whereas Microsoft Distributed Transaction Coordinator (DTC) is required to manage the external transaction.

For our order-processing server, the only resources that we need to update are managed by MSMQ, and so we need only an internal transaction. Later, in the next chapter when we consider the back-end systems, we spend more time considering an external transaction.

Order-Confirmation Architecture

So far, the customer has requested price and availability information about a particular book and supplied his or her billing and shipping information on an electronic form. In the inquiry workflow of Chapters 6 and 7, we used that information to gain approval for the purchase using the supplied credit card information and the details about the book. At the conclusion of the workflow, we left the user with a message box that said something like "Book xyz that you requested is available for immediate shipping at a price of $n." The user must now choose one of two push buttons: OK and Cancel, as shown in Figure 8.2.

Figure 8.2

Client interface for order confirmation.

If the user selects Cancel, no processing is required by the order-processing server, so we do not need to build a workflow here to handle it. In Chapter 5, "Inquiry Workflow: Client to Server," we associate some code with this button to reset the fields of the entry form and prepare for a new inquiry.

If the user selects OK, the order-processing server is responsible for managing the order, thereby ensuring that all elements of the unit of work either occur together or not at all. Our order-processing server is an entirely new application that can run independently of the inquire server.

We have chosen to make our server "stateless"; that is, it will not remember anything about the previous inquiry workflow. Instead, we will maintain all information about the request in the client application. This approach is preferable to others because the data from the inquiry is transient and relevant only if the client program is active. As a consequence, our server can be more straightforward.

Thus, although at first glance the server may appear to simply be receiving a confirm order message, the server actually receives all the data that was sent in the inquiry workflow.

With that explanation of the circumstances surrounding the execution of the order workflow, let's consider its steps and behavior. The flowchart in Figure 8.3 shows the process steps to be executed by the client program.

We have already said that the steps of this workflow need to be executed together or not at all. Because we are expecting our programs to manage a unit of work, MSMQ requires us to use transactional messages and queues. As we have already said, these are going to guarantee that the data gets to the appropriate destination queue once, and once only. This approach allows us to decouple our client application from the remainder of the order processing. Because MSMQ guarantees the once and once-only delivery of the message, we can commit to the customer that the order is complete as soon as the message is sent from the client to the server.

Figure 8.3

Client process steps required by order-confirmation workflow.

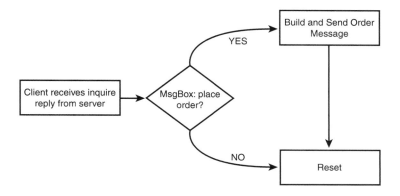

The server then receives its input message from a transactional queue named TReceiveQ and pushes messages to transactional queues for the credit card agency and the warehouse. All three steps must occur together, or they can't occur at all. If a failure occurs, the original confirmation message remains on the queue to be retried later.

You will have noticed that we have not mentioned reply processing. The reason is that we won't be doing any in the confirmation workflow. We are using the guarantee of the delivery of the messages to decouple the generation of the request from the processing of it. In Chapter 10, "Delivery Confirmation and Audit," Chapter 11, "Processing the Journal Queues," and Chapter 12, "Customer Service Application," we use the acknowledgment features of MSMQ to notify us if something catastrophic happens to our message.

In the next section, we consider in detail the steps of the order workflow as they affect the client and the server, and we modify and build new programs to implement those steps.

Application Architecture—Order-Processing Server

The flowchart in Figure 8.4 details the process steps our order-processing server takes in support of the order workflow. When the order-processing server starts, it attempts to create its input queue if one does not already exist, starts a unit of work, and then enables notification on this queue with an unlimited time-out. The queue that is created has the transactional property set for handling transactional messages. For now, we do nothing more than receive the message from the queue.

Figure 8.4

Flowchart for order-processing server.

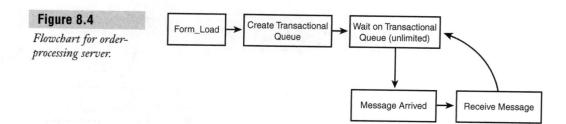

We made a design choice with respect to the input queue for the order-processing server and what happens to the queue when the program ends. MSMQ's guarantee of message delivery means that the nature of the workflow can be such that the final confirmation of the order is given to the customer even before the server has picked up the message. The consequence of this approach is that to confirm the order, all we need is a suitable input queue.

Our options were:

- To have the MSMQ administrator create and manage the input queue. In this case before the server can be run on a particular machine, the queue must be created. In addition, certain machines must be designated as servers for receipt of orders. As a consequence of this choice, messages build up on this queue until a server program is running to process them.

- To have the program create the input queue. This option does not preclude use of the preceding option and may be seen as a fail-safe measure if the program is started on a new machine. This option also helps to ensure that the ServiceTypeGUID property of the queue is set correctly. If the administrator creates the queue, this property must be set manually by typing it into the definition of the queue.

- To delete the queue if no server process is running to monitor it. This choice may result in the client being unable to submit an order, which would then defeat the purpose of using message queuing for this application. The power of message queuing is its capability to decouple applications.

- To have the MSMQ administrator delete the queue when it becomes redundant. By allowing the administrator to determine which queues are active, the administrator can control where new orders are routed.

In our example, we are going to create the queue either from the program or from MSMQ Explorer and delete the queue only from MSMQ Explorer.

You may also have noticed that this workflow has nothing whatsoever to do with the previous inquiry workflow. We will build an entirely separate program to process order requests. This technique gives the application administrator greater flexibility as to where and how many instances of the different server processes are running. For instance, if tests show that for every order that is confirmed we receive three inquiries and that each inquiry takes twice as long to process as an order, we may decide to run six instances of the order-processing server to handle inquiries and only one to process inquires.

The following pseudocode, shown in Listing 8.1, shows the program logic for the server program in our order-processing workflow.

Listing 8.1   Pseudocode for the Order-Processing Server

```
1    BEGIN
2        IF ( exists( OrderQ ) ) THEN
3                OpenQ( OrderQ )
4        ELSE
5                CreateQ( OrderQ, PUBLIC, TRANSACTIONAL )
6                OpenQ( OrderQ )
7        DO FOREVER
8                TxnID = BeginTxn()
9                OrderMsg = GetMsg( OrderQ, WAIT = UNLIMITED, TxnID )
10               IF NOT OK THEN
11               AbortTxn( TxnID )
12               ELSE
13                       CommitTxn( TxnID )
14       END
15   END
```

Our new server program will, like the inquiry server, be a long-running process. It will be set up to receive messages automatically. Once again we will build a VB project with a minimal user interface so that you can see what is going on. Figure 8.5 shows a picture of our form.

Figure 8.5

Example of order-processing server program.

Create a new VB project, using the instructions in Chapter 2, "Introducing Our Example: Designing the Solution." Call the project Order and the main form Main. On the main form add a list box control called MessageHistory.

We must add code for three events. The first is the form load event, during which we will attempt to create the input queue and enable notification on it, and the second is the arrival of a message. We will do some cleanup processing during the `form unload` event. In the following sections, we add the appropriate code to these events.

Form Load Event

When our confirmation server starts, it will create a queue onto which it will receive orders if one doesn't already exist on the machine on which it is running. If a queue does exist, the confirmation server will attempt to open it. Because the client and the server are decoupled, the client can queue orders when the server is not running and still confirm the order to the customer. Therefore, when the server starts up (after it has been run once), there are likely to be messages for it to process.

Double-click on the main form to display its code form. We will create and open the queue and enable event notification on it.

CreateQ()

We've created queues a few times now, but this time we need to create a transactional queue. The only difference between this CreateQ and those created in Chapters 3-7 is that the `transactional` property is set by setting the `IsTransactional` parameter of the `Create` method to `True`, as shown in line 11 of Listing 8.2. Note that we have created a new `ServiceTypeGUID` for use with all OrderQs (remember, GUIDGen will create a new one for you).

Listing 8.2   Code to Create the Transactional Input Queue

```
1 Private Sub Form_Load()
2
3     On Error GoTo ErrorHandler
4
5     ' Create Local Queue
6     Set TReceiveQInfo = New MSMQQueueInfo
7     TReceiveQInfo.PathName = ".\Transaction_Server_Queue"
8
9     ' Specific ServiceType for Transaction Queues
10     TReceiveQInfo.ServiceTypeGuid = "{CCD602C0-2E9F-11D3-A0AD-04D4B6000000}"
11     TReceiveQInfo.Create IsTransactional:=True
12     MessageHistory.AddItem "Transaction Queue: " + TReceiveQInfo.PathName
```

The next step is to open and enable notification on this queue. We again open the queue for receive access. We use a new event object for this queue. Listing 8.3 shows the rest of the code that we will add to the `form load` event at this time.

Listing 8.3   Code to Wait for an Order Message

```
14   ' Open Q
15   Set TReceiveQ = TReceiveQInfo.Open(1, 0)
16
17   ' Wait on Q
18   Set TQEvent = New MSMQEvent
19   TReceiveQ.EnableNotification TQEvent
20
21   Exit Sub
```

Finally, we need to include our error handler. This error handler is much like the error handlers from our inquire applications and needs no further explanation. It is shown in Listing 8.4.

Listing 8.4   Code for the Transaction Server Form Load Error Handler

```
23 ErrorHandler:
24
25 If Err.Number = MQ_ERROR_QUEUE_EXISTS Then
26       Resume Next
27   End If
28
29 If Err.Number = MQ_ERROR_QUEUE_NOT_FOUND Then
30       Err.Clear
31       DoEvents
32       Resume
33   End If
34
35 MessageHistory.AddItem "Error #" & Err.Number & ": " & Err.Description
36
37 End Sub
```

Message Arrived Event

When we get notified of a message arriving on the input queue we must:

1. Create a new MSMQ internal transaction.
2. Read the message from the queue within the unit of work.
3. Process the message.
4. Commit the unit of work.
5. Re-enable notification on the input queue.

Double-click on the main form to display its code form. After the code that you created for the form load event, create a new subroutine for the event handler. The subroutine is called vTReceiveQEvent_Arrived, as outlined in Listing 8.5.

Listing 8.5   `Arrived` Event Handler

```
1    Private Sub TQEvent_Arrived(ByVal vTReceiveQ As Object,
➡ ByVal Cursor As Long)
2        'Begin Internal Transaction
3        'Receive message from input queue
4        'Process the message
5        'Commit the transaction
6        'Enable notification on the input queue
7    Exit Sub
```

Begin Internal Transaction

We are going to introduce two new objects to support our unit-of-work management: the MSMQTransactionDispenser and the MSMQTransaction.

The MSMQTransactionDispenser creates new MSMQ internal transaction objects. It has one method, BeginTransaction and no properties. The BeginTransaction method creates a new MSMQTransaction object.

The MSMQTransaction object represents a managed unit of work and is supplied as a parameter on invocations of the send and receive methods, as you will see in a moment. The MSMQTransaction object has two methods: Commit and Abort. Commit completes the unit of work, and Abort rolls back any updates made to MSMQ resources under the transaction instance.

Listing 8.6 shows the code that we will add to the event handler to set up the transaction object.

Listing 8.6   Code to Begin a Transaction

```
1  Private Sub TQEvent_Arrived(ByVal IReceiveQ As Object, ByVal Cursor As Long)
2
3      On Error GoTo ErrorHandler
4      Main.SetFocus
5
6      ' Begin Transaction
7      Set TransDisp = New MSMQTransactionDispenser
8      Set Transaction = New MSMQTransaction
9      Set Transaction = TransDisp.BeginTransaction
10     MessageHistory.AddItem "Beginning transaction"
```

Receive Message from Input Queue

Receiving a message from the queue is much the same as it was in previous chapters of the book. Listing 8.7 shows our example.

Listing 8.7   Code to Get a Message

```
12 ' Get Message
13   Set Message = TReceiveQ.Receive (, , ,10000)
14    ' This should not time out, but if it does...
15   If Message Is Nothing Then
16      MessageHistory.AddItem "Unable to get message off queue"
17      Set TQEvent = New MSMQEvent
18      TReceiveQ.EnableNotification TQEvent
19      Exit Sub
20   End If
21
22   MessageHistory.AddItem "Message received: "
23   MessageHistory.AddItem "      " & Message.Body
```

Commit the Transaction

After the elements in the unit of work have completed successfully, we can commit the transaction, thereby making the changes effective. Until the transaction is committed, the input message is still held on the input queue (albeit in an "invisible" state) and whatever other messages may have been sent are not available to be received from their destination queues.

Completing the transaction is as easy as calling the `Commit` method of the transaction object, as we show in Listing 8.8.

Listing 8.8   Code to Commit the Transaction

```
25 ' Commit the transaction
26   Transaction.Commit
```

Re-Enable Notification on the Input Queue

Reenabling notification on the input queue is the same as it was for the `form load` event earlier in this chapter. Listing 8.9 shows the code to be added to the end of our event handler. Notice that we also have to re-enable event notification in case we exit the subroutine through the error handler.

Listing 8.9   Error Trapping and Reenabling Event Notification

```
28     GoTo Wait
29
30     Exit Sub
31
32 ErrorHandler:
33     MessageHistory.AddItem "Error #" & Err.Number & ": " & Err.Description
34
35 Wait:
36     Set TQEvent = New MSMQEvent
37     TReceiveQ.EnableNotification TQEvent
38
39 End Sub
```

8

Form Unload Event

When the program ends, all we have to do is close any MSMQ objects that are open. For now, the only open object is the input queue. Remember, we are not deleting the queue because we want clients to be able to submit orders even while the server is down.

You can add the code in Listing 8.10 by simply typing it into the Code window.

Listing 8.10   Code for the `form_unload` Event

```
1 Private Sub Form_QueryUnload(Cancel As Integer, UnloadMode As Integer)
2 '***** When the user exits, we confirm the exit and close the order queue
3
4    On Error GoTo ErrorHandler
5
6    Dim i As Integer
7
8    i = MsgBox("Do you want to exit?", vbYesNo + vbQuestion, "Order Server")
9        If i = vbNo Then
10            Cancel = 1
11        Else
12            TReceiveQ.Close
13            Unload Me
14            End
15        End If
16
17    Exit Sub
18
19 ErrorHandler:
20    Resume Next
21
22 End Sub
```

Application Architecture—Order-Processing Client

In Chapter 5, we left the client displaying a message box with the response to the customer's inquiry and two push buttons: OK and Cancel. We added code to the Cancel push button in Chapter 5. In this chapter, we are adding the code for the Confirm button. The work performed in Chapter 7, "Automating the Inquiry Workflow," to automate receipt of the response does not affect the flow of the application.

We now need to perform the following steps:

1. Locate a suitable input queue for an order-processing server, such as the one we just built.

2. Open the transactional queue.

3. Create the order message containing all the information about the customer, the order, and the price of the book the customer wants to purchase.

4. Send the message to the transactional queue.

5. Display an order-confirmation message for the user.

6. Reset the entry fields of the Order Entry window in preparation for the next customer.

Reload the VB project containing the client application.

Locate and Open the Server Queue

The first step is to locate a suitable order queue. We will add the code to find an order queue to the form_load processing. If a suitable queue is not available, then the client won't start.

Double-click on the main form to display its code form. At the moment, the procedure locates the inquiry queue for the order-processing server and displays a selection box if more than one is found. Immediately after the server's inquiry queue is opened, we need to locate and open the order queue for the order-processing server.

The steps are much the same as they were in Chapter 5 when we added the code to locate the server's inquiry queue. We will open the first queue that matches the search argument. We will, again, base our search on the ServiceTypeGUID property.

The first step is to establish the search index by using the LookupQueue method of the MSMQQuery object. We supply the ServiceTypeGUID that we want to match as a parameter to the LookupQueue method. This action gives us a MSMQQueueInfos object.

The next step is to reset the index cursor to the first queue found by using the Reset method of the MSMQQueueInfos object.

We then get the properties of a single queue by assigning the properties of the queue that the index cursor is pointing at to a MSMQQueueInfo object.

Finally, we use the Open method of the MSMQQueueInfo object to return to us a MSMQQueue object to which we can send messages.

The code shown Listing 8.11 locates all queues with the ServiceTypeGUID that we assigned to the server's order queue and opens the first one in the list that is returned. If no queues are found, the client is terminated.

8

Listing 8.11 Code to Locate the Server's Order Queue

```
1 ' Return a transactional queue
2   Set QList = New MSMQQueueInfos
3   Set QListQuery = New MSMQQuery
4   Set TSendQInfo = New MSMQQueueInfo
5   Set QList = QListQuery.LookupQueue(ServiceTypeGuid:= _
              "{CCD602C0-2E9F-11D3-A0AD-04D4B6000000}")
6   QList.Reset
7   Set TSendQInfo = QList.Next
8   If TSendQInfo Is Nothing Then
9       intPress = MsgBox("e-books server unavailable at this time.",
        ➥ vbInformation, "Client")
10      End
11  End If
12  QueueList.AddItem "Transaction queue: " & TSendQInfo.PathName
13
14  Exit Sub
```

Create the Order Message

As we stated earlier, we have decided that our server is to be stateless. That is, it remembers nothing about the transactions that it is processing, merely acting as a passthrough and hiding from the client the complexities of the network required to process the request. Because the order step requires information about the customer and the book he or she wants to purchase, we must send to the server all the information again. In addition, we must send the price of the book so that the correct information can be sent to the billing system, unlike the arbitrary amount used for the credit check earlier.

We will build and send this message when the user presses the OK button at the end of the inquiry workflow. Remember that the user is given a message box with OK or Cancel; our code picks up if the user clicks OK. We simply call a function SubmitOrder and encapsulate all the code we need to submit an order within that function. Most of the code shown in Listing 8.12 is identical to the code we used on the Submit button in Chapter 5. Note that we have added the actual price of the book to the end of the message. If you are unsure about the steps in this code segment, please refer to Chapter 5. In Listing 8.13, the call of the SubmitOrder function from within the event handler is shown in bold.

Listing 8.12 Code to Build the Order Message

```
1 Private Function SubmitOrder()
2 'This function is called when the user confirms an order after
3 'they have inquired about the book availability.
4 'It sends the transactional order message.
5
6 On Error GoTo ErrorHandler
```

```
7
8    '************************
9    'Open transactional queue
10
11   Set TSendQ = TSendQInfo.Open(MQ_SEND_ACCESS, MQ_DENY_NONE)
12   MessageHistory.AddItem "Transaction Queue opened for send"
13
14   '*********************
15   'Create data structure
16
17   Dim Order As New OrderInfo
18
19 With Order
20       .LastName = txtLastName.Text
21       .FirstName = txtFirstName.Text
22       .Address = txtAddressOne.Text
23       .Address2 = txtAddressTwo.Text
24       .City = txtCity.Text
25       .State = txtState.Text
26       .ZIP = txtZIP.Text
27       .CCNumber = txtCreditCardNumber.Text
28       .BookTitle = txtBookTitle.Text
29       .AuthorLast = txtBookAuthorLast.Text
30       .AuthorFirst = txtBookAuthorFirst.Text
31   End With
32
33   '*********************
34   'Build and send message
35
36   Set Message = New MSMQMessage
37   Message.Label = "Book Order Message"
38
39 ' Include Price in Message
40   Dim Dollar As String
41   Dollar = Right$(ReplyMessage, 6)
42   If Left$(Dollar, 1) = "$" Then
43       Dollar = Right$(ReplyMessage, 5)
44   End If
45   Dim Body As String
46   Body = Order.Serialize & StrConv(Dollar, vbFromUnicode) & _
         StrConv(Len(Dollar), vbFromUnicode)
47   Message.Body = Body
48   MessageHistory.AddItem "Order message created"
```

Listing 8.13   Code to Call the SubmitOrder Function

```
1 ' Submit the order?
2   intPress = MsgBox("Submit order?", vbOKCancel, "Client")
3   If intPress = 1 Then
4       Call SubmitOrder
5       intPress = MsgBox("Order submitted", vbOKOnly, "Client")
```

continues

Listing 8.13 continued

```
6    Else
7        ' They changed their mind
8        intPress = MsgBox("Order not submitted at this time.",
     ➥ vbInformation, "Client")
9    End If
```

Send the Order Message

Our design requires the order workflow to ensure that messages are delivered once and once only. We have started to show how the server protects the integrity of the workflow by managing the unit of work between order receipt and the billing and dispatching of the order. To coordinate the update of several MSMQ resources at the same time, those resources must be transactional. (In this case, we are concerned with the queues.) Transactional queues can only hold messages for which the transactional property is set, and transactional messages can be sent and received only as part of a unit of work. When we built the server earlier in this chapter, we showed you how to begin a managed unit of work, or transaction, and pass the transaction pointer to each resource update as it occurs.

In the case of the client submitting the order to the server, only one MSMQ resource is to be updated: the server's order input queue.

MSMQ offers a simpler way to process a transactional message when only one message is to be sent or received in the unit of work.

Because the only action associated with this process step is the send, instead of wrapping the entire process in a transaction, we simply use a parameter on the Send method, MQ_SINGLE_MESSAGE. This approach allows MSMQ to put a single transactional message onto a transactional queue and immediately commit the update, instead of creating MSMQTransaction and MSMQTransactionDispenser objects and using the Commit method.

The other parameters available to control the transactional behavior of the Send method are as follows:

- MQ_NO_TRANSACTION — The send is not part of a transaction.
- MQ_MTS_TRANSACTION — The current Microsoft Transaction Server (MTS) transaction is used to send the message.
- MQ_SINGLE_MESSAGE — Sends a single message as a transaction.
- MQ_XA_TRANSACTION — The send is part of an externally coordinated transaction.
- NULL — The message is not sent as part of a transaction.

Listing 8.14 shows the code to send our transactional order. It is a continuation of Listing 8.12.

Listing 8.14   Code to Send a Single Transactional Message

```
47
48      'Send as part of the transaction
49      Message.Send TSendQ, MQ_SINGLE_MESSAGE
50      MessageHistory.AddItem "Transaction message sent"
51
52      intPress = MsgBox("Your order has been confirmed. Thanks!", vbOKOnly,
        ➥ "Client")
53
54      TSendQ.Close
55      MessageHistory.AddItem "Queues closed"
56
57      cmdSubmit.Enabled = True
58
59 Exit Function
60
61 ErrorHandler:
62      If Err.Number = MQ_ERROR_QUEUE_EXISTS Then
63          Resume Next
64      End If
65
66      intPress = MsgBox _
        ("We're sorry, your order could not be processed at this time.", _
        vbOKOnly, "Client")
67
68 End Function
```

Display Confirmation of Order and Reset the Entry Form

As we have said before, the fact that MSMQ is assuring the delivery of the order means that we can confirm the order to the customer as soon as the message is successfully sent. The final steps for the code associated with our Confirm button are to display a confirmation message for the user and then, when the user clears the message, to clear or reset the fields on the entry form so that it is ready for the next customer.

Listing 8.15 shows the code to complete the order and reset the entry form.

Listing 8.15   Code to Complete the Order and Reset Entry Form

```
1 ' Submit the order?
2     intPress = MsgBox("Submit order?", vbOKCancel, "Client")
3     If intPress = 1 Then
4         Call SubmitOrder
5         intPress = MsgBox("Order submitted", vbOKOnly, "Client")
```

continues

Listing 8.15　continued

```
 6    Else
 7        ' They changed their mind
 8        intPress = MsgBox("Order not submitted at this time.",
        ➥ vbInformation, "Client")
 9    End If
10
11    ' Destroy the reply queue
12    IReplyQInfo.Delete
13
14    GoTo Reset
15
16 ErrorHandler:
17    MessageHistory.AddItem "Error: " & Err.Description
18
19 Reset:
20    Call clear_Click
21
22 End Sub
```

Testing the Programs

1. Start the server program built in this chapter to create the input queue; alternatively, create the queue by using MSMQ Explorer. If you create the queue with MSMQ Explorer, don't forget to correctly set the ServiceTypeGUID property.

2. End the server program.

3. Complete an inquiry workflow following the steps given at the end of Chapter 7 until the confirm/cancel message is displayed.

4. Press the Confirm button.

5. Using MSMQ Explorer, examine the queue and display the body of the message on it. You may need to press F5 first to refresh the display. You should see the details of the customer's order.

6. Restart the server. Notice that the message is removed from the queue and that the message history box is updated.

You have tested as much as we have built so far. In the next chapter, we extend the server to forward the dispatch and billing orders to the back-end systems.

Summary

This chapter has taken our applications to the next level. We have now incorporated more of the business benefits of MSMQ. By processing our messages transactionally, we achieve guaranteed and once and once-only message delivery. In a mission-critical environment, this transactional functionality plays an important role in processing information.

We introduced two new MSMQ objects: MSMQTransaction and MSMQTransactionDispenser. These two objects provide the capability to process messages under a unit of work. A few steps are necessary to accomplish this level of processing.

The queue to which the messages will be sent must be a transactional queue. This is a property of the queue and can be set by the administrator or an application. When the queue is available, the application needs to start or begin a unit of work. This "begin" step notes all the transactions that are associated with one another and groups them into one atomic unit of work. When all the transactions are executed (such as sending to one queue and receiving from another), the unit of work can be committed. If any of the transactions fail, the group of transactions are rolled back. It becomes an all-or-nothing fate.

In Chapter 9, "Order-Confirmation Workflow: Server to Back-End Systems," we complete our transactional workflow (steps 8 and 9 of the Concept Web). First, we build our order-processing back-end systems; then, we continue with our order-server application, processing the client's order message and sending off the appropriate messages to the warehouse and credit agency.

8

Chapter 9

Order-Confirmation Workflow: Server to Back-End Systems

e-books Order-Confirmation Workflow

When we left the confirmation workflow in Chapter 8, "Order-Confirmation Workflow: Client to Server," the server had received the order message but had not processed it. This chapter adds steps 8 and 9 in the Concept Web to our distributed application.

In this chapter, we build back-end programs to handle the dispatching of the order and the billing of the customer's credit card. We modify Chapter 8's server program so that now, after receiving the order-confirmation message, the server forwards the relevant pieces to the billing and distribution systems.

As it was with the message flow in Chapter 8, we are going to use the once-only delivery features of MSMQ to ensure that our messages reach their destinations. We will add to the unit of work that we started in our server the steps to forward the billing and dispatch messages to be back-end systems. Like the order input queue for the order-processing server, the dispatch and billing queues are transactional and, after being created, can be deleted only by the application administrator using MSMQ Explorer.

We build the back-end applications first, and then we modify the server built in Chapter 8. The client program does not change as a result of the steps we complete in this chapter.

As with the order-processing server in Chapter 8, we have chosen to break each back-end application into two programs, one for inquiry and one for order, for two very good reasons. One is simplicity, and the other is flexibility.

Simplicity is important because the simpler the implementation, the easier it is to maintain and enhance the program. Restricting the function of each program to manage only one input queue and perform one process helps us to describe the function of the program.

Flexibility is important because we cannot predict how the business use of this program will change over time. We might build different types of client applications that all use the same server programs. We would then expect to see many more hits on the inquiry program than on the order one, and so, would want to run more instances of the inquiry program.

At the end of this chapter, you will have all of the programs required to support the e-books application. Users will be able to inquire about price and availability and place an order for a book.

Application Architecture—Back-End Systems

Our back-end programs to bill the customer and dispatch the order are going to be very simple! Their only functions are to receive a transactional message and to update a log onscreen. In the real world, we would have databases to update and some additional back-end processing that would be part of an external transaction. We'll show you where this processing would go in our programs, and we'll use the hypothetical situation to introduce the elements required to support an external transaction (one that controls resources other than those of MSMQ).

If you don't have access to Microsoft Distributed Transaction Coordinator (DTC) to coordinate the external transaction, you can use an internal transaction, as we did for the order-processing server in Chapter 8.

The pseudocode shown in Listing 9.1 and all of the discussion that follows is for the warehouse application. When you are done with the warehouse dispatch program, repeat the steps for the credit card billing program.

Listing 9.1   Pseudocode for the Warehouse Dispatch Program

```
1    BEGIN
2    CreateQ( WarehouseQ, PUBLIC )
3    DO
4        TxnID = BeginExtTxn
5        OrderMsg = GetMsg( WarehouseQ, WAIT=UNLIMITED, REPLYQ = ResponseQ,
         ↪ TxnID )
6        IF OK THEN
```

```
7              ' Do other processing here, like DB updates
8              CommitExtTxn( TxnID )
9      END
10   END
```

When the program starts, we will create, if it does not exist, and open the input queue for the warehouse's dispatch program. The program does not delete the queue because the confirmation workflow runs outside the current execution instance. That is to say, it doesn't matter so much when the order is processed, only that it is processed. MSMQ is taking care of the safe storage and delivery of the message, so system unavailability need not affect our ability to do business. By having this queue available even when the dispatch program is not, we allow normal business to proceed. When the dispatch program is restarted later, it will process the pending orders before taking new ones.

 **Note**

If the application administrator stops the dispatch program and does not intend to restart it on the same machine within a reasonable time, then the administrator should at the same time delete the input queue by using MSMQ Explorer. Messages that are addressed to this queue are then written to the system's transactional dead-letter queue.

The dispatch program is a long-running process and is set up to automatically receive messages when they arrive on the input queue. For each message that is received, the dispatch program begins a new unit of work under which the program receives and processes the message. Because processing such a message is likely to require the update of other managed resources (such as a database), the transaction that we use in this case is externally managed.

Create a new VB project for the dispatch program. The process has a single list box on the form to display progress messages. Call the list box MessageHistory and the project Dispatcher. The program processes three separate events: starting, ending, and message arrival. In the following sections, we add code for each event to the project.

Form_Load Event

Double-click on the main form to display its code form. We will add code to create and open the input queue, receive and process any messages that are pending, and then enable notification on the queue for any messages that arrive subsequently.

9

Create and Open Input Queue

As with the inquiry case, we need to create a public queue the first time the application is run. We must create this queue to be transactional because the order-processing server puts messages on the queue as part of a unit of work. You must create a unique `ServiceTypeGUID` (using GUIDGen, as shown in Chapter 5, "Inquiry Workflow: Client to Server") for this new queue. To make a queue transactional, simply set the `IsTransactional` parameter on the `Create` method equal to `True` (as shown in line 14 of Listing 9.2).

Listing 9.2   Code to Create and Open a Transactional Queue

```
1 Private Sub Form_Load()
2
3 On Error GoTo ErrorHandler
4
5     '****************************
6     '* Create transactional queue
7
8     Set TReceiveQ = New MSMQQueue
9     Set TReceiveQInfo = New MSMQQueueInfo
10
11    TReceiveQInfo.PathName = ".\Transaction_Warehouse_Queue"
12    TReceiveQInfo.Label = "Warehouse Transaction Queue"
13    TReceiveQInfo.ServiceTypeGuid = "{443D0100-2F01-11d3-A0AE-CA8FB4000000}"
14    TReceiveQInfo.Create IsTransactional:=True
15    MessageHistory.AddItem "Transactional Queue: " & TReceiveQInfo.PathName
16
17    ' Open the queue for receive
18    Set TReceiveQ = TReceiveQInfo.Open(MQ_RECEIVE_ACCESS, MQ_DENY_NONE)
19    MessageHistory.AddItem "Queue opened for receive"
```

Enable Notification of Message Arrival

The final step in processing the form_load event is to enable the notification of message arrivals on the input queue. Listing 9.3 shows the sample code that we have added to the end of the form_load process.

Listing 9.3   Enable Notification of Messages Arriving

```
1 ' Enable event notification on the queue
2    Set TEvent = New MSMQEvent
3    TReceiveQ.EnableNotification TEvent
4    MessageHistory.AddItem "Waiting on queue"
5
6    Exit Sub
```

Message Arrived **Event**

The next thing for which we need to add code is the processing of a message that arrives on the input queue. This action occurs in the Event_Arrived subroutine.

The first step is to initiate the external transaction. To do so, we introduce a new MSMQ object: MSMQCoordinatedTransactionDispenser. Like its counterpart for internal transactions, MSMQTransactionDispenser, MSMQCoordinatedTransactionDispenser has only one method: BeginTransaction. Also like its internal counterpart, MSMQCoordinatedTransactionDispenser returns a MSMQTransaction object. (See Line 8 of Listing 9.4 for an example.)

The next step is to retrieve a message as shown in line 15 of Listing 9.4.

Processing of the message, in this example, involves nothing more than adding a line to the Message History list box. Lines 25 and 26 of Listing 9.4 show this step.

In the simple case that we have taken for this book, this action concludes the unit of work. In reality, you would probably update at least one database, and possibly more, to process the shipping order. Each update would make reference to the same transaction to facilitate the synchronization of the resources.

 Note

It is worth noting here that had this step indeed been the only step in the unit of work, we would not have needed to initiate a transaction at all. Instead, we could have set the MQ_SINGLE_MESSAGE parameter on the Receive method invocation. If we are going to add some real processing (like a SQL update) to the unit of work, however, we need to instantiate the transaction object.

Listing 9.4   Sample Code to Receive and Process Messages

```
1 Private Sub TEvent_Arrived(ByVal TReceiveQ As Object, ByVal Cursor As Long)
2    ' This is our event handler for our inquire receive queue
     ' (requests from client)
3
4    On Error GoTo ErrorHandler
5
6    ' Begin Transaction
7    Set CoorTransDisp = New MSMQCoordinatedTransactionDispenser
8    Set Transaction = CoorTransDisp.BeginTransaction
9
10    '*************
11    '* Get Message
12
13    warehouse.SetFocus
```

continues

Listing 9.4   continued

```
14    Set Message = New MSMQMessage
15    Set Message = TReceiveQ.Receive(ReceiveTimeout:=10000)
16    ' This should not timeout, but if it does...
17    If Message Is Nothing Then
18       MessageHistory.AddItem "Unable to get message off queue"
19       Set TEvent = New MSMQEvent
20       TReceiveQ.EnableNotification TEvent
21       Exit Sub
22    End If
23
24    ' Display the message
25    MessageHistory.AddItem "Message Arrived"
26    MessageHistory.AddItem Message.Body
```

After we have received the message and concluded any processing, we must commit the transaction by using the Commit method of the MSMQTransaction object (line 32 of Listing 9.5).

As everyone knows, a good coding practice is to code error handlers within the application logic. This approach enables you to better debug your code and/or display error messages to the end user. The code in Listing 9.5 is the complete code for the Arrived event handler.

Listing 9.5   Event_Arrived Subroutine

```
1 Private Sub TEvent_Arrived(ByVal TReceiveQ As Object, ByVal Cursor As Long)
2     ' This is our event handler for our inquire receive queue
      ' (requests from client)
3
4     On Error GoTo ErrorHandler
5
6     ' Begin Transaction
7     Set CoorTransDisp = New MSMQCoordinatedTransactionDispenser
8     Set Transaction = CoorTransDisp.BeginTransaction
9
10    '*************
11    '* Get Message
12
13    warehouse.SetFocus
14    Set Message = New MSMQMessage
15    Set Message = TReceiveQ.Receive(ReceiveTimeout:=10000)
16    ' This should not timeout, but if it does...
17    If Message Is Nothing Then
18       MessageHistory.AddItem "Unable to get message off queue"
19       Set TEvent = New MSMQEvent
20       TReceiveQ.EnableNotification TEvent
21       Exit Sub
22    End If
```

```
23
24     ' Display the expiry from the message
25     MessageHistory.AddItem "Message Arrived"
26     MessageHistory.AddItem Message.Body
27
28     '**********************
29     '* Query on database...
30
31     ' Commit Transaction
32     Transaction.Commit
33
34     ' Wait again
35     GoTo Wait
36
37 ErrorHandler:
38     If Err.Number = MQ_ERROR_QUEUE_NOT_FOUND Then
39         Err.Clear
40         DoEvents
41         Resume
42     End If
43
44     Transaction.Abort
45     MessageHistory.AddItem "Error: " & Err.Description
46
47 Wait:
48     ' Wait on Q -- reset the event handler
49     Set TEvent = New MSMQEvent
50     TReceiveQ.EnableNotification TEvent
51
52 End Sub
```

Form_unload Event

Finally, we add the code for the event that the dispatch program is ended. We do not delete the input queue, so the only cleanup we have to do is to close the open input queue.

Just type in the heading for the form_unload event subroutine.

 Note
The Form_QueryUnload events are so common that you can copy and paste them from one application to another, changing only which queues are affected and how (either closed or deleted).

Listing 9.6 shows the code that we added to our program to process the closing of the window.

Listing 9.6   Code for the `form_unload` Event

```
1 Private Sub Form_QueryUnload(Cancel As Integer, UnloadMode As Integer)
2    Dim i As Integer
3    On Error GoTo ErrorHandler
4    i = MsgBox("Do you want to exit?", vbYesNo + vbQuestion, "e-books
Warehouse")
5    If i = vbNo Then
6        Cancel = 1
7    Else
8
9        TReceiveQ.Close
10        Unload Me
12        End
13    End If
14    Exit Sub
15
16 ErrorHandler:
17    Resume Next
18
19 End Sub
```

Application Architecture—Order-Confirmation Server

Next, we turn our attention back to the order-processing server—in particular, to the program we built in Chapter 8 that received the confirmation message from the client but did nothing else. We need to change the processing of the Arrived event to include the forwarding of the billing and dispatch messages to the back-end systems.

Reload the server project that you created in Chapter 8 and find the code for the ReceiveMsg subroutine.

It should look like that shown in Listing 9.7.

Listing 9.7   Code for ReceiveMsg from Chapter 8

```
1 Private Sub TQEvent_Arrived(ByVal IReceiveQ As Object, ByVal Cursor As Long)
2
3    On Error GoTo ErrorHandler
4    Main.SetFocus
5
6    ' Begin Transaction
7    Set TransDisp = New MSMQTransactionDispenser
8    Set Transaction = New MSMQTransaction
9    Set Transaction = TransDisp.BeginTransaction
10    MessageHistory.AddItem "Beginning transaction"
11
```

```
12    ' Get Message
13    Set Message = TReceiveQ.Receive
14    ' This should not timeout, but if it does...
15    If Message Is Nothing Then
16      MessageHistory.AddItem "Unable to get message off queue"
17      Set TQEvent = New MSMQEvent
18      TReceiveQ.EnableNotification TQEvent
19      Exit Sub
20    End If
21
22    MessageHistory.AddItem "Message received: "
23    MessageHistory.AddItem "      " & Message.Body
```

This procedure now performs the following steps within a single, internal transaction:

1. Receive order confirmation
2. Build billing notice
3. Build dispatch notice
4. Send billing notice
5. Send dispatch notice

The code to build the billing and dispatch notices is shown in Listing 9.8. We have used much the same code as we did in Chapter 6, "Inquiry Workflow: Server to Back End," to extract the data from the input message and format it for the billing system. We have changed the amount sent to the credit agency to be the real cost of the book. As for the billing notice, this time we are also going to forward to the warehouse the customer's name and address for shipping the book. As before, we call the Parse function to build the messages.

To accurately pick up the price of the book from the message, we must do the following:

1. Get the price. The last byte of the message gives the length of the price. The price is either the next 5 or 6 bytes to the left of this number. Our first step is to get this number (line 20 of Listing 9.8).
2. Get rid of that number because it is not necessary for the back ends. We reassign our Body string to be the entire message body except the right-most byte (line 21).
3. Pick up the dollar amount from the message based on the length of the dollar amount we just determined (lines 22 to 28).
4. Determine the warehouse message, which consists of all the information about the client and the book (line 32), and determine the credit message, which consists of all the information about the client and the price of the book (line 33).

Listing 9.8 **Code to Build the Billing and Dispatch Notices**

```
1 Public Function Parse()
2
3    On Error GoTo ErrorHandler
4
5    Set WarehouseMessage = New MSMQMessage
6    Set CreditMessage = New MSMQMessage
7
8    'Message Parse
9    Dim CreditMessageBody As String
10   Dim WarehouseMessageBody As String
11   Dim DollarLen As String
12   Dim Dollar As String
13   Dim Body As String
14
15   ' This message include the price of the book.
16   ' The last number in the string is the length of the price --
17   '        either 6 bytes for $$$.$$ or five for $$.$$
18   Body = Message.Body
19   Body = StrConv(Body, vbUnicode)
20   DollarLen = Right$(Body, 1)
21   Body = Left$(Body, Len(Body) - 1)
22   If DollarLen = "5" Then
23       Dollar = Right$(Body, 5)
24   ElseIf DollarLen = "6" Then
25       Dollar = Right$(Body, 6)
26   Else
27       MessageHistory.AddItem "Invalid price returned"
28   End If
29
30   ' We know exactly which part of the message body pertains to which
     ' back-end process, so we simply pull out those parts of the
31   ' string and assign them to new string objects.
32   WarehouseMessageBody = Left(Body, Len(Body) - CLng(DollarLen))
33   CreditMessageBody = Left(Body, 152) & Dollar
34
35   WarehouseMessage.Body = WarehouseMessageBody
36   CreditMessage.Body = CreditMessageBody
37
38   Exit Function
39
40 ErrorHandler:
41   MessageHistory.AddItem "Error #" & Err.Number & ": " & Err.Description
42
43 End Function
```

We are then ready to send our messages to the back-end processes. The only difference from our other examples of the Send method is that this time we associate the send with the transaction object (as shown in Listing 9.9).

Listing 9.9   Code to Send the Billing and Dispatch Notices

```
1 ' Send the message
2    WarehouseMessage.Send TWarehouseQ, Transaction
3    CreditMessage.Send TCreditQ, Transaction
```

The final step is to commit the update of the resources, assuming that all was successful (or, in the ErrorHandler, abort the transaction). Listing 9.10 shows the code to complete the transaction. We use the `Commit` method of the `MSMQTransaction` object.

Listing 9.10   Code to Commit the Transaction

```
1 ' Commit the transaction
2    Transaction.Commit
3
4    GoTo Wait
5
6 ErrorHandler:
7    MessageHistory.AddItem "Error #" & Err.Number & ": " & Err.Description
8    Transaction.Abort
9
10 Wait:
11    Set TQEvent = New MSMQEvent
12    TReceiveQ.EnableNotification TQEvent
13
14 End Sub
```

Testing the Complete Application

You have now completed all the programs to support the inquiry and order workflows (steps 1 through 9 on the Concept Web).

To test them, follow the steps from the end of Chapter 7, "Automating the Inquiry Workflow," to complete the inquiry workflow through the user being presented with the Confirm/Cancel message box.

Then:

1. Start and stop the warehouse dispatch program to create its input queue.

2. Start and stop the credit card billing program to create its input queue.

3. Make sure that the order-confirmation server is not running but that its input queue exists. (This setup should be the case if you ran the tests at the end of Chapter 8. If not, start and stop the order-confirmation server to create its input queue.)

4. Press the client's Confirm button.

9

5. Verify that the message is written to the input queue of the order-confirmation server by using MSMQ Explorer.

6. Start the order-confirmation server.

7. Verify that the message is removed from the order-confirmation server's input queue and that messages are now waiting on the input queues for the billing and dispatch programs.

8. In turn, start the billing and dispatch programs and verify that the messages are removed from the input queues.

9. Accept the Order confirmed message on the client.

10. Order another book with each program running to start with. Watch how each window is updated as the workflows execute. (Be careful not to blink—the whole process doesn't last longer than a couple of seconds!)

Summary

Congratulations! At this point, you have built all the programs required to support steps 1 through 9 of the Concept Web. The user of your distributed application is able make an inquiry about a book and place an order for it. The programs have been constructed so that one or more servers can process input from several client programs and interface with a variety of back-end systems. You can try running different components on different machines and even running multiple instances of the different applications.

In the following chapters, we consider more techniques that can help ensure that orders are processed correctly, and we examine ways to track an order's progress through the order process.

Part 5

Advanced MSMQ Application Development: Acknowledgements

Chapter 10

Delivery Confirmation and Audit

This chapter as well as the two that follow are as much about the design of a robust, mission-critical business application as they are about programming. In fact, although we introduce a few new properties and system objects, the bulk of the programming tasks should be familiar.

Part 3, "Advanced MSMQ Application Development: Processing a Request," and Part 4, "Advanced MSMQ Application Development: Processing an Order," helped you build a business application to inquire and then confirm an order. Throughout the process we showed you how to manage two different types of data. The first was transient or "temporary"; nothing about the workflow changed the state of the business data. The second workflow did update the state of the databases and, as such, was required to be transactional. Now, in Part 5, "Advanced MSMQ Application Development: Acknowledgments," we turn our attention to this second workflow.

We've already explained, when you are using transactional messages and queues, MSMQ assures the once, and once-only, delivery of a message. Perhaps you take our word for it, perhaps you don't, but how many auditors will? In our workflow, money changes hands. At least two businesses (the bookstore and the credit card company) and possibly a third (a distributor) are involved, and that's before we count the customer. Auditors will require us to keep records of the billing transactions that we send to the credit card company and very likely to the warehouse or distributor. But even leaving the checks and balances aside, what about customer satisfaction? How can we become more proactive in delighting our customer in the event that something goes wrong with an order after it has been confirmed?

This part of the book discusses the topics of audit, delivery confirmation, and error notification. Remember that this discussion relates only to the "confirmation" workflow (steps 10 to 16 of our Concept Web) and, as such, relates to the programs built in Chapter 8, "Order Confirmation Workflow: Client to Server," and Chapter 9, "Order Confirmation Workflow: Server to Back-End Systems," of the book. In the following chapters we add to those programs and build a few new programs to help with the results in Chapters 11, "Processing the Journal Queues," and 12, "Customer Service Application."

Audit Logs

In our example, the credit agency requires a reliable mechanism to record each and every billing transaction that it receives from the bookstore. This step is important because it may later be necessary to demonstrate that the reason something was not billed was because it was never received. We do not want to leave the creation of this log to either the sending or receiving application.

MSMQ offers two types of journal queues that we can use to maintain audit logs automatically from within a program. The first is known as the machine journal, and the second is the target queue journal. A single message can be either "machine journaled" or "target journaled," but not both. If both are specified, target journaling takes precedence. Whichever journaling method is chosen, the journal entry is written when the message is removed from the target queue. The machine journal may be used when a message is sent from one machine to another (not when sending to a local queue, for obvious reasons). (This procedure is also referred to as "source journaling.") Each MSMQ server has one machine journal that is created when MSMQ is installed on the computer. The one machine journal may hold many different types of messages destined for many different target queues on any MSMQ machine.

When the target queue's journaling property is set to true, the target queue journal is populated when an application receives a message from the target queue. One queue journal exists for every queue that is defined. The target journal is automatically created when the target queue is created. Messages are automatically copied to this journal when they are read from the application queue if the properties are appropriately set. The target journal shares, in part, the format name of the target queue with which it is associated and takes on the entire format name with the suffix ;JOURNAL.

> You can view the machine journal by highlighting the machine name, which displays all the available queues in the right panel of MSMQ Explorer.
>
> Target journals are located as subset of the "normal" queue.

Your applications cannot write directly to either of these journals. They may only read from them. MSMQ never removes messages from either journal. It is up to your program to process them or the system administrator to purge them by using MSMQ Explorer.

Returning to the example, then, the credit card billing program will use target journaling to keep a copy of every message that it receives. For completeness, we must consider also the machine journal and how it may be used.

Creating Machine Journal Entries

Because we want a mechanism for the credit agency to record everything it receives, our example does not use the machine journal entry. However, if, instead, we wanted the store to record everything it sends, we would use the machine journal. This section considers what we would do if we wanted to create records on the machine journal. Note that both machine and target journaling cannot be used for the same message. When both are specified, only the target journal is written.

As we have already mentioned, a user-written program cannot send messages to the machine journal. It is therefore unnecessary (not to mention impossible) for the sending application to open the journal. After all, if we could add records to the journal, it wouldn't be an accurate record! So, if we are unable to open the journal and we can't send messages to it, how do we create entries on it?

Creating entries on the journal is actually very simple and only requires the setting of one more property of the `MSMQMessage` object that we are sending. The property is `Journal`.

The `Journal` property can take several values that are defined as constants in the ActiveX components:

> `MQMSG_JOURNAL_NONE`—The default.
>
> `MQMSG_JOURNAL`—The value we want, and the one that causes MSMQ to create a source journal entry every time the message is passed from one machine to another.
>
> `MQMSG_DEADLETTER`—This value causes the message to be written to the dead-letter queue of the machine that is currently holding the message if its time to be delivered or retrieved expires. This value may be used with `MQMSG_JOURNAL`. Undeliverable transactional messages are automatically journaled in the transactional dead-letter queue.

Listing 10.1 shows the code you can add to the program before sending a message to ensure that the message is copied to the machine journal queue.

Listing 10.1   Code to Enable Source Journaling on a Message

```
1    Message.Journal = MQMSG_JOURNAL
2    Message.Send vMyQ
```

It really is that easy! That's all our server application has to do to satisfy the auditors that every transaction is recorded. Well, almost. Someone has to read the journal and sort out all the records on it. Remember that every message that moves between this machine and the next (wherever it may be going) is recorded in the machine journal if this message property is set. To make it easy, we recommend the use of one more message property, that of message correlation ID, or CorrelationId. The CorrelationId property of the MSMQMessage object is a globally unique identifier (GUID) that the application may set when the message is sent. Use GUIDGen to create a new, unique GUID and use it in your order-processing server as the correlation ID for all messages sent to the credit agency. This practice allows a program that has been built to produce a report of all messages sent to the credit agency to pull only the appropriate records from the log. Listing 10.2 shows an example of the use of this property and how it would be set before the use of the Send method.

Listing 10.2   Code to Specify a CorrelationId for a Journaled Message

```
1    Message.Journal = MQMSG_JOURNAL
2    Message.CorrelationId = "{56AF59F0-3A2D-11d3-A0C3-00A024A5BFC5}"
3    Message.Send vMyQ
```

Creating Target Journal Entries

As with the machine journal, a user application cannot send messages to a target journal queue. Our auditors (we are the credit agency now) want a mechanism to show exactly what was received from the queue. Instead, the property belongs to the target queue. Every message received from the queue is logged to the queue journal if the Journal property of the queue is set.

The Journal property of the queue can take one of two values:

> MQ_JOURNAL_NONE—The default.
>
> MQ_JOURNAL—The value we want and the one that causes MSMQ to automatically create a journal copy of each message that an application receives from the queue.

The Journal property may be set by the application when the queue is created, and in this case it will be. Therefore, for target journaling you must enable the property on the queue MSMQQueueInfo object. Listing 10.3 shows how the Journal property might be set on the MSMQQueueInfo object before the Create method is called.

Listing 10.3   Code to Specify Target Journaling on a Queue

```
1    TReceiveQInfo.Journal = MQ_JOURNAL
2    TReceiveQ = TReceiveQInfo.Create
```

If the queue were a static queue, that is, one defined by an administrator through MSMQ Explorer, then the property would be set by using the panel interface. Figure 10.1 shows the check box on the Advanced tab of the Queue Properties dialog box that allows you to enable queue journaling. Another option allows you to set the maximum size of that journal.

Figure 10.1

Enabling a queue journal via the Queue Properties dialog box.

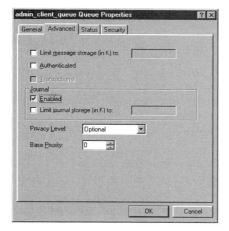

Whether the queue is created by the programmer or the administrator, when the Journal property is set, each message that is received from the queue is written to the queue journal automatically. Because the only messages written to this queue are billing transactions, sorting by type of journal message is not necessary when the audit report is produced.

Chapter 11 includes an example of an application to produce this audit report.

Delivery Confirmation and Error Notification

At the conclusion of Part IV, the customer received a confirmation as soon as MSMQ received the 'order' command. We are using the transactional features of MSMQ to guarantee the delivery of the order to the warehouse. It is now that paranoia enters our design. We are going to build some processing to keep the bookstore's customer service manager happy. After all, if you had to deal with irate customers calling a week after receiving a "confirmation" but not a book, would you trust MSMQ to deliver the message?

10

What we need is a log of all the messages that are sent from the store to the warehouse and a mechanism for recording when the warehouse has processed them. Ideally, we want to use an automated process, and at the end of the business day we want to show the customer service manager that the log contains no outstanding orders.

EXCURSION

The Types of Acknowledgement Message

Before we continue, let's take a moment to consider the different types of acknowledgments that are available and how we request they be sent. Using the acknowledgment feature requires two steps. We first have to request the kinds of acknowledgments we want to receive, and then we have to tell MSMQ where to write the acknowledgment messages. MSMQ automatically sets the correlation ID of the acknowledgment message to the ID of the original message.

Acknowledgments are requested for a specific message and are therefore requested by setting the `Ack` property of the `MSMQMessage` object before it is sent to the queue. The possible values for the `Ack` property are as follows:

- `MQMSG_ACKNOWLEDGMENT_NONE`—The default.
- `MQMSG_ACKNOWLEDGMENT_FULL_RECEIVE`—Posts a positive or negative acknowledgment depending on whether or not an application retrieves the message from the queue before the message expires. This value is the one we want.
- `MQMSG_ACKNOWLEDGMENT_FULL_REACH_QUEUE`—Posts a positive or negative acknowledgment depending on whether or not the message is written to the final destination queue successfully before the message expires.
- `MQMSG_ACKNOWLEDGMENT_NACK_RECEIVE`—Posts a negative acknowledgment if the message is not received from the queue before the message expires.
- `MQMSG_ACKNOWLEDGMENT_NACK_REACH_QUEUE`—Posts a negative acknowledgment if the message is not written to the destination queue before the message expires.

We tell MSMQ which queue to write the acknowledgment messages to by using the `AdminQueueInfo` property of the `MSMQMessage` object. This queue must already exist, so we must either create it from our program or have a MSMQ administrator create it for us from MSMQ Explorer.of the `MSMQMessage`

The first piece of our design requires the sender—in this case, the order entry system (the client application)—to create a record of the order that it places (a status message). This step is Step 11 in the Concept Web. The client must then request positive acknowledgment that the server has processed the order (Concept Web step 12). The next step is for the order-processing server to create a record (again, a status message) of the dispatch order that it places with the warehouse (Concept Web step 14). The order-processing server will also request positive acknowledgment that the warehouse has processed the dispatch order (Concept Web step 15). So, taking the client application first, the flowchart in Figure 10.2 shows the steps that we need to perform.

Figure 10.2

Flowchart showing the client process steps for order tracking.

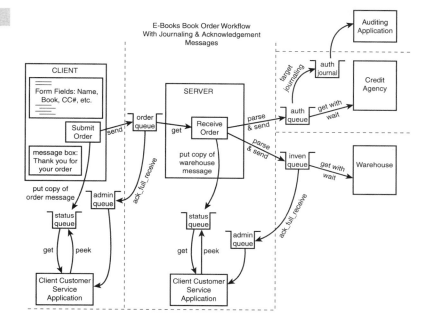

When we put a message on the order queue, we also put a corresponding message on a new queue that we use to track the status of an order. We refer to this queue as the "status" queue (this term is not a MSMQ term, rather just our term for this customer service application-specific queue). We will perform both queue updates as a single unit of work (so that either they both happen or neither of them happens). Both messages are transactional, so they will be recovered automatically in the event of a system failure before the unit of work is completed.

We also need a mechanism to match the status record to the order message. We'll use the CorrelationId property of the message to provide this function. When a message is sent to a queue, MSMQ always generates a unique ID for the message. Every message has a unique ID, and the application program cannot set it. The CorrelationId property has the same format (that is, it is a GUID) and can be set by the application. After a message is written to a queue and the send is successful, MSMQ returns to the program the ID of the message that was created by MSMQ. The ID property of the MSMQMessage object that was sent is then set to the actual ID of the message that was put on the queue. We copy this ID into the CorrelationId property of the status message and write the status message to the status queue.

10

The pseudocode in Listing 10.4 illustrates the process we just described. (This listing modifies the pseudocode we introduced for the Confirm button in Chapter 8.)

Listing 10.4 Pseudocode for the Confirm Order Workflow

```
1    CreateQ( StatusQ, TRANSACTIONAL )
     ...
     ...
2    LocateQ( OrderQ )
3    BeginTxn( TxnId )
4        BuildMsg( OrderMsg, BookTitle, CustomerName, CustomerAddress,
         ➥ CreditCard )
5        SendMsg( OrderQ, OrderMsg, TxnId )
6        IF NOT OK THEN
7            AbortTxn( TxnId )
8            MessageBox( 'We are sorry, we cannot complete your order.' )
9        ELSE
10           Buildmsg( StatusMsg )
11           StatusMsg.Body = OrderMsg.Body
12           StatusMsg.CorrelationId = OrderMsg.Id
13           SendMsg( StatusQ, OrderMsg, TxnId )
14           IF NOT OK THEN
15               AbortTxn( TxnId )
16               MessageBox( 'We are sorry, we cannot complete your order.' )
17           ELSE
18               CommitTxn( TxnId )
19               IF OK THEN
20                   MessageBox( 'Your order is confirmed. Thank You.' )
21               ELSE
22                   MessageBox( 'We are sorry, we cannot complete your order.' )
23   EndTxn( TxnId )
```

This modification of the client program allows us to create copies of all the orders in a status queue. The exact data written to the queue obviously depends on the information in the body of the message. We have chosen to write the same message body to the status queue as we are writing to the order queue.

Order Tracking—Client to Server

Reload the client project from Chapter 8. We will modify the behavior of the form_load process and the Confirm Order button.

Create the Admin and Status Queues

When we request that MSMQ generate acknowledgment messages, we must also provide the name of a queue to which those messages will be sent. The information concerning this queue (the MSMQQueueInfo object that describes it) is passed in the AdminQueueInfo property of the MSMQMessage object. Because these queues are providing information about the total activity on this client workstation, all orders should be logged and tracked on the same pair of queues.

Before we can send the status message or request acknowledgment of the delivery, we must create the queues to which the messages will be sent if those queues do not already exist. We do this step in the form_load procedure. Listing 10.5 shows the code that we will add immediately after we have opened the server's regular input queue. Note also that we have created new ServiceTypeGUIDs for the admin (line 5) and status (line 12) queues.

Listing 10.5   Code to Create Admin and Status Queues on the Client

```
1       '*********************
2       'Create Admin Q
3       Set AdminQInfo = New MSMQQueueInfo
4       AdminQInfo.PathName = ".\admin_client_queue"
5       AdminQInfo.ServiceTypeGuid = "{10E294A0-3878-11d3-A0BF-00A024A5BFC5}"
6       AdminQInfo.Create
7       QueueList.AddItem "Admin queue: " & AdminQInfo.PathName
8       '*********************
9       'Create Status Q
10      Set StatusQInfo = New MSMQQueueInfo
11      StatusQInfo.PathName = ".\status_client_queue"
12      StatusQInfo.ServiceTypeGuid = "{702F2A10-389A-11d3-A0BF-
        ➡ 00A024A5BFC5}"
13      StatusQInfo.Create IsTransactional:=True
14      QueueList.AddItem "Status queue: " & StatusQInfo.PathName
```

Create the Tracking Messages

The next step is to change the code that we added to process the Confirm button. In Chapter 8 we were sending a single message to a transactional queue, and so we did not need to build and manage an entire unit of work.

In this chapter we must send the order-confirmation and status messages as a single unit of work, and so we require an internal transaction object. We are sending the order-confirmation message to the server first. Then, the status message is sent. Either both or neither will appear on their respective target queues, ensuring that we preserve the integrity of the order-tracking system. The status message takes the MSMQ-supplied ID of the order message for its own correlation ID. This action helps us match status and confirmation messages in Chapter 12 when we build the customer service program. We execute the following steps:

1. Begin an internal transaction.
2. Send the order-confirmation message as before, requesting that acknowledgments be sent and to which queue.
3. Extract the MSMQ-generated ID from the order-confirmation message that was sent and copy the ID to the Correlation ID field.

10

4. Send the order-confirmation message to the status queue. No acknowledgments should be sent concerning this message

5. Commit the update of both queues.

Listing 10.6 shows the code that we have added to the Commit button to send both the order-confirmation and status messages as a single unit of work.

Listing 10.6   Code to Begin an Internal Transaction

```
1       Set TransDisp = New MSMQTransactionDispenser
2       Set Transaction = TransDisp.BeginTransaction
3       MessageHistory.AddItem "Beginning transaction"
```

Listing 10.7 shows the code to build and send the order-confirmation message. The bold text shows what has changed from the code in Chapter 8. Line 14 shows how we request confirmation of message delivery to the receiving application, and line 16 shows how we name the queue to which such acknowledgments should be sent. We have modified line 19, the Send, to point to the transaction object that we are now using instead of the Send taking the MS_SINGLE_TRANSACTION parameter as it did in Chapter 8.

Listing 10.7   Code to Build and Send the Order-Confirmation Message

```
1       Set Message = New MSMQMessage
2       Message.Label = "Book Order Message"

3       ' Include Price in Message
4       Dim Dollar As String
5       Dollar = Right$(ReplyMessage, 6)
6       If Left$(Dollar, 1) = "$" Then
7       Dollar = Right$(ReplyMessage, 5)
8       End If
9       Dim Body As String
10      Body = Order.Serialize & StrConv(Dollar, vbFromUnicode) & _
11      StrConv(Len(Dollar), vbFromUnicode)
12      Message.Body = Body

13      ' Set the ack property of the message
14      Message.Ack = MQMSG_ACKNOWLEDGMENT_FULL_RECEIVE

15      ' Tell MSMQ where to put the ack message
16      Set Message.AdminQueueInfo = AdminQInfo

17      MessageHistory.AddItem "Message created"

18      ' Send as part of the transaction
19      Message.Send TSendQ, Transaction
20      MessageHistory.AddItem "Transaction message sent"
```

The next step is to build and send the copy of the order-confirmation message to the status-tracking queue. Listing 10.8 shows the code that we have added to build and send the status-tracking message. Line 7 copies the content of the order-confirmation message into the status-tracking message. This step provides a complete record of the customer's order should it go astray. Line 12 copies into the status-tracking message's correlation ID property the MSMQ-generated ID of the order-confirmation message. MSMQ automatically puts the ID of the order-confirmation message into the Correlation ID field of any acknowledgment messages that it sends. The customer service program matches status and acknowledgment messages by their correlation IDs.

Listing 10.8   Code to Copy the Message to the Status Queue

```
1     ' Send status message
2     Set StatusQ = StatusQInfo.Open(MQ_SEND_ACCESS, MQ_DENY_NONE)
3     MessageHistory.AddItem "Status queue opened"

4     Set StatusMessage = New MSMQMessage
5     StatusMessage.Label = "Book Order Status Message"

6     ' Set the body equal to the transaction message body
7     StatusMessage.Body = Message.Body

8     ' Set the correlationID equal to the message ID. The acknowledgement
9     ' message coorelationID for the transaction message will also equal
10    ' the transaction message ID. MSMQ does this for us. This way we will just
11    ' compare correlID's when we create the customer service application.
12    StatusMessage.CorrelationId = Message.Id

13    ' Send as part of a UOW
14    StatusMessage.Send StatusQ, Transaction
15    MessageHistory.AddItem "Status message sent"
16    ' Finally, commit the transaction when both order and status
      ' messages are gone
17    Transaction.Commit
```

The final step to be added, shown in line 17, is to commit the internal transaction. Again, we did not have to do this step in Chapter 8 because we sent only one message as part of the unit of work.

To summarize, then, the client program has been modified to request positive feedback when the message is received from the destination queue. The feedback messages are written to a new queue, AdminQ, which is monitored by the customer service application that we will build in Chapter 12. The client has been further modified to write a copy of each order to a StatusQ, which is also used by the customer service application in Chapter 12. Both the AdminQ and the StatusQ reside on the local machine on which the client application is running. The customer

10

service application will be run against this pair of queues to produce a report showing which orders are outstanding (there shouldn't be any) at the end of the day.

Order Tracking—Server to Warehouse

The second piece of the acknowledgment path concerns workflow steps 14 and 15 in the Concept Web and requires that we do exactly the same thing between the server and warehouse applications as we just did between the client and the server. As in the client case, when an order is sent to the warehouse, we will generate a copy of the order and store it on the ServerStatusQ. We'll request acknowledgment messages be sent to the ServerAdminQ.

The first step is to reload the server project last modified in Chapter 9 and display the code for the form_load event. (Double-click on the main form to display the code for the form_load event. Add the code in Listing 10.9 to create and open the status and admin queues if they don't already exist.

Listing 10.9   Code to Create and Open the Status and Admin Queues

```
1     '**********************
2     'Create Admin Q
3     Set AdminQInfo = New MSMQQueueInfo
4     AdminQInfo.PathName = ".\admin_server_queue"
5     AdminQInfo.ServiceTypeGuid = "{7FEAEC10-3AC0-11d3-A0C4-00A024A5BFC5}"
6     AdminQInfo.Create IsTransactional := TRUE
7     MessageHistory.AddItem "Admin queue: " & AdminQInfo.PathName
8     '**********************
9     'Create Status Q
10    Set StatusQInfo = New MSMQQueueInfo
11    StatusQInfo.PathName = ".\status_server_queue"
12    StatusQInfo.ServiceTypeGuid = "{7FEAEC11-3AC0-11d3-A0C4-00A024A5BFC5}"
13    StatusQInfo.Create IsTransactional:=True
14    MessageHistory.AddItem "Status queue: " & StatusQInfo.PathName
```

Listing 10.10 shows, in bold, the code to be added to the Arrived event handler to request that acknowledgments be generated by MSMQ and to name the queue to which they are to be sent. In addition to the other operations that are part of the existing internal unit of work that was built in Chapter 9, we are going to add the Send to the status queue.

Listing 10.10   Code to Request Acknowledgments and Store Tracking Message

```
1     ' Set the acknowledgement properties of the warehouse message
2     WarehouseMessage.Ack = MQMSG_ACKNOWLEDGMENT_FULL_RECEIVE
3     Set WarehouseMessage.AdminQueueInfo = AdminQInfo

4     ' Send the messages
5     WarehouseMessage.Send TWarehouseQ, Transaction
```

```
6      CreditMessage.Send TCreditQ, Transaction

7      ' Send status message
8      ' Open the queue
9      Set StatusQ = StatusQInfo.Open(MQ_SEND_ACCESS, MQ_DENY_NONE)
10     MessageHistory.AddItem "Status queue opened"

11     ' Build the message
12     Set StatusMessage = New MSMQMessage
13     StatusMessage.Label = "Book Order Status Message"
14     StatusMessage.Body = WarehouseMessage.Body
15     StatusMessage.CorrelationId = WarehouseMessage.Id

16     ' Send the message
17     StatusMessage.Send StatusQ, Transaction
18     MessageHistory.AddItem "Status message sent"
```

Testing

Run through the complete order process from a new inquiry right through to confirming the order. Then, use MSMQ Explorer to look at the client and server status and admin queues. One message should appear on each queue for each time you confirm an order.

Taking the client queues first, look at the properties of the messages and note that the correlation IDs are identical. This information is important in Chapter 12, "Customer Service Application," when we build the Customer Service program to process these queues.

Look next at the server status and admin queues and verify that the message on each carries the same correlation ID.

The last queue to check is the target journal for the credit card billing program. Use MSMQ Explorer to find the billing queue and double-click on its journal. You should see a single message (if you ordered only one book). Display the body of the message, and you should see that it contains an exact copy of what your server sent to the billing program.

Summary

This chapter has provided more than just MSMQ application logic. We were able to incorporate additional business rules into our messaging applications. Auditing and report tracking are important concepts in designing enterprise applications.

We introduced new properties on the MSMQMessage object: Journal and Ack. The Journal property provides a means to create journal entries in one of two journals:

machine and target queue journals. We can use the journaling feature to store and record auditing information.

The Ack property of a message specifies the kind of acknowledgment report an application desires. The Ack property is used with the AdminQueue property, which specifies the name of the queue that receives the report messages.

These features were combined in our application to provide order tracking. The information was retained for several sources, such as auditors and customer queries.

In the following chapters, we are going to build the applications that process the journal and acknowledgment messages that we just created. In Chapter 11 we create the credit agency audit application that reads the journal messages of the credit agency's order queue. In Chapter 12 we create the customer service application that reads both the acknowledgment messages and status messages, comparing them to determine the status of an order.

Chapter 11

Processing the Journal Queues

In Chapter 10, "Delivery Confirmation and Audit," we modified the programs and queues associated with the order-processing workflow to create system journal entries. We introduced machine and target journals. These elements are system queues to which MSMQ can write messages according to the properties of the queue or the message.

A target journal exists for each defined queue in the MSMQ Enterprise. If the queue property Journal is set to MQ_JOURNAL, every message that is delivered to the receiving program is copied to the target journal. MSMQ never removes messages from the target journal. It is up to your program or MSMQ administrator to manage this queue.

Only one machine journal exists for each node (independent client, primary or backup site controller, primary enterprise controller, or routing server) in the MSMQ Enterprise. A copy of every message for which this property is set to MQMSG_JOURNAL is written to the machine journal of the system from which it was sent, unless the Journal property of the target queue is also set to MQ_JOURNAL.

Chapter 10 showed you how the machine journal entries would be created for messages between the order-processing server and the billing program. We did not implement this function, choosing instead to use target journaling for these messages. Target journaling has allowed us to keep a complete set of every billing message received by the billing program.

As we did in Chapter 10, we cover both the machine and target journals in this chapter. In this case, we do not do anything to receive messages from the machine journal because we have not actually written anything to that journal.

We are going to build a new program to read the target journal of the billing program. This program completes process step 10 from the Concept Web. The program reads the target journal and produces a report detailing all the billing requests that have been received.

Processing the Machine Journal

This section explains how to access the machine journal to read messages from it. The discussion is hypothetical. We have not created any entries on the machine journal queue.

In our hypothetical case, then, the machine journal contains messages that were transmitted to the credit agency machine and for which machine journaling was active. To differentiate between messages that may be written to this queue by other applications, the order-processing server sets either the correlation ID or the app-specific ID to a globally unique identifier (GUID) used to identify billing orders.

To open the machine journal, you must use a special format name that requires the GUID of the machine that hosts the particular machine journal. The syntax for such a format name is "MACHINE=MachineGuid;JOURNAL" (as shown in line 6 of Listing 11.1).

You can obtain the GUID of the machine by using the MSMQApplication object. The MSMQApplication object has only a single method associated with it: MachineIdOfMachineName. The method takes as a single parameter the name of the machine for which the GUID is required. This name is the same as the Windows computer name.

The code segment in Listing 11.1 shows how an application can open the machine journal to read the messages on the it. Remember, an application can never directly write messages to the machine journal.

Listing 11.1　Code to Open the Machine Journal Queue

```
1    Dim MachineID As String
2    Dim App As MSMQApplication
3    Set App = New MSMQApplication
4    Set JournalQInfo = New MSMQQueueInfo
5    MachineID = App.MachineIdOfMachineName("machinename")
6    JournalQInfo.FormatName = "MACHINE=" & MachineID & ";JOURNAL"
7    Set JournalQ = JournalQInfo.Open(MQ_RECEIVE_ACCESS, MQ_DENY_NONE)
8    List1.AddItem "Local machine journal opened."
```

In fact, because the MSMQApplication object is an application component, it does not have to be explicitly referenced. The code segment in Listing 11.1 could be simplified to that shown in Listing 11.2.

Listing 11.2   Code to Open the Machine Journal Queue

```
1 Dim MachineID As String
2    Set JournalQInfo = New MSMQQueueInfo
3    MachineID = MachineIdOfMachineName("machinename")
4    JournalQInfo.FormatName = "MACHINE=" & MachineID & ";JOURNAL"
5    Set JournalQ = JournalQInfo.Open(MQ_RECEIVE_ACCESS, MQ_DENY_NONE)
6    List1.AddItem "Opened queue for receive"
7    List1.AddItem JournalQInfo.FormatName
```

When the machine journal is open, the application can read from the journal just as the application can read from any other queue.

Processing the Target Journal

The target journal for the billing queue contains copies of every message that was written to the credit agency's billing queue. We need a program to read the messages from this queue and produce an audit report detailing the day's activity.

To recap, MSMQ automatically created these journal entries when the original message was read from the target queue. A property of the queue determines whether or not the message is written to the journal. (See Chapter 10 for details.)

The pseudocode in Listing 11.3 shows how a program reads the target journal queue and writes a record to a flat file.

Listing 11.3   Pseudocode to Produce an Audit Log from Journal Queue Entries

```
1    BEGIN
2        OpenQ( BillingQ;JOURNAL )
3        OpenFile( AuditLog )
4        While BillingQ;JOURNAL is not empty
5            TxnId = BeginTxn()
6            JournalMsg = GetMsg( BillingQ;JOURNAL, TxnId )
7            IF WriteFile( AuditLog, JournalMsg, APPEND ) is OK
8                CommitTxn( TxnId )
9            ELSE
10                   AbortTxn( TxnId )
11        END While
12   END
```

We start off by opening the target journal queue and the file the user has specified (lines 2 and 3). Then in a loop (bounded by lines 4 and 11), we receive a message and write it to a file within a unit of work. In line 8 we commit the transaction if both the receive from the queue and the write to the file are successful. This step ensures that if the program were to fail after reading the message but before writing the log record, the audit message would be rolled back onto the journal queue. The result of a failure between writing the log record and the "commit" would be that the log record would exist and the journal message would be rolled back onto the queue for later processing. In other words, the potential exists for the audit report to contain duplicate records. This possibility is better than losing a record altogether. In reality the log might be written to a database that could be synchronized, removing the window of doubt altogether.

> **Note**
>
> The use of a database is the preferred approach because of the database's capability to participate with a transaction monitor. A common occurrence is the use of Microsoft's SQL Server with MSMQ. MSMQ makes strong use of the Microsoft Distributed Transaction Coordinator to manage the external unit of work between SQL Server and MSMQ.

Create a new VB project and call it Audit. Name the main form Main. The program is going to process all the messages on the journal queue and then stop. Unlike other processes that we have written, Audit is not a long-running process.

Build the form shown in Figure 11.1. We will add a list box to the form into which we will write the history, and we will add a push button named cmdStart that we will use to start the journal queue processing. We will allow the user to specify the name of the file to which the report is written by using the entry field named ExportPath. All the code for this program is associated with the Start button. Double-click on the button to display its code form.

Figure 11.1

The audit program main panel.

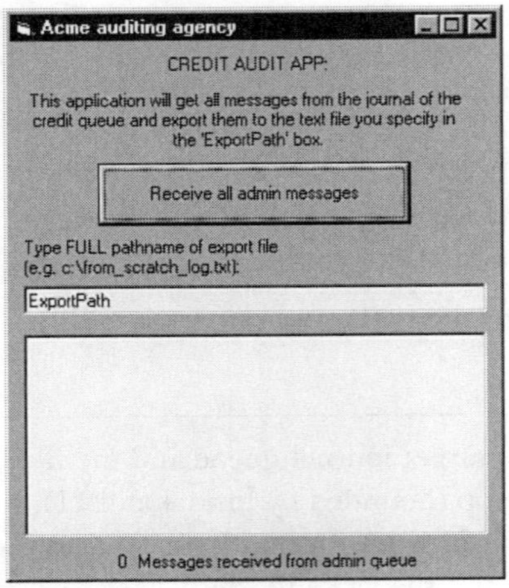

> **Acme auditing agency**
>
> CREDIT AUDIT APP:
>
> This application will get all messages from the journal of the credit queue and export them to the text file you specify in the 'ExportPath' box.
>
> [Receive all admin messages]
>
> Type FULL pathname of export file
> (e.g. c:\from_scratch_log.txt):
>
> ExportPath
>
> 0 Messages received from admin queue

Open the Journal

The first step is to open the target journal for the billing program's input queue. The target journal must be opened by using, in part, the GUID of the target queue. The GUID of the target queue is available as one of the target queue's properties, the QueueGUID property of the MSMQQueueInfo component.

The code in Listing 11.4 opens a queue's journal if you know the queue's pathname. If you do not know the queue's pathname, you could use the LookupQueue method of MSMQQuery to locate the billing queue, as we did in Chapter 9, "Order Confirmation Workflow: Server to Back-End Systems."

Listing 11.4   Code Segment to Open the Target Journal Queue

```
1    Dim TargetQInfo As New MSMQQueueInfo
2    Dim JournalQInfo As New MSMQQueueInfo
3    Dim JournalQ As New MSMQQueue
4    TargetQInfo.PathName = ".\QueuePathName"
5    TargetQInfo.Refresh
6    JournalQInfo.FormatName = TargetQInfo.FormatName & ";JOURNAL"
7    Set JournalQ = JournalQInfo.Open( MQ_RECEIVE_ACCESS, MQ_DENY_NONE )
```

In Listing 11.4 the first three lines contain the familiar statements to create the MSMQ objects that we need. Note that we create two MSMQQueueInfo objects: one for the target queue itself and the other for its journal queue. As we said earlier, we open the journal queue based on the format name of the queue for which it is the journal.

The first step is to obtain the format name of the target queue. We set the PathName property of the MSMQQueueInfo object to the pathname of the target queue. In line 4 of our example, this information is hard-coded into the program, but you could locate this queue by using the Lookup method to find the pathname. When the PathName property is set, we use the Refresh method of the MSMQQueueInfo object to populate, from Message Queue Information Store (MQIS), the other properties of the target queue, particularly the FormatName. The FormatName property of the journal queue is exactly the same as that of the target queue with ;JOURNAL appended to it. Finally, in lines 6 and 7, we copy the FormatName of the target queue, with the ;JOURNAL appended, to the FormatName property of the journal queue and open the journal queue.

Open the Target File

The next step is to open a file, named by the user, into which we will write the audit records. If the file already exists, we will overwrite the existing content. Listing 11.5 shows the code that we add to the Start button after we have opened the journal queue.

11

Listing 11.5 Code to Open the File

```
1    Dim n As String
2    n = 0
3    Dim strPath As String
4    strPath = ExportPath.Text
5    Dim fso, fil
6    Set fso = CreateObject("Scripting.FileSystemObject")
7    Set fil = fso.CreateTextFile(strPath, True)
8    fil.WriteLine (Format(Now, "ddddd ttttt"))
```

To create our flat file, we are going to use some built-in VB objects. The object we are concerned about in particular is the FileSystemObject, located in the Microsoft Scripting Runtime library reference; the actual file, located in the system32 folder, is scrrun.dll. You must add this library to your project before attempting to reference this object.

In line 5 we declare the objects fso and fil. In line 6 we declare our fso object as a FileSystemObject by using the CreateObject method. In line 7 we make our fil object a text file by using the CreateTextFile method of the FileSystemObject. Finally, in line 9 we simply put a date/time stamp at the top of the file.

Receive and Process a Journal Message

The bulk of the processing is to receive each message from the target journal, in turn, and write a record for each to the output file. We perform both operations within a MSMQ internal unit of work because any transaction manager cannot manage the file system write. (If we were using a database for the audit log, we could use an external transaction object to coordinate both updates.)

The code in Listing 11.6 receives and processes one message from the queue. We explain these steps before we add the loop to receive all messages from the journal queue, in the final section of this chapter.

Listing 11.6 Code to Receive and Log One Journal Message

```
1    On Error GoTo ErrorHandler
2    Dim JournalMessage As MSMQMessage
3    Dim Transaction As MSMQTransaction
4    Dim TransDisp As MSMQTransactionDispenser
5    Set TransDisp = New MSMQTransactionDispenser
6    Set Transaction = TransDisp.BeginTransaction
7    Set JournalMessage = JournalQ.Receive(ReceiveTimeout:=5000)
8    If JournalMessage Is Nothing Then
9        MessageHistory.AddItem "No admin messages in queue"
10       Transaction.Abort
11       Exit Sub
12   Else
```

```
13          MessageHistory.AddItem JournalMessage.Body
14          fil.WriteLine (JournalMessage.Body)
15          Transaction.Commit
16      End If
17      Exit Sub
18      ErrorHandler:
19          MessageHistory.AddItem Err.Description
20          Transaction.Abort
21          MessageHistory.AddItem "Transaction aborted"
22      End Sub
```

Line 1 sets up the process to call our error handler in case a call returns an error. If an error occurs, we want to roll back onto the target journal any message that we are currently processing. We use the Abort method of the MSMQTransaction object to do so, as you can see in line 19.

In lines 2, 3 and 4, we declare our MSMQ objects. We initiate an internal transaction in lines 5 and 6.

Lines 7 through 16 receive and process a message from the journal queue. First, in line 7, we receive the message from the journal queue as part of the coordinated unit of work. If no messages are available, we abort the transaction and exit the subroutine (lines 8–11). If a message is available, we write the body of the message to the form's list box, MessageHistory, and to the file we opened. The write to the file is not under the control of the transaction manager, but if the write operation returns an error, the ErrorHandler routine aborts the unit of work and leaves the journal message on the queue for next time. If the write to the file works, line 15 commits the unit of work and thereby removes the message completely from the journal queue.

If the program were to terminate between lines 14 and 15, MSMQ would automatically abort the uncommitted transaction, rolling the message back onto the journal queue for processing at a later time. In this case the log record is eventually written twice. The window for this error is extremely small, and logging the record twice is better than not logging it at all.

Listing 11.6 processes just one message from the queue. We want to get all the available messages, so the next section takes this code and builds a loop around it to process all messages on the journal queue.

Receive and Process All Journal Messages

Working with the code to process a single message (see Listing 11.6), we need to build a loop that exits when there are no more messages on the journal queue. Listing 11.7 shows this code. The lines we added to create the loop are shown in bold type. We simply use a While loop that continues as long as we receive a message from the queue (lines 12–25 of Listing 11.7). If we do not receive a message from the queue, we exit the loop and finish the processing of the messages (lines 16 and 17). We are also updating a count of the messages we received from the journal queue (lines 9 and 21) and later displaying that count in a label control (line 22).

Listing 11.7   Code to Process All Messages on the Journal Queue

```
1     Set JournalMessage = JournalQ.Receive(ReceiveTimeout:=5000)
2     If JournalMessage Is Nothing Then
3         MessageHistory.AddItem "No Journal messages in queue"
4         Transaction.Abort
5         Exit Sub
6     Else
7         MessageHistory.AddItem JournalMessage.Body
8         fil.WriteLine (JournalMessage.Body)
9         n = n + 1
10        Label2.Caption = n
11        Transaction.Commit
12        While Not JournalMessage Is Nothing
13            Set TransDisp = New MSMQTransactionDispenser
14            Set Transaction = TransDisp.BeginTransaction
15            Set JournalMessage = JournalQ.Receive(ReceiveTimeout:=5000)
16            If JournalMessage Is Nothing Then
17                GoTo Done
18            Else
19                MessageHistory.AddItem JournalMessage.Body
20                fil.WriteLine (JournalMessage.Body)
21                n = n + 1
22                Label2.Caption = n
23                Transaction.Commit
24            End If
25        Wend
26    End If
27
28 Done:
29    MessageHistory.AddItem ""
30    MessageHistory.AddItem "Files retrieved from Journal queue"
31    MessageHistory.AddItem "Files exported to: " & strPath
32
33    MessageHistory.AddItem "Transactions committed"
34    Screen.MousePointer = vbDefault
35
36    Exit Sub
37
38 ErrorHandler:
39    Transaction.Abort
40    MessageHistory.AddItem "Transaction aborted"
41    MessageHistory.AddItem Err.Description
42
43 End Sub
```

Summary

This chapter has presented the logic to process journal messages. Journal messages enable us to track all the messages that pass between MSMQ nodes or are removed from a queue.

We showed the steps necessary to open and process messages from the journal queue. The following syntax specifies the format name of journal queue: MACHINE=MachineGuid;JOURNAL. The MachineGuid is extracted by using the MSMQApplication object. This object provides a single method for extracting the machine's identification (GUID).

Next we are going to build the customer service applications that are responsible for checking acknowledgments against requests. You will see how to browse, or peek, at messages so that the application can view a queue and read each message non-destructively.

11

Customer Service Application

In Chapter 11, "Processing the Journal Queues," we modified our order-entry and order-processing systems to write a record to a status queue and request acknowledgment of the delivery of the order message each time an order is submitted to the server and the warehouse, respectively. Focusing on the client, as we did in Chapter 11, this chapter explains the process of comparing the acknowledgment messages with the messages on the status queue to produce a record of the transactions that were not processed.

In Chapter 9, "Order Confirmation Workflow: Server to Back-End Systems," our client application creates an order message that is submitted to the order queue. The same unit of work copies the ID of the order message into the correlation ID of a status message and writes the status message to the status queue. The bodies of the order and status messages are identical. The client application also requests that positive acknowledgments be generated for the order message when it is picked up by the order processing server. MSMQ generates the acknowledgment messages automatically, copying the ID of the original message to the correlation ID of the acknowledgment messages, and sends the message to a queue we specify (in this case, the admin queue).

Each client workstation needs two queues: the status queue, containing the status messages we generated, and the admin queue, containing acknowledgment messages generated by MSMQ. Each message on the status queue has a unique correlation ID, and a corresponding receipt acknowledgment (identical correlation ID) should appear on the admin queue.

The purpose, then, of this chapter is to build an application that reads messages from the admin queue and removes the corresponding copy of the order from the status queue. Browsing the status queue allows the customer service manager to see at any time a complete list of the unprocessed orders.

Customer Service Application Architecture

Listing 12.1 shows the pseudocode for the customer service application. This application opens both the admin and status queues and picks a message off the admin queue. The application then searches the status queue for a message whose correlation ID matches that of the acknowledgment and removes that message from the queue. For completeness, we could write some of the body of the message to a record in a file, but we'll leave that complexity out of our example! (We simply display the results in a ListBox.)

At any one time, the status queue contains copies of all the orders that have yet to be confirmed.

Listing 12.1   Pseudocode for the Customer Service Application

```
1     BEGIN
2             OpenQ( AdminQ )
3             OpenQ( StatusQ )
4             DO
5                 ResetBrowseCursor( StatusQ )
6                     AdminMsg = GetMsg( AdminQ, READ, WAIT=unlimited )
7                     WHILE ( NOT END OF QUEUE( StatusQ ) )
8                         StatusMsg = GetMsg( StatusQ, BROWSE )
9                         IF ( StatusMsg.CorrelationId =
                       ➥ AdminMsg.CorrelationId ) THEN
10                            GetMsg( StatusQ, READ )
11                        break
12                        ELSE
13                        IncrementBrowseCursor( StatusQ )
14                    END-WHILE
15            END
16     END
```

This example has introduced the need to browse the messages on the queue, instead of reading them destructively. We now focus on introducing the methods to perform this function.

Browsing the Status Queue

To achieve our browse of the status queue, we are going to teach an old dog some new tricks: We are going to call the Peek, PeekCurrent, and PeekNext methods on the MSMQQueue object. Why all three, you ask? Well, just as with the Receive method, there is an implied cursor position in the queue when we attempt to perform a Peek. We must look at the first message in the queue and then work through the queue, one message at a time, until we have looked at every message (or until we find our admin message match). Our procedure is as follows:

1. We perform a Peek on the first message in the queue by calling the Peek method on the MSMQQueue object, as shown in Listing 12.2.

Listing 12.2   Source for Peeking at the First Message in the Queue

```
1       'Peek at first message in status queue
2       Set StatusMessage = StatusQ.Peek(ReceiveTimeout:=10000)
```

2. We check to see whether this message is the one we want (the message that corresponds to our admin message). If it is not, we do a PeekCurrent to look at the second message in the queue. Remember that the cursor moved when we performed the Peek. Now we must call the PeekCurrent method before we can call PeekNext (see Listing 12.3).

Listing 12.3   Source for Peeking at the Message at the Current Cursor Position

```
1       'PeekCurrent must be used before PeekNext can be used
2       Set StatusMessage = StatusQ.PeekCurrent(ReceiveTimeout:=10000)
```

3. We continue by calling the PeekNext method until we arrive at the end of the queue (see Listing 12.4).

Listing 12.4   Source for Peeking at the Next Message in a Queue

```
1       'Otherwise, we peek at the next message
2       Set StatusMessage = StatusQ.PeekNext(ReceiveTimeout:=10000)
```

As you might imagine, the actual Visual Basic (VB) logic to perform all these steps correctly is relatively extensive. Do not worry; we walk you through it. Figure 12.1 shows the form appearance of our client customer service application.

The first thing you should notice is the ListView control that makes up most of the form. We added this special control so that we could display all the data from the message to the user of the customer service application. To use this component and for the project to reference it, we must add the Microsoft Windows Common Controls component set to the project (press Ctrl+T to add components). (We kept the default name of ListView1 for our ListView. We also have a ListBox named List1.) We then add the column headers in our Form_Load subroutine. Listing 12.5 shows the global declarations section of our code, Listing 12.6 shows the Exit button code, and Listing 12.7 gives the Form_Load code. Notice how in the form load we

12

first populate the ListView control (lines 5–21 in Listing 12.7); we then find and open both the admin queue (lines 23–38) and the status queue (lines 40–56). We must know the service type GUID for both of these queues to use as the locate parameter. We then open them both for receive (receive access allows both peeking and receiving).

Figure 12.1

Client customer service application at form load.

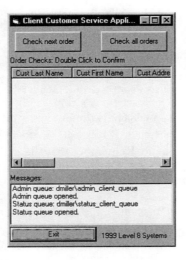

 **Note**

If you are using VB 5.0, the control set that includes the ListView control is still called Microsoft Windows Common Controls. However, Service Pack 2.0 for VB must be installed for the control set to be available.

Listing 12.5   Source for the Customer Service Application

```
1  '******************************
2  'Global declaration of objects
3  '******************************
4
5  Option Explicit
6  Dim AdminQ As MSMQQueue               'said 'admin' queue
7  Dim AdminQInfo As MSMQQueueInfo
8  Dim AdminMessage As MSMQMessage       'said 'admin' message
9  Dim StatusQ As MSMQQueue              'status queue
10   Dim StatusQInfo As MSMQQueueInfo
11 Dim StatusMessage As MSMQMessage      'status message
12 Dim StatusQList As MSMQQueueInfos     'QueueInfos object for status queue
13 Dim StatusQListQuery As MSMQQuery     'Query for status queue
14 Dim AdminQList As MSMQQueueInfos      'QueueInfos object for admin queue
15 Dim AdminQListQuery As MSMQQuery      'Query for admin queue
16
```

```
17 'Transaction objects we will be using in this workflow
18 Dim Transaction As MSMQTransaction
19 Dim TransDisp As MSMQTransactionDispenser
20
21 'VB objects we will be using
22 Dim intPress As Integer
23 Dim strStatusMessageID As String
24 Dim strAdminMessageID As String
25 Dim n As Integer
26 Dim Counter As Long
```

Listing 12.6   Source for the Customer Service Application Exit Button

```
1        Private Sub cmdExit_Click()
2            Unload Me
3            End
4        End Sub
```

Listing 12.7   Source for the Customer Service Application Form Load

```
1 Private Sub Form_Load()
2
3 On Error GoTo ErrorHandler
4
5     'Populate our ListView control's columns
6     With ListView1
7         .ColumnHeaders.Add , , "Cust Last Name"
8         .ColumnHeaders.Add , , "Cust First Name"
9         .ColumnHeaders.Add , , "Cust Address One"
10        .ColumnHeaders.Add , , "Cust Address Two"
11        .ColumnHeaders.Add , , "Cust City"
12        .ColumnHeaders.Add , , "Cust State"
13        .ColumnHeaders.Add , , "Cust ZIP"
14        .ColumnHeaders.Add , , "Cust CC Number"
15        .ColumnHeaders.Add , , "Book Title"
16        .ColumnHeaders.Add , , "Auth Last Name"
17        .ColumnHeaders.Add , , "Auth First Name"
18
19        .View = lvwReport
20        .LabelEdit = lvwManual
21    End With
22
23    'Find  and open the admin queue for receive
24    'The client creates this queue and places
25    'acknowledgements on it.
26
27    Set AdminQListQuery = New MSMQQuery
28
29    Set AdminQList = AdminQListQuery.LookupQueue_
                (ServiceTypeGuid:="{10E294A0-3878-11d3-A0BF-00A024A5BFC5}")
```

12

continues

Listing 12.7   continued

```
30    AdminQList.Reset
31    Set AdminQInfo = AdminQList.Next
32    If AdminQInfo Is Nothing Then
33        intPress = MsgBox("Customer service queues unavailable at this
      ➡ time.",                 vbInformation, "Client customer service
      ➡ application")
34        End
35    End If
36    List1.AddItem "Admin queue: " & AdminQInfo.PathName
37    Set AdminQ = AdminQInfo.Open(MQ_RECEIVE_ACCESS, MQ_DENY_NONE)
38    List1.AddItem "Admin queue opened."
39
40  'Find and open the status queue for peek/receive
41  'The client also created this queue and puts
42  'duplicates of the order messages on this queue
43  'before it commits its order transaction.
44
45    Set StatusQListQuery = New MSMQQuery
46
47    Set StatusQList = StatusQListQuery.LookupQueue _
              (ServiceTypeGuid:="{702F2A10-389A-11d3-A0BF-00A024A5BFC5}")
48    StatusQList.Reset
49    Set StatusQInfo = StatusQList.Next
50    If StatusQInfo Is Nothing Then
51        intPress = MsgBox("Customer service queues unavailable at this
      ➡ time.", _
              vbInformation, "Client customer service application")
52        End
53    End If
54    List1.AddItem "Status queue: " & StatusQInfo.PathName
55    Set StatusQ = StatusQInfo.Open(MQ_RECEIVE_ACCESS, MQ_DENY_NONE)
56    List1.AddItem "Status queue opened."
57
58    Exit Sub
59
60  ErrorHandler:
61    List1.AddItem "Error: " & Err.Description
62
63  End Sub
```

The real intelligence in this application comes with the code to actually check the status of an order. The first thing we do is pull the first message off the admin queue. This message may or may not be the one we want to check. Later we will build a command to check every admin message; at that point if we do not see the message we are looking for, the order processing server has not yet received the message. This code is nothing new; simply notice how we are wrapping the entire process in a transaction—this way we do not lose any admin messages if the application fails somewhere within the processing. We set new instances of our MSMQTransactionDispenser and MSMQTransaction objects (lines 17 and 18 of

Listing 12.8). Then we receive the first message off the admin queue (line 22). If we fail to get a message, we must abort the transaction (lines 23–29).

Listing 12.8   The `cmdPerformCheck` Command Button Code

```
1 Private Sub cmdPerformCheck_Click()
2 'Will get first message off of the admin queue,
3 'find it's match on the status queue,
4 'pull that message off, and display confirmation
5
6 Screen.MousePointer = vbHourglass
7 On Error GoTo ErrorHandler
8
9  'n is our test to see if we have done PeekCurrent.
10 'We cannot do PeekNext until we have done PeekCurrent
11 n = 1
12
13 'Set transaction objects and begin the transaction.
14 'We are wrapping this in a transaction so that in the case we
15 'don't find a correspoding status message, the admin message
16 'will be rolled back onto the admin queue.
17 Set TransDisp = New MSMQTransactionDispenser
18 Set Transaction = TransDisp.BeginTransaction
19 List1.AddItem "Beginning transaction"
20
21 'Get admin message
22     Set AdminMessage = AdminQ.Receive(ReceiveTimeout:=10000)
23         If AdminMessage Is Nothing Then
24             intPress = MsgBox("No admin message at this time.", _
                        vbInformation, "Client customer service application")
25             Transaction.Abort
26             List1.AddItem "Transaction aborted"
27             Screen.MousePointer = vbDefault
28             Exit Sub
29         End If
```

The next step is to peek at the first message on the status queue. We perform a `Peek` on the queue object in line 2 of Listing 12.9. If no message is on the queue, then we must abort the transaction (lines 2–9).

Listing 12.9   The `cmdPerformCheck` Command Button Code (continued)

```
1 'Peek at first message in status queue
2    Set StatusMessage = StatusQ.Peek(ReceiveTimeout:=10000)
3        If StatusMessage Is Nothing Then
4            intPress = MsgBox("No status message at this time.", _
                        vbInformation, "Client customer service application")
5            Transaction.Abort
6            List1.AddItem "Transaction aborted"
7            Screen.MousePointer = vbDefault
8            Exit Sub
9        End If
```

12

The next step is to compare the CorrelationIds of both messages. If they are the same, then that status message can be confirmed as received by the order processing server. Again, the code to convert the strings in lines 2–8 of Listing 12.10 is not new. We have encapsulated the code for confirmation at a point within the subroutine defined as Confirm. (We discuss the confirm code later.) You can see in line 11 that if the IDs match, we go to the confirm line.

Listing 12.10   **The cmdPerformCheck Command Button Code (continued)**

```
1  'Convert CorrID's to strings we can compare (conversion is one byte at a time)
2    For Counter = LBound(StatusMessage.CorrelationId) To _
            UBound(StatusMessage.CorrelationId)
3       strStatusMessageID = strStatusMessageID & _
                    Hex(StatusMessage.CorrelationId(Counter))
4    Next Counter
5
6    For Counter = LBound(AdminMessage.CorrelationId) To _
            UBound(AdminMessage.CorrelationId)
7       strAdminMessageID = strAdminMessageID & _
                    Hex(AdminMessage.CorrelationId(Counter))
8    Next Counter
9
10    'Compare ID's: Do these message correspond with each other?
11    If strStatusMessageID = strAdminMessageID Then GoTo Confirm
```

If we do not find the correlating status message to match the admin message, the next step is to continue browsing through the queue. We were able to use the Peek method to look at (but not remove) the first message on the queue, but to continue we must now use the PeekCurrent method. We use a tester to determine whether we have already performed a PeekCurrent within this loop (the While Not loop is defined in line 2 of Listing 12.11). The tester is simply n. When n is equal to 1 (line 3), we know we are passing through this loop for the first time and that we need to call a PeekCurrent.

Listing 12.11   **The cmdPerformCheck Command Button Code (continued)**

```
1  'If not, continue checking StatusQ for corresponding message
2    While Not strStatusMessageID = strAdminMessageID
3       If n = 1 Then
4          'PeekCurrent must be used before PeekNext can be used
5          Set StatusMessage = StatusQ.PeekCurrent(ReceiveTimeout:=10000)
```

If n is not equal to 1, then we know that we have already called a PeekCurrent and that we now must call the PeekNext method of the queue object (line 2 of Listing 12.12). From now on we will be able to call the PeekNext method (we reset the tester object in line 23). At this time we also convert the ID (lines 14–17). Again, if we do not find a message at all, we abort the transaction (lines 6–12).

Listing 12.12   The `cmdPerformCheck` **Command Button Code (continued)**

```
1  'Otherwise, we peek at the next message
2       Else: Set StatusMessage = StatusQ.PeekNext(ReceiveTimeout:=10000)
3       End If
4
5       'If we never found a corresponding status message, bail.
6       If StatusMessage Is Nothing Then
7           intPress = MsgBox("No status message at this time.", _
                      vbInformation, "Client customer service application")
8           Transaction.Abort
9           List1.AddItem "Transaction aborted"
10          Screen.MousePointer = vbDefault
11          Exit Sub
12      End If
13
14      'Again convert the status message CorrId
15      For Counter = LBound(StatusMessage.CorrelationId) To _
                   UBound(StatusMessage.CorrelationId)
16          strStatusMessageID = strStatusMessageID & _
                          Hex(StatusMessage.CorrelationId(Counter))
17      Next Counter
18
19      'Again compare
20      If strStatusMessageID = strAdminMessageID Then GoTo Confirm
21
22      'Next time around we will perform PeekNext instead of PeekCurrent
23      n = 2
24
25  Wend
```

Next is the Confirm step. We first pick up off the status queue the message at the current cursor position by using the `ReceiveCurrent` method of the queue object (line 3 of Listing 12.13). We moved the cursor during the peeking routine and left the cursor at the position of the desired message when we found the corresponding message and stopped browsing. After we receive the message, we simply populate the ListView control with the different portions of the message (lines 11–23). Finally, we commit the transaction in line 26. In addition, in the case of an uncontrolled-for error, we must abort the transaction (line 33, in the error handler).

Listing 12.13   The `cmdPerformCheck` **Command Button Code (continued)**

```
1 Confirm:
2   'StatusMessage corresponds with AdminMessage, so we will pick it up off the
➥queue
3   Set StatusMessage = StatusQ.ReceiveCurrent
4
5   'Adding the different portions of the message (cust name, address, etc.)
6   'to the corresponding columns in our ListView control.
```

12

continues

Listing 12.13   continued

```
7     Dim lvItem As ListItem
8     Dim order As String
9     order = StrConv(StatusMessage.Body, vbUnicode)
10     Set lvItem = ListView1.ListItems.Add
11     With lvItem
12         .Text = Left$(order, 25)
13         .SubItems(1) = Mid$(order, 26, 25)
14         .SubItems(2) = Mid$(order, 51, 25)
15         .SubItems(3) = Mid$(order, 76, 25)
16         .SubItems(4) = Mid$(order, 101, 25)
17         .SubItems(5) = Mid$(order, 126, 2)
18         .SubItems(6) = Mid$(order, 128, 9)
19         .SubItems(7) = Mid$(order, 137, 16)
20         .SubItems(8) = Mid$(order, 153, 25)
21         .SubItems(9) = Mid$(order, 178, 25)
22         .SubItems(10) = Mid$(order, 203, 25)
23     End With
24
25     'Commit the transaction
26     Transaction.Commit
27     List1.AddItem "Transaction committed"
28     Screen.MousePointer = vbDefault
29     Exit Sub
30
31 ErrorHandler:
32     'Abort the transaction on failure
33     Transaction.Abort
34     List1.AddItem "Transaction aborted"
35     List1.AddItem Err.Description
36     Screen.MousePointer = vbDefault
37
38 End Sub
```

That is all of the code for the cmdPerformCheck command. Next we will create a command that checks every admin message on the admin queue for its corresponding status message. We accomplish this task with a Do loop. This step adds some more logic to the code. First we must have some exits from the loop that come whenever we do not receive an admin message or have no status message at which to peek. In the cmdPerformCheck command, we simply bailed on the transaction and exited the subroutine. This time, however, we may have simply arrived at the end of the admin queue's messages. We therefore have added another test, x, to this routine (lines 10–11 of Listing 12.14). x tells us whether we are passing through the entire loop for the first time. If it is our first time through the loop, then we bail just as before (lines 28–33). If it is not, then we have at least checked one message from the admin and status queues. We commit our transaction before exiting (lines 34–39).

The only other code to add is the loop itself, in lines 15 and 127. Listing 12.14 shows the complete code for this command; the portions that differ from the `cmdPerformCheck` appear in bold.

Listing 12.14　The `cmdPerformCheck` **Command Button Code (continued)**

```
1 Private Sub Command1_Click()
2 'This command does the exact same thing as above, but
3 'puts it in a loop so that it will pull every admin
4 'message and compare it to its status message.
5
6 Screen.MousePointer = vbHourglass
7 On Error GoTo ErrorHandler
8
9 'x is our test to see if we've been through the entire loop yet or not
10 Dim x As Integer
11 x = 1
12
13 n = 1
14
15 Do
16
17     'Each time through the loop is a transaction so that
18     'we do not lose any admin messages
19         Set TransDisp = New MSMQTransactionDispenser
20         Set Transaction = TransDisp.BeginTransaction
21
22     'Get admin message
23         Set AdminMessage = AdminQ.Receive(ReceiveTimeout:=10000)
24             If AdminMessage Is Nothing Then
25             'If this is the very first time we've done this, then there
26             'is nothing at all to check. Otherwise, we have just reached
27             'the end of the queue and are done.
28                 If x = 1 Then
29                     intPress = MsgBox("No admin message at this time.", _
                            vbInformation, "Client customer service
                            ➥ application")
30                     Transaction.Abort
31                     List1.AddItem "Transaction aborted"
32                     Screen.MousePointer = vbDefault
33                     Exit Sub
34                 Else
35                     intPress = MsgBox("Order Checks received", _
                            vbInformation, "Client customer service
                            ➥ application")
36                     Transaction.Commit
37                     List1.AddItem "Transaction committed"
38                     Screen.MousePointer = vbDefault
39                     Exit Sub
40                 End If
```

continues

12

Listing 12.14 continued

```
41              End If
42
43      'Peek at first message in status queue
44          Set StatusMessage = StatusQ.Peek(ReceiveTimeout:=10000)
45              'If we don't get a status message, we must roll back this
46              'transaction to keep the admin message on the queue
47              If StatusMessage Is Nothing Then
48                  intPress = MsgBox("No status message at this time", _
                        vbInformation, "Client customer service application")
49                  Transaction.Abort
50                  List1.AddItem "Transaction aborted"
51                  Screen.MousePointer = vbDefault
52                  Exit Sub
53              End If
54
55      'At this point we have at least one message to check
56          x = 2
57
58      'Convert CorrID's to strings we can compare
59          For Counter = LBound(StatusMessage.CorrelationId) To _
                        UBound(StatusMessage.CorrelationId)
60              strStatusMessageID = strStatusMessageID & _
                            Hex(StatusMessage.CorrelationId(Counter))
61          Next Counter
62
63          For Counter = LBound(AdminMessage.CorrelationId) To _
                        UBound(AdminMessage.CorrelationId)
64              strAdminMessageID = strAdminMessageID & _
                            Hex(AdminMessage.CorrelationId(Counter))
65          Next Counter
66
67      'Compare ID's: Do these messages correspond with each other?
68          If strStatusMessageID = strAdminMessageID Then GoTo Confirm
69
70          'Otherwise, continue checking StatusQ for corresponding message
71          While Not strStatusMessageID = strAdminMessageID
72              If n = 1 Then
73                  'PeekCurrent must be used before PeekNext can be used
74                  Set StatusMessage = StatusQ.PeekCurrent(ReceiveTimeout:=10000)
75
76              'Otherwise, we peek at the next message
77              Else: Set StatusMessage = StatusQ.PeekNext(ReceiveTimeout:=10000)
78              End If
79
80              'If we never found a corresponding status message, bail.
81              If StatusMessage Is Nothing Then
82                  intPress = MsgBox("No status message at this time.", _
                            vbInformation, "Client customer service
                            ➥ application")
83                  Transaction.Abort
```

```
84                       List1.AddItem "Transaction aborted"
85                       Screen.MousePointer = vbDefault
86                       Exit Sub
87                 End If
88
89                 'Again convert the ID's
90                 For Counter = LBound(StatusMessage.CorrelationId) To _
                             UBound(StatusMessage.CorrelationId)
91                       strStatusMessageID = strStatusMessageID & _
                                   Hex(StatusMessage.CorrelationId(Counter))
92                 Next Counter
93
94                 'Again compare
95                 If strStatusMessageID = strAdminMessageID Then GoTo Confirm
96
97                 n = 2
98
99          Wend
100
101 Confirm:
102     'StatusMessage corresponds with AdminMessage, so we will pick it up off
        'the queue.
103     Set StatusMessage = StatusQ.ReceiveCurrent
104
105     'Adding the appropriate portion of the message to the ListView columns
106     Dim lvItem As ListItem
107     Dim order As String
108     order = StrConv(StatusMessage.Body, vbUnicode)
109        Set lvItem = ListView1.ListItems.Add
110        With lvItem
111           .Text = Left$(order, 25)
112           .SubItems(1) = Mid$(order, 26, 25)
113           .SubItems(2) = Mid$(order, 51, 25)
114           .SubItems(3) = Mid$(order, 76, 25)
115           .SubItems(4) = Mid$(order, 101, 25)
116           .SubItems(5) = Mid$(order, 126, 2)
117           .SubItems(6) = Mid$(order, 128, 9)
118           .SubItems(7) = Mid$(order, 137, 16)
119           .SubItems(8) = Mid$(order, 153, 25)
120           .SubItems(9) = Mid$(order, 178, 25)
121           .SubItems(10) = Mid$(order, 203, 25)
122        End With
123
124     'Commit the transaction
125     Transaction.Commit
126
127 Loop
128
129 List1.AddItem "Transactions committed"
130 Screen.MousePointer = vbDefault
131 Exit Sub
```

12

continues

Listing 12.14 continued

```
132
133 ErrorHandler:
134     intPress = MsgBox("Error: " & Err.Description, _
                    vbExclamation, "Client customer service applicaiton")
135     Transaction.Abort
136     List1.AddItem "Transaction aborted"
137     Screen.MousePointer = vbDefault
138
139 End Sub
```

The last step needed to complete the client customer service application is to add just a little more functionality. This portion, in a real situation, would be relatively complex, with database updates and/or perhaps more messages being sent to other nodes. However, we are simply going to create a MessageBox that simulates a confirmation of one of the orders displayed in the ListView. Whichever entry the user double-clicks on is displayed in a YesNoCancel MessageBox along with the question Confirm order for. . .? This feature necessitates a ListView1_DblClick() subroutine. Listing 12.15 shows the code.

Listing 12.15 The `cmdPerformCheck` Command Button Code (continued)

```
1       Private Sub ListView1_DblClick()
2       ' In real life there would be work done here...
3           strPress = MsgBox("Confirm order for: " & vbCrLf & _
              ListView1.SelectedItem & vbCrLf & _
                ListView1.SelectedItem.SubItems(1) & vbCrLf & _
                ListView1.SelectedItem.SubItems(2) & vbCrLf & _
                ListView1.SelectedItem.SubItems(3) & vbCrLf & _
                ListView1.SelectedItem.SubItems(4) & vbCrLf & _
                ListView1.SelectedItem.SubItems(5) & vbCrLf & _
                ListView1.SelectedItem.SubItems(6) & vbCrLf & _
                ListView1.SelectedItem.SubItems(7) & vbCrLf & _
                ListView1.SelectedItem.SubItems(8) & vbCrLf & _
                ListView1.SelectedItem.SubItems(9) & vbCrLf & _
                ListView1.SelectedItem.SubItems(10) _
                , vbYesNoCancel, "Client Customer Service Application")
4
5       End Sub
```

That is it! You have completed the client customer service application. You will remember, however, that the server node also needs a customer service application. Only two small changes are required to transform the current application into the server customer service application: We need to modify the GUIDs used in the LookUpQueue arguments in the form load. Change them to the GUIDs assigned to the admin and status queues the server creates. If we are distributing this application across many client and server machines, we could either assign identical GUIDs to the admin and status queues on each machine or use a different identifier, such as label.

Testing

You should be able to test this application right away because you already ran a single order workflow when you tested the audit application. Therefore, messages should be waiting for this customer service application on the status and admin queues. For debugging purposes, you may want to submit many orders to load up those queues. That way you do not need to run a transaction every time you need to test this customer service application.

Summary

Now in addition to relying on the transactional processing capabilities of MSMQ to responsibly carry out our orders, we can use its acknowledgment features to monitor its success and provide information to our customers on the status of their orders. In the future, we might even centralize this customer service operation, allowing a central user to check on queues throughout the order process from one location. Or we might set up local applications to run continuously, writing to a central repository of order status information for the customer service agents to access.

In this chapter you learned the functionally to browse a queue using the `Peek`, `PeekCurrent`, and `PeekNext` methods of the queue object, and you were also able to use the `ReceiveCurrent` method of the queue object to retrieve the message at the current cursor position.

There you have it! Congratulations, you have successfully completed your first MSMQ-based, distributed application. If you have run everything on one machine up to this point, you will probably want to experiment with the use of a more complete MSMQ Enterprise. We are going to leave our e-books example here. In the following chapters, we discuss some of the advanced features of MSMQ and how to extend MSMQ beyond Windows NT.

12

Part 6

Advanced Topics

Chapter 13

Advanced MSMQ Topics

Security Features

For many business applications to be considered "robust," the data transfer between them must be secure. But the term *secure* has many meanings. The various aspects of a secure system cover elements such as authentication, privacy, integrity, nonrepudiation, and access control.

Authentication is the process of verifying that the message came from whom it claims to have come. In our example, the warehouse needs to be sure it is receiving dispatch messages only from a valid order-processing server.

Privacy is the process of ensuring that only the intended recipient of a message can read its contents. In our example, we want the customer's credit card information to remain private.

Integrity is the process of ensuring that the message that was sent is the message that was received. In our example, we want to ensure that the warehouse receives the correct dispatch message. We want to be sure that no one could have tampered with the message while it was en route.

Nonrepudiation is the process of ensuring that the sender cannot deny sending the message. In our example, the credit card company wants to ensure that the order-processing server cannot deny sending the billing transaction.

Access control is the process of making sure that only those who have been given permission have access to certain resources, such as queues. In our example, the order-processing server wants to ensure that only valid users can send messages to its inquiry queue.

We have already stated that MSMQ is integrated with Windows NT platform tools, such as the security manager. But what does this integration mean to designers of distributed applications, and how do we take advantage of these features from our application?

First of all, we need to make a distinction between a workgroup and a domain environment. When MSMQ is deployed in a workgroup environment, very little is offered in the way of security. It is not possible to differentiate between users, and so usually everyone has full access control to everything, including the primary enterprise controller (PEC). In a domain environment, the full object-level security features are available to the administrator, and so access to individual objects can be restricted by an individual user or group of users.

MSMQ uses the RSA security model. That is, a pair of keys—one public and one private—preserves the security of the data. Only the corresponding keys may be used to lock and unlock a message. The public key may be shared among all the nodes, but the private key is held only on the node to which it belongs.

RSA is a public key cryptosystem that offers facilities for both encryption and digital signatures (authentication). Ron Rivest, Adi Shamir, and Leonard Adleman developed RSA, hence the designation RSA for Rivest, Shamir, and Adleman.

For authentication the sender uses its own private key to encrypt the message. Any receiver may use the public key of the sender to decrypt the message. Because only the sender knows its private key, the receiver can be sure of where the message came from. This arrangement also takes care of the nonrepudiation of the message. It is impossible for anyone else to have sent it, so the sender cannot later deny having done so.

To ensure the privacy of the data, the sender uses the receiver's public key to encrypt the message, and the receiver uses its own private key to decrypt the message. Because only the intended receiver has access to the private key, only the intended receiver can unpack the message. Note that this process does not say anything about the integrity of the message. Although the original message could not have been tampered with, it could be intercepted and replaced. Authentication and encryption must be used together to guarantee the integrity of the message. Figure 13.1 illustrates how the flow of encryption is implemented in sending messages.

As mentioned earlier, MSMQ uses the RSA model of public and private keys to authenticate and encrypt messages. These keys, or "certificates" as they are known in Windows NT, are registered pieces of information that are created when MSMQ is installed on a particular machine. Each machine has a unique pair of private and public keys. If one is used to lock the information, the other must be used to unlock it. The keys that are generated in this manner are known as internal keys. Internal certificates use only the Security ID (SID) information for encoding the message.

Figure 13.1

Sending encrypted messages.

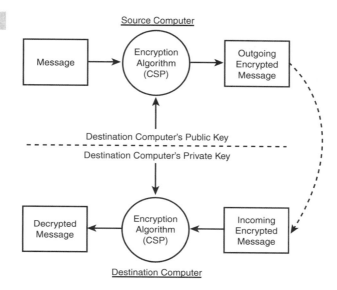

Note A SID is a unique name that identifies the logged on user to the security system.

The MSMQ control applet administers a computer's certificates. This applet is located in the Windows NT Control Panel and is described as MS Message Queue in the available list of icons. You can use the control applet to register, view, or remove a computer's certificates. These certificates are stored and maintained in the copy of the Microsoft Message Queue Information Store (MQIS) with which the machine is associated.

Figure 13.2 shows a picture of the MS Message Queue control applet's main panel.

Figure 13.2

MS Message Queue control applet.

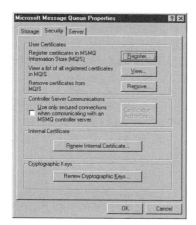

Encryption keys should be renewed periodically, for example, every 6 months. They can be renewed by selecting the Renew Cryptographic Keys button on the Security tab of the MSMQ Control Panel applet. Note that any encrypted messages that have been sent but not received before selecting this option cannot be read. This process creates a new pair of private and public keys for the computer and publishes the public key to the MQIS. If you suspect that the keys have become compromised, they should be renewed immediately.

You will not be able to replicate the server's key information. The keys in the server's MQIS can not be exposed during transfer. Instead, you must use a MSMQ-supplied application called mqsrvkey to manually copy the keys onto diskette for distribution. Follow these steps:

1. On the server where the keys have been renewed, at a command prompt enter:

   ```
   mqsrvkey filename
   ```

2. Copy the generated file to a floppy disk.

3. On each subordinate server, run the following command from the command line:

   ```
   mqsrvkey a:filename
   ```

4. This command installs the new key into the server and allows the replication requests to be accepted.

If Windows 95 or Windows NT is reinstalled on a MSMQ machine, you must use the MSMQ Control Panel applet to remove the existing internal certificate and register a new certificate for the machine. The reason is that a unique SID is created each time you register a certificate (which is actually another GUID) and that value is stored in the MQIS. The value stored in the MQIS must then match the value from the sending computer so that the operation can complete successfully when the receiving application authenticates the message.

If you want to use more stringent security, external certificates are available from various certificate vendors on the Web (example, Verisign digitalid.verisign.com). These certificates are stored in the Internet Explorer (IE) store (as opposed to the MQIS) and require the use of IE v3.0 or later. Regardless of the type, all certificates appear the same to a MSMQ application programmer.

In the following sections, we talk about using the features of MSMQ to achieve message authentication, message encryption, and object access control.

13

Authentication

Authentication provides the assurance that the message came from a specific source. Therefore, someone cannot "fake" receiving a message, and the sender cannot deny sending it.

When used with encryption, MSMQ authentication also provides the assurance that the data was transported between applications without alteration. In addition to the receiver having confidence that the message came from a known source, authentication used with encryption assures that the sender cannot later deny sending the message (nonrepudiation).

MSMQ handles authentication automatically when an application requests that a message be sent that way. It is specified as a property of the MSMQMessage object, AuthLevel.

The AuthLevel property of the MSMQMessage object can take one of two possible values:

- MQMSG_AUTH_LEVEL_NONE, the default—The message is not to be authenticated by MSMQ.
- MQMSG_AUTH_LEVEL_ALWAYS—The message is to be authenticated by MSMQ.

In addition to messages carrying a property, you can also indicate in the definition of a queue whether or not it can receive authenticated messages. In the e-books example, the warehouse might want to set its queue to receive only authenticated messages, preventing any unknown source from sending the application a message.

It is worth noting that MSMQ verifies message authentication when the message is placed on the target queue. To the receiving application, all messages are the same. Thus to ensure that we receive only authentic messages (if this option is desired), we must set the property of the input queue to allow it to receive only authentic messages.

The queue property may be set either from MSMQ Explorer or by the program that creates or modifies its properties. The Authenticate property of the MSMQQueueInfo object sets the security on the queue and can be used with either the Create or Update methods of the MSMQQueueInfo object.

The Authenticate property can have one of the following values:

- MQ_AUTHENTICATE_NONE, the default—The queue accepts both authenticated and nonauthenticated messages.
- MQ_AUTHENTICATE—The queue accepts only authenticated messages.

Although the receiving application does not participate in the authentication of the message, the receiving application can determine whether or not the message is authenticated. Of course, this feature is relevant only if the queue accepts both authenticated and nonauthenticated messages. The IsAuthenticated property of the MSMQMessage object contains this information and is a read-only property available to the application after it has received the message. The IsAuthenticated property can have one of two values:

- TRUE—The message is authenticated.
- FALSE—The message is not authenticated.

Figure 13.3 shows what happens to a message as it travels from the sending computer.

Figure 13.3

Authentication at the sender.

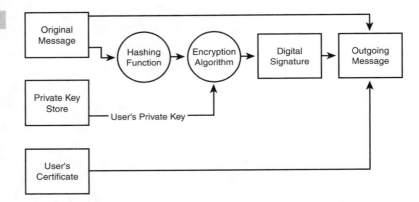

- A hashing function (MD5, by default) is applied to various properties of the message being sent, creating a message digest.
- The message digest is encrypted by using the sending user's private key. The result of the encryption is known as a digital signature.

The receiving MSMQ computer performs the following steps to authenticate a message, as shown in Figure 13.4.

- The receiver applies the same hashing function, MD5 in this case, to the same properties of the incoming message as were applied to the original message, again producing the message digest.
- The receiver uses the sender's public key to decrypt the digital signature and to recover the message digest that the sender created.
- If the two message digests are the same, then the identity of the sender has been verified.

Figure 13.4

Authentication at the receiver.

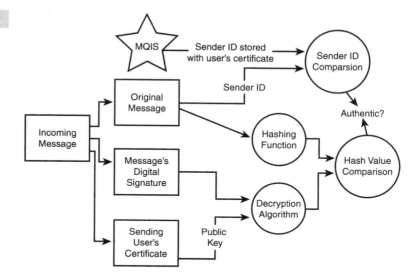

The hashing function that is used to produce the message digest can be changed from the default by using the HashAlgorithm property of the MSMQMessage object. The property can be set to any of the values defined by the ALG_ID data type in wincrypt.h. The default is CALG_MD5. A copy of wincrypt.h is supplied with the installation of C or C++ compiler. For example, if you are using Microsoft's Visual Studio set, wincrypt.h is under \Program Files\Microsoft Visual Studio\VC98\Include.

Encryption

Encryption is the process of ensuring that the contents of a message remain private between the sender and the receiver.

Like authentication, encryption is done automatically by MSMQ, when requested by the programmer. Also like authentication, you can set a property of a target queue to indicate that only encrypted messages can be sent to it.

The PrivLevel property of the MSMQMessage object indicates whether or not MSMQ should encrypt a message. The property may be assigned one of the following values:

- MQMSG_PRIV_LEVEL_NONE, the default—MSMQ is not to encrypt the message.
- MQMSG_PRIV_LEVEL_BODY—MSMQ is to encrypt the body of the message.

The MSMQQueueInfo object offers the same property that may be used to specify in the queue definition whether or not a queue can receive encrypted messages. The privacy level of a queue may be set when it is created with the Create method of the MSMQQueueInfo object and altered later by using the Update method of the same object.

In the case of the `MSMQQueueInfo` object, the `PrivLevel` property can take one of three values:

- `MQ_PRIV_LEVEL_OPTIONAL`, the default—The queue can receive either encrypted or nonencryted ("clear") messages.
- `MQ_PRIV_LEVEL_NONE`—The queue can receive only clear messages.
- `MQ_PRIV_LEVEL_BODY`—The queue can receive only encrypted messages.

MSMQ performs the encryption/decryption of messages as they pass through the network. Messages are written to their target queue unencrypted.

Figure 13.5 summarizes the encryption process. The message is encrypted by the sender, using the public key of the intended recipient. The message is then unlocked by the recipient, using its own private key. Only the intended recipient has access to this key, so the message remains private.

Figure 13.5

The encryption process.

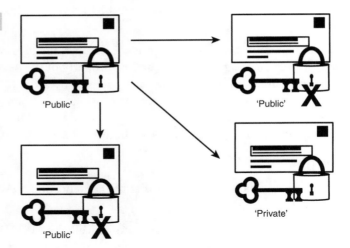

The sending node retrieves from the MQIS the public key of the intended recipient. When locked with this key, the data can be unlocked only with the corresponding private key.

MSMQ, by default, uses the RC2 encryption algorithm, part of the RSA security model, for encrypting and decrypting messages. You can use the `EncryptAlgorithm` property of the `MSMQMessage` object to vary this default setting. The property may be set to one of the following options:

- `MQMSG_RC2`, the default
- `MQMSG_RC4`

The encryption of MSMQ messages is carried out by a cryptographic service provider (CSP). By default, MSMQ uses Microsoft Base Cryptographic Provider version 1.0, which must be installed on all computers that will send or receive encrypted messages. This CSP is installed by default with Windows NT version 4 and Internet Explorer version 3 and higher.

Details about the Microsoft CryptoAPI, with which CSPs can be developed, along with information for cryptography and public key encryption, can be found at the Microsoft Web site or in the MSMQ SDK.

Access Control

Access Control has nothing to do with RSA keys and is simply the process of allowing the MSMQ administrator to control which user can perform which action. For example, you may control who can add or remove servers and who can read from or write to a particular queue.

The security settings panel for any given MSMQ object can be accessed by highlighting the object in MSMQ Explorer and clicking the right mouse button to display the Objects menu. From the Objects menu, choose Properties and then select the Security tab. Click the Permissions button to display a panel similar to that shown in Figure 13.6. This panel shows the users and the groups who have access to the selected object and the nature of that access.

Figure 13.6

Object permissions list.

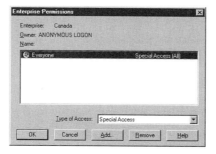

This panel in Figure 13.6 should look very familiar to a Windows NT administrator and serves to emphasize the tight integration that MSMQ has with Windows NT. The administrator is able to use this panel to set the access that different users and groups have to the selected object.

The following sections identify the security options available for each MSMQ object and explain what the options mean in terms of the actions that users can perform.

Enterprise Security Options

By default, all users have read access to the PEC. The enterprise administrator (the user who installed the enterprise) has full control.

Figure 13.7 shows the Special tab and the security options that are available for the PEC.

Figure 13.7

Security options available for the PEC.

Read access allows the user to

- Retrieve the enterprise permissions settings *(Get Permissions)*
- Register certificates in the MQIS *(Create User)*

Write access allows the user to

- Retrieve the enterprise permissions settings *(Get Permissions)*
- Register certificates in the MQIS *(Create User)*
- Create sites *(Create Site)*
- Create connected networks *(Create CN)*

Site Security Options

By default, all users have write access to a site. The site administrator (the user who installed the site) has full control.

Figure 13.8 shows the options that are available if Special access is selected for a user.

Read access allows the user to

- Retrieve the site's permissions settings *(Get Permissions)*

Write access allows the user to

- Retrieve the site's permissions settings *(Get Permissions)*
- Install a computer in the site *(Create Computer)*

Figure 13.8

Security options available for the primary site controller.

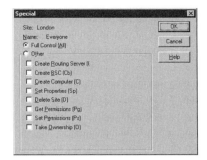

Connected Network Security Options

By default, all users have read access for a connected network. The connected network administrator (the user who created the connected network) has full control.

Figure 13.9 shows the security options that are available for a connected network. Of particular note is the Open Connector option. Having permission for this option allows you use MSMQ outside the MSMQ infrastructure. Examples of such connectors are the MSMQ-MQSeries Bridge (discussed later) and the interface to Microsoft's Exchange Server (MAPI interface).

Figure 13.9

Security options available for the connected network.

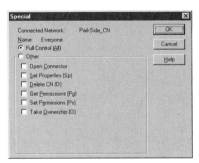

Read access allows the user to

- Retrieve a connected network's permissions settings *(Get Permissions)*

Write access allows the user to

- Retrieve a connected network's permissions *settings (Get Permissions)*

Individual Computer Security Options

Access permissions for a computer relate to the user's ability to create and delete MSMQ objects on that node. The computer can be any machine in the MSMQ network, including the PEC, primary site controller (PSC), backup site controller (BSC), routing server (RS), or independent clients.

By default, everyone has write permission for a computer. The computer administrator (the user who installed the computer) has full control permission.

Figure 13.10 shows the detailed options available.

Figure 13.10

Security options available for a computer.

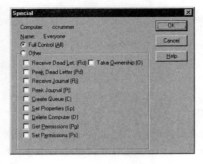

Read access allows the user to

- Receive messages from the computer's journal queue (*Receive Journal, Peek Journal*)
- Receive messages from the computer's dead letter queue (*Receive Dead Letter, Peak Dead Letter*)
- Retrieve the computer's permissions settings (*Get Permissions*)

Write access allows the user to

- Retrieve the computer's permissions settings (*Get Permissions*)
- Create queues on the computer (*Create Queue*)

Queue Security Options

By default, everyone has send access to a queue. The queue administrator (the user who created the queue) has full control.

Figure 13.11 shows the access options associated with a queue.

Figure 13.11

Security options available for a queue.

Send access allows the user to

- Retrieve the queue's properties *(Get Properties)*
- Retrieve the queue's permissions *(Get Permissions)*
- Send messages to the queue *(Send Message)*

Receive access allows the user to

- Retrieve the queue's properties *(Get Properties)*
- Retrieve the queue's permissions *(Get Permissions)*
- View messages from the queue *(Peek Message)*
- Receive messages from the queue *(Receive Message, Receive Journal)*

Optimization

This section outlines some additional benefits that can be realized by setting up a loosely coupled application infrastructure, such as that provided by MSMQ. By enabling certain properties on some MSMQ machines, you can affect the delivery of a message. You can influence the path taken to deliver it, the nodes it passes through, and what happens in the event a particular node or link is not available.

Dynamic Routing

The description of PSCs in Chapter 1, "An Overview of Message Queuing and MSMQ," introduced the term *sites*. So, with all our sites established and ready to work, we now need to connect everything. Sites are linked to other sites through communication sessions called site links.

Intersite routing is the process of sending messages between sites on these links. MSMQ calculates intersite routing based on relative numbers that administrators assign to site links. These numbers, called site link costs, represent the cost of communication on that link. This cost is not drawn from your bank account! It is a cost you associate with the delivery time, resource consumption, and reliability in the delivery of a message.

You set site link costs when you install new sites. If you have only two sites, choose any value above zero. If you have three or more sites and the cost of routing between sites is more or less equal, use the same value for each site link. However, if you have three or more sites and the cost of routing between sites is not equal, use site link costs to define the difference in the routing costs. You can also use site link costs to persuade MSMQ to favor one route over another.

For example, in Figure 13.12 suppose you have two sites, A and B, that are connected by a high-speed link via an intermediate RS, Site C. An additional site, Site D, is available. This site, however, is overseas and is connected to Site B by a low-speed link.

Figure 13.12

Dynamic routing link costs.

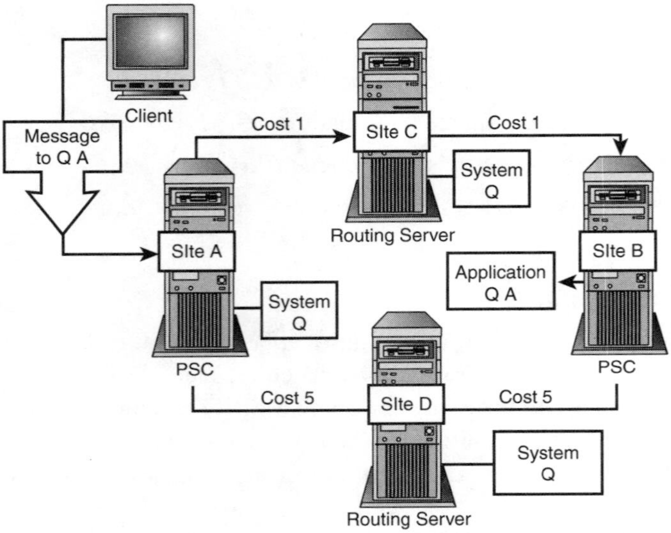

In Figure 13.12, you can see that the cost from Site A to Site B through Site C is much lower than the cost is through Site D. The route through Site D, then, is taken only if the route through Site C is unavailable.

If something should happen to the network link between Site A and Site C, MSMQ would use the next cheapest alternative route to deliver the messages. In this case messages would travel via Site D, even though the site cost is more. The link is available, and MSMQ will deliver (as shown in Figure 13.13).

As a rule, each connected site should have an alternative route in the event of a network failure—especially in a time-critical environment. In Figure 13.13 a message was routed to Site B because of the lower link cost between Site A and Site C.

However, in Figure 13.14, if the link between Site C and Site B is down and no alternative route exists between the sites, the message remains in a temporary system-controlled queue at Site C. An administrator must be familiar with the potential routings and holding queues of the enterprise. Site C has the capacity to then send the message to Site B when the connection is reestablished; thus the message is still delivered. Delivery becomes a matter of when, instead of whether. Without alternative routing, messages may be delayed in arriving at their intended destination.

Figure 13.13

Dynamic routing with fail over.

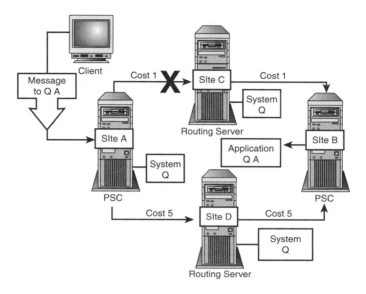

Figure 13.14

Dynamic routing without alternative routing.

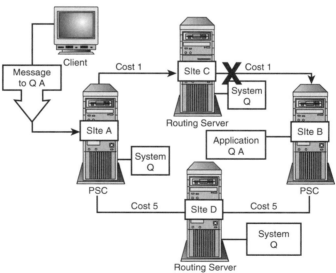

Load Balancing

With some insight into dynamic routing, we can now appreciate the power of load balancing. Load balancing is how an administrator can control the load on a network by dictating the direction in which messages should go. The diagram in Figure 13.15 closely resembles that in Figure 13.12. In Figure 13.15, we have request type messages traveling from Site A to Site C to Site B and reply messages traveling via the bottom path, from Site B to Site D to Site A. Whether or not the messages actually go the way we told them to depends on network status. If load balancing is of the utmost importance, we should probably also determine alternative routes to maintain the load balancing in the event of a disconnected network (as discussed in the preceding section).

Figure 13.15

Load balancing.

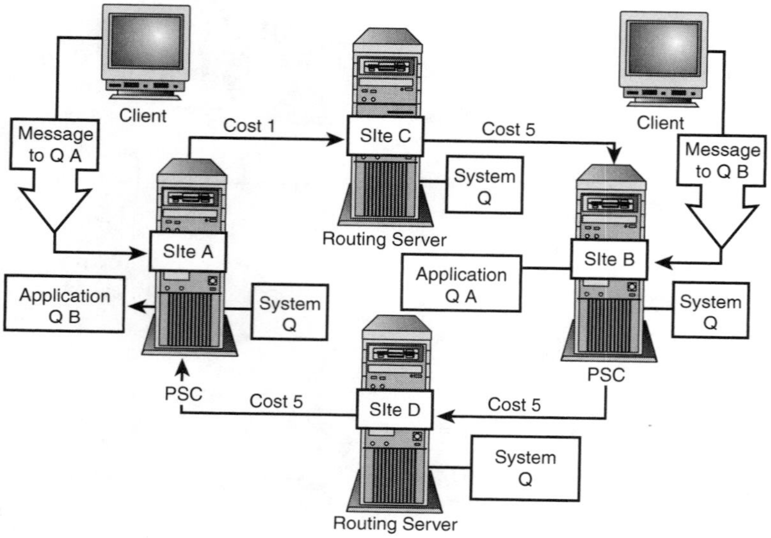

Load balancing is especially powerful in a request/reply model. Usually the model notes a 1:1 relationship. That is, one request expects one reply. Balancing messages via alternative paths extends the flexibility of MSMQ to savings in performance, response time, resources (CPU usage), and network bandwidth.

We can leverage the network redundancy offered by dynamic routing to facilitate load balancing. If two routes exist between two nodes, each with similar site costs, we can use load balancing during normal operation to spread the burden and increase network performance. However, in the event one connection becomes unavailable, MSMQ simply routes the additional traffic down the single pipe. Performance may be affected, but the messages get to their destination. When the failed connection is restored, MSMQ again balances the network load across the available pipes.

Session Concentration

MSMQ servers can be designated as in routing servers (InRSs) or out routing servers (OutRSs), and these MSMQ servers (also known as site gates) can be used to control the flow of messages and provide session concentration.

13

As your message queuing enterprise begins to send a lot of messages, you may experience bottlenecks on some of the servers. Bottlenecks can develop, for example, when many MSMQ clients (dependant or independent) are connecting to a specific MSMQ server and expecting processing acknowledgments in return. This situation can lead to severe delays in the turnaround time of the messages.

We can alleviate some of the congestion by providing a level of dynamic routing: having inbound client requests take one path (InRS) and sending replies via a different server (OutRS). InRS and OutRS are still MSMQ RSs, but they just serve a different kind of function from each other.

In Figure 13.16 we can see how many session links can be saved by using a routing server. Without a RS, you would need 36 sessions to exchange messages with other independent clients. With a RS, the required number of sessions is reduced to seven.

Figure 13.16

Session concentration.

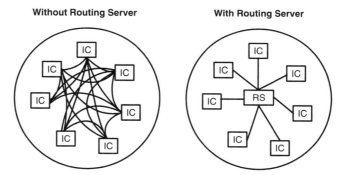

Only MSMQ-independent clients can be configured to have either InRSs or OutRSs. MSMQ dependent clients and MSMQ servers cannot be configured to use InRSs or OutRSs.

Fail-Over Support

The BSC provides fail-over support for a MSMQ server. The BSC contains a read-only copy of the MQIS. The BSC allows applications that are currently running to continue in case the server to which they are connected becomes unavailable. The MQIS copy remains read-only, so applications cannot create queues. Also worth noting is that messages stored on the physical queues hosted by the failed server are not available until the server is restored. If they were express messages en route when the server failed, they will be lost forever.

MSMQ Event Logging

One of the best ways to track operations completed by MSMQ is to enable event logging. Event logging is a standard Windows NT operation used in normal day-to-day activities. Network administrators generally use event logging to watch who is doing what. MSMQ again uses this core Windows NT technology for its own purposes.

For MSMQ computers installed on Windows 95/98, events are recorded in the Msmqlog.txt file, located in C:\Program Files\Msmq\Storage\Msmqlog.txt.

In NT, all the events are captured in the Windows NT event log. These events can be viewed by using the Event Viewer under Start, Programs, Administration Tools, Event Viewer.

A few procedures and considerations need to be made within NT to record the appropriate audit events.

- The administrator must enable File and Object Access auditing on the computer to audit. This feature is enabled within Start, Programs, Administration Tools, User Manager. When the User Manger window appears, choose Audit from the Policies menu. File and Object Access auditing must also be enabled on the controller servers where MQIS will carry out the operation.

- The user account under which the MSMQ service runs must have the Generate Security Audits right to write messages to the security log. If this right is not enabled, a warning message is written to the application log.

  This right can be enabled from within the Windows NT User Manager, in the User Rights Policy section. A little trick is necessary to enable this function. As seen Figure 13.17, you must select the Show Advanced User Rights check box to display the Generate Security Audits item in the selection list.

  The local system account, where the MSMQ service runs by default, has this required right.

Figure 13.17

Setting the Generate Security Audits rights.

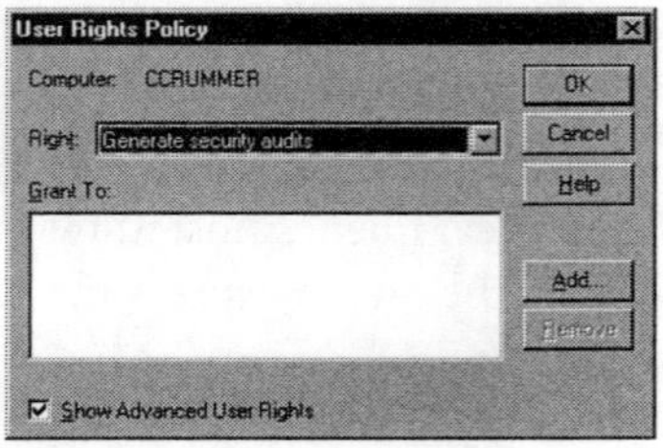

- When using MSMQ Explorer to manage the audit policy, the user must have the Manage auditing and security log right on the MSMQ controller server. This right is enabled very much as shown in Figure 13.17, but you do not need to select the Show Advanced User Rights check box.

  The audit log messages are written in the event log of the server that performs the operation, which may not be the server that owns the object.

  All queue operations except for Read Message and Peek Message are performed by a MSMQ controller server, and the audit messages are stored on that same server. However, in the case of a read or peek, the audit messages are generated on the computer where the queue resides.

With the Windows NT procedures now out of the way, we can start to configure the MSMQ events we want to log. We can specify the properties of each MSMQ object by right clicking on the object and then selecting Properties, Security, Auditing. The Audit Events window affiliated with that MSMQ object is then displayed.

Figure 13.18 show the audit properties for the enterprise.

Figure 13.18

Enterprise audit properties.

As with the security permissions, we can select which userId or group we want to add.

The Audit window for the enterprise allows us to capture both the success and failure of events affiliated with it. Notice how the events look similar to security permissions. Coincidence? I don't think so!

The Site Auditing properties panel is displayed in Figure 13.19. This panel allows monitoring of the events occurring within a site.

Figure 13.19

Site Auditing properties.

The Computer Auditing panel allows you to watch events that relate to the operations within a computer. Figure 13.20 shows the events available for audit.

Figure 13.20

Computer Auditing properties.

Connected networks also have auditing available. Figure 13.21 shows the events available for audit.

The last MSMQ object to audit is the Queue object. Figure 13.22 shows the details associated with logging the use of queues.

Now that you have selected the audit events that you want to monitor, you can see them in the Event Viewer. Each audited event, whether it is a success or failure, is recorded in the event log of the appropriate computer as an open entry and a close entry.

By double-clicking on an open entry, further information about the event, including details of the user who initiated it, are displayed in a second window. Figure 13.23 what the Event Viewer looks like for a MSMQ audited event.

Figure 13.21

Connected Network Auditing properties.

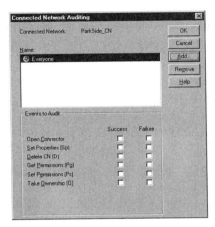

Figure 13.22

Queue Auditing properties.

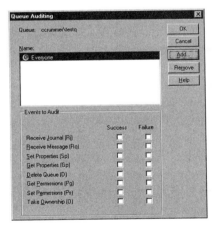

Figure 13.23

Example of an event view.

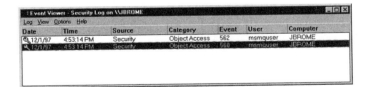

Performance Monitor

We have described several methods for sending messages. One thing you might be wondering about is how to monitor all these messages. How can I ensure that I'm receiving the best performance possible? A good question. Well, again back to the fact that MSMQ is integrated with Windows NT, the Performance Monitor that is supplied with the operating system and can record and monitor message traffic.

Located within the properties of a computer, queue, or the MQIS (right-click on any machine or queue name and select Properties, Status) and the performance statistics for the object. Figure 13.24 shows what the screen may look like. The following list describes some of the information available in the Status tab.

- The total number of bytes of all messages in all the queues that are currently stored on that one machine.

- Total messages in all queues—incoming and outgoing messages per second.

- In regard to the earlier section on dynamic routing and session concentration, the tab maintains a count of the connected sessions. This value helps you determine whether you require more RSs to alleviate the magnitude of concurrent sessions.

Figure 13.24

Statistics for a computer.

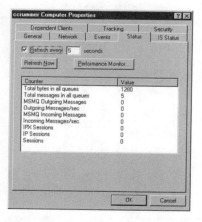

If the values displayed in the window are not sufficient, you can click the Performance Monitor button to start the Performance Monitor application. To track the necessary statistics, you need to configure the Performance Monitor. As shown in Figure 13.25, you can select various objects to monitor. Figure 13.25 is showing the available counters for the MSMQ IS object. You can tailor what you want to see happening with the MQIS.

Figure 13.25

Performance Monitor configuration.

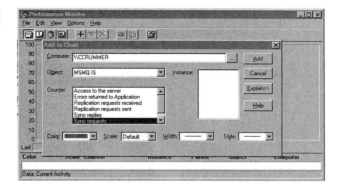

The overall values that are derived from the Performance Monitor indicate whether everything is moving at an appropriate pace or whether some issues need to be addressed. As mentioned earlier, the monitoring statistics can indicate whether you require additional RSs. Other counters to watch could include the number of messages on a particular queue and seeing whether the messages are being retrieved in sufficient time.

The Performance Monitor can record the statistics in a log file, which can be viewed later, or you can view the results via a progressive chart monitor.

Summary

This chapter has covered some important topics that were not incorporated into the programming example.

You have learned about security, and we suggest that you try to provide a secure connection between the order-processing server and the warehouse, using both encryption and authentication.

You might also try setting up a more extensive MSMQ Enterprise for your store and running multiple clients and servers. You can also experiment with the fail-over features and dynamic routing when links or servers are unavailable.

Chapter 14

Extending MSMQ to Non-Windows Platforms

Early in Chapter 1, "An Overview of Message Queuing and MSMQ," we mentioned that MSMQ is part of a technology solution being used in many environments to integrate business processes. The reality of such integration is that it must encompass a variety of operating system platforms. Thus we must integrate our applications with others running on MVS OS/390, UNIX, OS/400, Digital VMS, and Tandem, to name a few.

This chapter outlines two options that are available to you to extend MSMQ to such a heterogeneous network. In addition, the chapter includes a discussion of taking your enterprise applications and viewing the layer above the messaging technology and also introduces the concept of enterprise application integration (EAI). EAI is the process that incorporates various business systems and their underlying technologies.

Geneva Message Queuing

Geneva Message Queuing is an external gateway for MSMQ. Geneva Message Queuing extends the capabilities of MSMQ from Windows NT to other operating systems and enables you to connect systems such as UNIX, mid-range, and mainframes to a MSMQ enterprise network.

Geneva Message Queuing provides a fast and reliable message queuing interface between Windows NT and other operating systems. Geneva Message Queuing enables all your applications to use MSMQ store-and-forward messaging. This technology allows applications to communicate across a network even if the applications are not running at the same time.

Developed by Level 8 Systems, Inc., in collaboration with Microsoft Corporation, Geneva Message Queuing works with MSMQ in the simplest and most efficient way possible. Figure 14.1 shows how Geneva Message Queuing interfaces with the MSMQ machines.

 Note   For more information of Level 8 Systems, Inc. and its Geneva Message Queuing product, visit www.level8.com.

Figure 14.1

Geneva Message Queuing architectural overview.

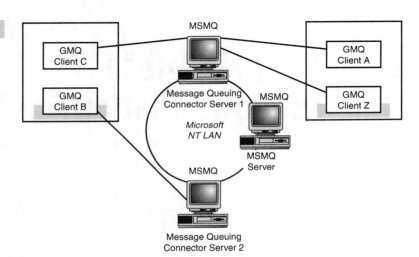

A Geneva Message Queuing installation comprises server and client components. The Geneva Message Queuing clients are installed on non-Windows systems and communicate with the Geneva Message Queuing server. The Geneva Message Queuing server is installed on at least one Windows NT system in the network and provides the interface with MSMQ.

The Geneva Message Queuing monitor is supplied as a component of Geneva Message Queuing to enable the system administrator to observe and control Geneva Message Queuing message traffic passing through the Geneva Message Queuing server.

Figure 14.2 shows the Geneva Message Queuing monitor. The monitor allows you to select the server you want to monitor. The monitor can be used to administer more than one installation of Geneva Message Queuing server. In fact, you can install the Geneva Message Queuing monitor on a separate server whose sole purpose is to watch Geneva Message Queuing server machines.

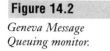

Figure 14.2

Geneva Message Queuing monitor.

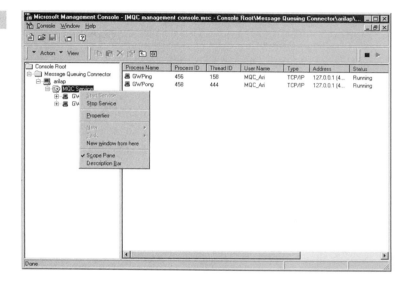

14

Using the Geneva Message Queuing Application Programming Interface (API), you can write application programs for non-Windows platforms that access the MSMQ message queues.

The API is designed to be as similar as possible to that of MSMQ running in its native Windows environment. The Geneva Message Queuing API is available in a various languages; however, ActiveX is not one of them because it is available only for Windows platforms! The supported languages are C, C++, COBOL, and RPG. The specific support varies by platform. RPG, for instance, is available only for the AS/400. Whatever the language selection, the principal features of MSMQ are the same as those available to Geneva Message Queuing programs.

Figure 14.3 shows how version 1.0 (v1.0) of Geneva Message Queuing works. You can see from the diagram that it behaves in a manner very similar to the MSMQ-dependent client. Geneva Message Queuing v1.0 relies upon the MSMQ server to host the queues that it has access to. Without a connection to a server, a Geneva Message Queuing program cannot perform the queuing function.

This restricted behavior is removed in v2.0, which supports queues on the Geneva Message Queuing machine (non-Windows machine). Geneva Message Queuing v2.0 behaves in much the same way as a MSMQ independent client. Figure 14.4 shows the level of independence achieved with v2.0. With local store and forwarding, non-Windows platforms can achieve true asynchronous processing. Now the non-Windows platforms have local queues and a queue manager. Here are some additional features in v2.0:

- Transactional support now includes the capability to send, receive, and update external resources under the same unit of work.

- Callback support allows applications that go beyond request/reply models. Callback functionality allows for nonblocking or nonpolling applications to be constructed in an event-driven model.

- Management of the infrastructure has been strengthened to support Web management and the Geneva Message Queuing monitor has been deployed under the Microsoft Management Console (MMC).

Figure 14.3

Geneva Message Queuing API execution overview.

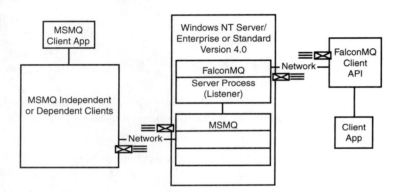

Figure 14.4

Geneva Message Queuing v2.0 architecture overview.

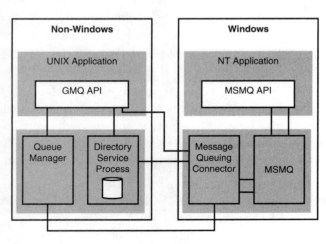

To summarize, Geneva Message Queuing allows you to do MSMQ on non-Windows platforms. By this point you should realize that you may need to do some processing outside of your Windows environment. If so, Geneva Message Queuing is the only

Microsoft-recognized solution for providing this functionality. If you are interested in more information on Geneva Message Queuing, an evaluation copy, and an online demonstration of the product, visit the Level 8 Systems Web site at `www.level8.com`.

MSMQ to MQSeries Bridge

Now that we have discussed connecting MSMQ to non-Windows platforms, we need to talk about connecting MSMQ to IBM's MQSeries.

MQSeries is IBM's message queuing product. MQSeries has a strong presence in the middleware market, and companies wanting to maintain their investment in MQSeries need to connect it to MSMQ.

Preserving the investment is the intent of the MSMQ-MQSeries Bridge. This product (originally developed and released by Level 8 Systems, Inc., as the FalconMQ Bridge) is now a Microsoft product that is available with Microsoft SNA Server, SP2.

With the MSMQ-MQSeries Bridge, MSMQ and IBM's MQSeries applications can send messages to each other across the different message queuing systems. MSMQ-MQSeries Bridge achieves this functionality by mapping the messages and data fields of the sending system, and the values associated with those fields, to the fields and values of the receiving environment. After the mapping and conversion, MSMQ-MQSeries Bridge completes the process by routing the message across the combined MSMQ and MQSeries networks. Figure 14.5 shows how the two messaging products communicate.

Figure 14.5

Bridge architecture.

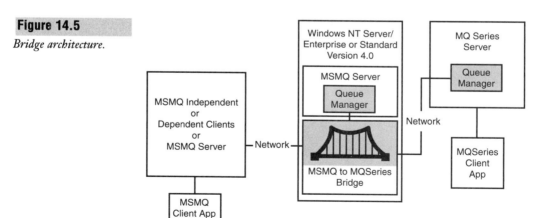

The MSMQ-MQSeries Bridge has two components. The MSMQ-MQSeries Bridge itself converts and transmits messages between the two messaging environments. The other component is MSMQ-MQSeries Bridge Explorer. Bridge Explorer configures and monitors the bridge. Figure 14.6 shows a screen from MSMQ-MQSeries Bridge Explorer.

Figure 14.6

Bridge Explorer.

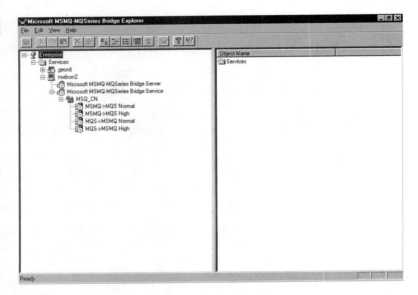

The architecture behind the MSMQ-MQSeries Bridge requires a little further explanation. MSMQ can communicate with outside resources such as other primary enterprise controllers (PECs), and Microsoft's Exchange Server through the MSMQ Connector. This communication feature allows information (messages) to be sent in and out of a MSMQ infrastructure. The Bridge uses the MSMQ Connector.

MSMQ Connector allows MSMQ-based applications to communicate with computers (called foreign computers) that use other messaging systems. MSMQ Connector uses foreign connected networks and foreign queues to communicate with foreign computers.

Creating a foreign computer is straightforward. First you must create a foreign connected network, as follows:

- Right-click on the enterprise (at the top of your MSMQ Explorer) to display the menu for the PEC.
- From the menu, select New, CN to create a new connected network.
- Provide a name and specify the type of CN you want to create, as shown in Figure 14.7. You can choose to establish a connection between nodes running MSMQ on a different protocol or between nodes running a foreign queuing system, such as IBM MQSeries.

Figure 14.7

Creating a foreign connected network.

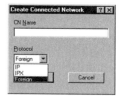

After the foreign connected network is created, you need to create a foreign computer. The foreign computer represents the MQSeries Queue Manager. If you are not familiar with IBM's MQSeries product, a Queue Manager is a single node that hosts queues. It is similar to a *computer* in MSMQ terminology.

To create a foreign computer:

- Right-click on the Site icon (the yellow building icon, not the PSC machine).
- Select New and then click on Foreign Computer. A screen similar to the one in Figure 14.8 appears.
- Enter the name of the foreign computer (which is the same name as your MQSeries Queue Manager).
- Select the connected network to which the foreign computer belongs.
- Click the Add button to add the connection and then click OK.

Figure 14.8

Creating a foreign computer.

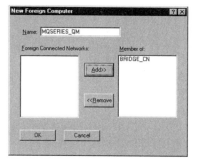

To enable all the foreign aspects of MSMQ, we need to enable the Open Connector security permission.

1. Right-click on the foreign connected network that was just created in the MSMQ Explorer.
2. Select Properties from the list provided.
3. Click on the Security tab.
4. Click the Permissions button.

5. Double-click on the group for which you want to enable communication with the foreign connected network.

6. Enable the Open Connector. Figure 14.9 shows the panel in which this option is set.

Figure 14.9

Enabling the Open Connector.

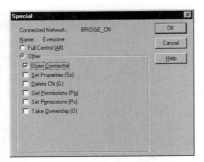

This step concludes the MSMQ configuration required to communicate with any foreign system, including another MSMQ Enterprise. For the specifics of configuring either the foreign system or the connection to it refer to the product documentation for the bridge or foreign system.

 **Note**

If you are interested in using the MSMQ-MQSeries Bridge, Microsoft provides it at no charge. You can download the product from the Microsoft Web site on the SNA Server SP2 Web page. Within the page, specify the file 40sp2mq.exe for download. After the bridge is installed, follow the tutorial to configure and set up an infrastructure between MSMQ and MQSeries. (This product was developed and marketed by Level 8 Systems. The product was sold and licensed to Microsoft in early 1998.)

Enterprise Application Integration (EAI)

In this rapidly changing, information-driven marketplace, the ability to respond quickly to new business opportunities and changing business requirements is vital for business success. E-commerce, mergers, acquisitions, global competition, and changing customer demands are just a few of the business drivers that are forcing information technology (IT) organizations to find cost-effective ways to work smarter.

Enterprise applications have been developed and deployed on many computing architectures over the last 30 years, including mainframe, client/server, and Web-based architectures. Each platform supports different application development tools and programming languages, such as COBOL, C++, Visual Basic, and Java and runs on a variety of operating systems, including MVS, UNIX, Windows, and OS/400. To add to the complexity, many organizations have multiple, often inconsistent, versions of business information (such as customer databases, inventory, or shipping information) scattered across disparate applications. Figure 14.10 shows a highly simplified illustration of the problem. Many different systems are connected by using point-to-point solutions.

Figure 14.10

Point-to-point systems.

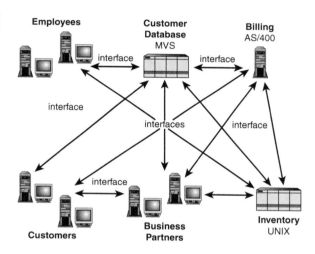

Business Trends

Four trends are driving an unprecedented demand for application integration:

- Corporations are recognizing that, to improve their business processes and rapidly change them in response to dynamic business conditions, they must make their applications work together.
- Corporations are adopting best-of-breed application strategies.
- Corporations are experiencing an increase in mergers, acquisitions, and reorganizations.
- Corporations are expressing a desire to develop closer links with customers, suppliers, and partners.

Hence companies want to fully leverage their application investments by seamlessly integrating and consolidating disparate applications and extending access to new customers, suppliers, and partners. Application integration enables companies to streamline and optimize their business processes, thereby increasing customer service, productivity, and profitability.

Geneva Integrator

Geneva is a family of products from Level 8 Systems, Inc., that simplifies the integration of n-tier Windows applications, e-commerce systems, and legacy systems. Geneva Integration Server is the core component of the system that lets you define integration rules—including transaction flows, data transformations, and adapters for connecting systems with little or no programming—manage these rules in a central repository, and use them throughout your IT infrastructure.

These features significantly reduce both initial development costs and long-term maintenance costs by providing a comprehensive set of tools for quickly connecting systems within the enterprise and for "Internet-enabling" them to conduct both business-to-consumer and business-to-business e-commerce.

Application integration involves rationalizing and restructuring these systems so they can work together effectively and complete the restructuring as quickly as possible and for the lowest possible cost. Figure 14.11 outlines how Geneva Integrator is serving as the common information bus. Applications first connect to Geneva Integrator; then Geneva Integrator processes and distributes information based on user-defined business rules.

Figure 14.11

Application integration goal.

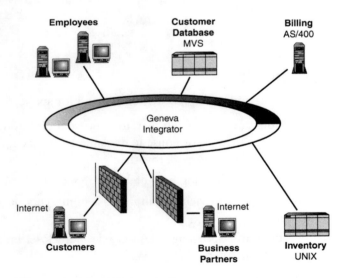

At the heart of Geneva Integrator is the transaction flow request-processing engine. Geneva Integrator receives requests from client applications, server programs, external parties, and so on and processes them according to a transaction flow.

A transaction flow consists of a series of steps in which each step performs an action such as sending/receiving messages, performing data transformations, accessing databases, encrypting/decrypting messages, executing other flows, handling a transaction, performing content-based routing, executing scripted actions, and invoking user-defined steps. The use of transaction flows reduces the time to market when you need to respond to changing business conditions quickly.

Geneva Integrator is tightly integrated with Windows Distributed interNet Application (DNA) technologies including Component Object Module (COM), Distributed Component Object Module (DCOM), Microsoft Transaction Server (MTS), OLE DB, MSMQ, Microsoft Management Console, and System Management Services and fully supports Microsoft's BizTalk e-commerce vision.

Architectural Environments

Geneva Integrator adapts to your environment, rather than forcing you to adapt to its architecture. Geneva Integrator is capable of supporting a wide range of common application and system architectures including

- Event-driven, publish/subscribe
- Three-tier and *n*-tier architecture
- Hub and spoke architecture
- Peer-to-peer, distributed processing
- Services-based, distributed architecture
- Straight-through processing
- Web-based and thin-client architectures
- E-commerce and supply-chain integration

Geneva Integrator enables you to integrate legacy systems, third-party applications, and business applications so that consolidated business information can be delivered to any information consumer.

Also, Geneva Integrator enables companies to easily integrate the legacy applications that implement their mission-critical business processes. Geneva Integrator delivers the industrial-strength performance, scalability, security, reliability, and manageability required to integrate applications under the most demanding conditions.

Metadata

Metadata-driven processing is one of the most important concepts of Geneva Integrator. Metadata-driven processing has two aspects: getting all data into a metadata-rich state and controlling the processing behavior of the infrastructure by using metadata that can be changed by application developers.

In simple terms, metadata is data that describes data. The longer answer is that metadata is definitional data that provides information about or documentation of other data managed within an application or environment.

Metadata is stored in the Geneva Integrator Repository as eXtensible Markup Language (XML) based files (the actual data store can be flat files, RDBMS, directory service, and so on). Geneva reads the metadata and transforms it so that it can be put into a Geneva Message Object,_the standard metadata-rich generic container used throughout Geneva.

Geneva Integrator includes a central configuration tool to facilitate metadata management across multiple Geneva Integrator nodes, and the actual location of the metadata is up to application designers.

Metadata text files can be edited in a text editor, a standard (XML) editor, or the Geneva Integrator-dedicated metadata editors integrated with Microsoft Management Console (MMC). Figure 14.12 is a screen shot of the Geneva Integrator Management Console.

Figure 14.12

Geneva Integrator Management Console.

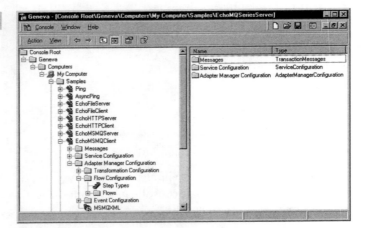

Adapters and Integration Services API

External systems connect to Geneva Integrator by using the Geneva Integrator API or a Geneva Integrator adapter. External systems are any business application that needs to use Geneva Integrator, such as

- Client applications
- Message queuing systems
- Databases (for example, SQL, Sybase, Oracle)
- Web browsers, Java applets, Web servers

- Legacy applications (mainframe, UNIX, NT, AS/400, and so on)
- Real-time data feeds
- File systems
- Directory services

There are two ways for these systems to access Geneva Integrator:

- Geneva Integrator API—External systems capable of using COM/DCOM can access Geneva Integrator by directly calling the API. Java programs can access Geneva Integrator by using the Geneva/Java API.

- Adapters—Adapters are Geneva Integrator components that provide access to Geneva Integrator for external systems that cannot call the API directly.

Figure 14.13 shows how Geneva Integrator ties together different protocols, formats, and adapters. Figure 14.13 also illustrates the use of the Geneva Message Object, which was explained earlier in the "Metadata" section.

Figure 14.13

Geneva Integrator with formats, protocols, and adapters.

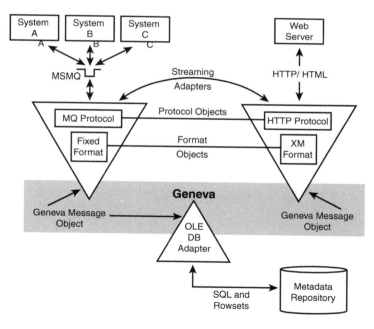

Geneva Integrator is one of few products on the market today that solves true business needs. The requirements that are specified and the complexity of these operations are accomplished by using the component-based architecture in Geneva Integrator.

For more information on Geneva Integrator, visit the Level 8 Systems Web site at
www.level8.com.

Summary

In today's increasingly complex business enterprise, the need to exchange information between disparate systems is an important factor for operational success. Furthermore, a key issue in the deployment of new and complex applications is integration with existing systems, applications, and network infrastructure.

You have learned something about foreign systems. We suggest that you try installing a second MSMQ Enterprise and running the credit agency on it. You will have to use direct format names to identify the target queues.

With the material that has been provided in Geneva Message Queuing, MSMQ-MQSeries Bridge, and Geneva Integrator, you can appreciate that systems may need more than just message queuing.

The concept of messaging (on which you are now an expert) has become an industry standard in connecting applications, disparate operating systems and messaging technologies. You need to understand that messaging is just one layer that addresses only specific needs.

We hope that by this stage your ability to apply this technology is bounded only by your imagination. In addition, we hope that you have enjoyed working through this book as much as we enjoyed putting it together, and we wish you success in your next MSMQ and enterprisewide project!

Part 7

Appendixes

ActiveX Component Reference

This section provides a reference summary of each ActiveX component and its associated methods and properties. A comprehensive reference for each component, including the complete set of allowed values for the various properties, can be found in the online help for MSMQ.

MSMQApplication

The MSMQApplication object obtains the machine GUID, given a machine's name. It is required when you wish to access a system queue, such as the machine journal queue.

MachineIdOfMachineName — the one method associated with the MSMQApplication object—gives a specific machine identifier. Here's an example:

```
machineId=MachineIdOfMachineName("MachineName")As String
```

MSMQCoordinatedTransactionDispenser

MSMQCoordinatedTransactionDispenser maintains an external unit of work. When an MSMQ application needs to write or send to a queue as well as update a database, this component allows both elements of the transaction to be completed as one unit of work. Microsoft's Distributed Transaction Coordinator (DTC) maintains the resource handles to both MSMQ and SQL servers.

MSMQCoordinatedTransactionDispenser has one method, BeginTransaction, which creates an MSMQTransaction object and starts the atomic unit of work. Here's an example:

```
Set MSMQTransaction = MSMQCoordinatedTransactionDispenser.BeginTransaction
```

You should also see MSMQTransactionDispenser.

MSMQMessage

MSMQMessage provides the message construction and delivery mechanisms. Several properties can uniquely define, provide security, or deliver methods of the message.

Table A.1 lists the properties associated with the MSMQMessage object.

Table A.1 MSMQMessage **Properties**

Property	What It Does
Ack	Indicates the type of acknowledgment message MSMQ posts: messages related to reporting, discussed in Chapter 11.
AdminQueueInfo	Contains a description of the queue used for acknowledgment messages: application defined.
AppSpecific	Contains application-specific and generated information such as message classes.
ArrivedTime	Indicates the time when the message was successfully written to the queue.
AuthLevel	Indicates if the message must be authenticated when it arrives at the queue.
Body	Contains the body, or content, of a message; can be any byte array.
BodyLength	Contains the length of the message body in bytes (Unicode bytes).
Class	Indicates message type as a normal MSMQ message, an acknowledgment message, or a report message; read-only.
CorrelationID	Contains a 20-byte correlation identifier for a message.
Delivery	Indicates how MSMQ will deliver the message, express or recoverable. If it is a transactional message, MSMQ automatically sets the delivery mechanism to recoverable.
DestinationQueueInfo	Contains a description of the destination queue for a message.
EncryptAlgorithm	Indicates the encryption algorithm to encrypt the message.
HashAlgorithm	Indicates the hash algorithm used to encrypt the message.
Id	Contains an MSMQ-generated 20-byte identifier (GUID) for the message; read-only.

Property	What It Does
IsAuthenticated	Indicates whether or not the message was authenticated by MSMQ; read-only.
Journal	Indicates whether or not the message is to be journaled (for example, in an administration queue) when the message is sent, or sent to a dead letter queue if the message could not be sent.
Label	Contains a descriptive label for the message.
MaxTimeToReachQueue	Indicates, in seconds, a time limit for the message to reach the queue.
MaxTimeToReceive	Indicates, in seconds, a time limit for the message to be retrieved from the target queue. This limit includes delivery time plus the time it takes to be retrieved by an application.
Priority	Indicates a message's priority from zero to seven (three is the default). Lower numbers indicate lower priority; higher numbers indicate higher priority.
PrivLevel	Indicates whether or not the message is encrypted (private) or public.
ResponseQueueInfo	Contains a description of a queue to which responses to this message should be sent
SenderCertificate	Contains the security certificate used to authenticate messages.
SenderID	Contains an identifier for the sending application.
SenderIDType	Indicates the Security ID (SID) found by MSMQ. In the future, other sender identifiers may be available beyond the SID. The SID is simply a unique value used to identify a user or a group that is assigned to a user when he or she logs on.
SentTime	Indicates the time when a message was sent.
SourceMachineGuid	Contains the GUID of the machine from which the message was sent.
Trace	When using the trace facilities, this property indicates where the report messages are sent (for example, an administration queue).

Two methods are available for MSMQMessage:

- AttachCurrentSecurityContext retrieves security information from a certificate. Here's an example:

```
MSMQMessage.AttachCurrentSecurityContext
```

- Send sends the current message to a queue. Here's an example:

```
MSMQMessage.Send (DestinationQueue, [pTransaction])
```

The pTransaction variable is optional. It can be an MSMQTransaction object or a constant:

- MQ_NO_TRANSACTION
- MQ_MTS_TRANSACTION, the default, which is a Microsoft Transaction Server transaction
- MQ_SINGLE_MESSAGE, which sends a single message as a transaction
- MQ_XA_TRANSACTION, which specifies that the call is part of an externally coordinated transaction

MSMQQuery

The MSMQQuery object queries the MQIS (Message Queue Information Store) for public queues, placing the results in MSMQQuery in an MSMQQueueInfos object.

One method is associated with MSMQQuery. The LookupQueue method returns to the MSMQQueueInfos object a list of public queues. This list is based on the following queue properties: queue identifier, service type, label, create time, and/or modify time. Here's an example:

```
MSMQQuery.LookupQueue ([QueueGuid] [, ServiceTypeGuid]
                       [, Label] [, CreateTime] [, ModifyTime]
                       [, RelServiceType] [, RelLabel]
                       [, RelCreateTime] MSMQQuery [, RelModifyTime])
```

MSMQQueue

The MSMQQueue object represents an MSMQ queue (whether it is a private or public queue). At any given moment, this object refers to a particular position in the queue.

Table A.2 lists the properties associated with the MSMQQueue object.

Table A.2   MSMQQueue Properties

Property	What It Does
Access	Indicates how you want to open the queue: send, receive, and/or peek.
Handle	Contains the handle of the opened queue. The value of the handle changes for each instance of the queue (each time it is opened); read-only.
IsOpen	Indicates whether or not the queue is open; read-only.
QueueInfo	Contains the initial settings for the MSMQQueueInfo object used to open the queue; read-only.
ShareMode	Indicates whether the queue can be opened for sending, peeking, and/or retrieving messages.

The methods available for MSMQQueue are as follow:

- Close closes an instance of a queue; releases the handle thread. Here's an example:

  MSMQQueue.Close

- EnableNotification starts event notification in the application so that it can asynchronously read messages from the queue. Here's an example:

  MSMQQueue.EnableNotification Eventobject

- Peek returns the first message from the queue, but does not destructively remove the message from the queue. Here's an example:

  MSMQMessage = MSMQQueue.Peek

- PeekCurrent returns the current message (based on the implied cursor position). Here's an example:

  MSMQMessage = MSMQQueue.PeekCurrent

- PeekNext returns the next message. Here's an example:

  MSMQMessage = MSMQQueue.PeekNext

- Receive reads the first message in the queue, destructively removing the message from the queue upon completion. Here's an example:

  MSMQMessage = MSMQQueue.Receive

- ReceiveCurrent retrieves the message at the current cursor position. Here's an example:

  MSMQMessage = MSMQQueue.ReceiveCurrent

- Reset returns the cursor to the top of the queue. Here's an example:

  MSMQQueue.Reset

MSMQQueueInfo

MSMQQueueInfo provides queue management. One MSMQQueueInfo object represents one queue. Its properties are returned from a query, or the developer can determine them.

Table A.3 lists the properties associated with MSMQQueueInfo.

Table A.3 MSMQQueueInfo **Properties**

Property	What It Does
Authenticate	Determines whether the queue accepts only authenticated messages.
BasePriority	Determines a priority for a message being sent to queues.
CreateTime	Tells at what time the queue was created; read-only.
FormatName	Must be set before the queue can be opened; by default, it is the pathname of the queue.
IsTransactional	Designates whether the queue supports transactional-based processing (UOW); read-only.
IsWorldReadable	Specifies whether everyone can read from the queue; read-only.
Journal	Specifies whether messages retrieved from the queue are stored in a queue journal.
JournalQuota	Gives the maximum size of a queue journal (in K).
Label	Descriptive label name for the queue. The label provides a reference variable for a queue; used to further detail the queue's function (other than the queue name itself).
ModifyTime	States the last time the properties of the queue were modified; read-only.
Pathname	Determines the location of the queue from the name of the computer where the queue is placed and the name of the queue. Also specifies whether the queue is public or private; required.
PrivLevel	The privacy level of the queue. Supports private (encrypted) messages, nonprivate messages, or both.
QueueGuid	The global unique identifier for the queue; read-only.
Quota	Gives the maximum size of a queue (in K). Allows you to specify the maximum amount of message accumulation.
ServiceTypeGuid	Gives the queue's service type, which can be used to identify the queue, for example, for a specific task. The service type can be specified when the queue is created by the application.

The methods available for MSMQQueueInfo are as follows:

- Create creates an MSMQ queue. Here's an example:

```
MSMQQueueInfo.Create IsTransactional:=True, IsWorldReadable:=True Queuename
```

IsTransactional defaults to False. When True, the queue is a transaction queue. All messages sent to or read from a transaction queue must be done as part of a transaction.

IsWorldReadable defaults to False—only the owner can read the messages. When True, everyone can read the messages in the queue and in its journal.

The only queue property required to create the queue is PathName. This property tells MSMQ where to store the queue's messages, whether the queue is public or private, and the name of the queue.

- Delete deletes an MSMQ queue. Here's an example:

  ```
  MSMQQueueInfo.Delete Queuename
  ```

  Deleting the queue does not delete the MSMQQueueInfo object, only the existing queue.

- Open opens a queue for sending, peeking, and/or receiving. Here's an example:

  ```
  Set MSMQQueueInfo = MSMQQueue.Open (MQ_SEND_ACCESS, MQ_DENY_NONE)
  ```

  Access can be set to one of the following:

  MQ_PEEK_ACCESS—Messages can be viewed, but they cannot be removed from the queue.

  MQ_SEND_ACCESS—Messages can only be sent to the queue.

  MQ_RECEIVE_ACCESS—Messages can be retrieved from the queue or peeked at.

- Refresh refreshes the values of the MSMQQueueInfo object properties, which are read from the MQIS for public queues or from the local computer for private queues. Here's an example:

  ```
  MSMQQueueInfo.Refresh
  ```

- Update updates the MQIS or the local computer with the current values of the MSMQQueueInfo properties. Here's an example:

  ```
  MSMQQueueInfo.Update
  ```

MSMQQueueInfos

MSMQQueueInfos is a list of queues created by using LookupQueue.

Two methods are associated with MSMQQueueInfos: Next and Reset.

- The Next method returns the next queue in the list. Here's an example:

  ```
  MSMQQueueInfos.Next
  ```

- Reset returns to the first queue in the list. Here's an example:

  ```
  MSMQQueueInfos.Reset
  ```

MSMQTransaction

MSMQTransaction notes that the message is one element of a single unit of work. The management of the message is maintained by an internal or external transaction coordinator and works with MSMQCoordinatedTransactionDispenser and/or MSMQTransactionDispenser components.

The MSMQTransaction object has only one property. The underlying Transaction object is used to complete the transaction.

Two methods are associated with MSMQTransaction:

- Abort terminates the MSMQTransaction; rolls the message back off the queue in the case of the Send method; or places the message back onto the queue, in the case of the Receive method. Here's an example:

  ```
  MSMQTransaction.Abort
  ```

- Commit commits the MSMQTransaction; makes the message visible to other applications, in the case of the Send method; or permanently deletes the message from the queue in the case of the Receive method. Here's an example:

  ```
  MSMQTransaction.Commit
  ```

MSMQTransactionDispenser

MSMQTransactionDispenser provides transactional processing for a unit of work that is controlled within MSMQ. This procedure is also known as internal transactional processing. Microsoft's Transaction Server (MTS) is used to maintain this atomic unit of work.

One method is available with MSMQTransactionDispenser:

- BeginTransaction creates an MSMQTransaction object and starts a distributed unit of work that spans across one or more external resources (processes outside MSMQ, like SQL Server). Here's an example:

  ```
  Set MSMQTransaction = MSMQTransactionDispenser.BeginTransaction
  ```

You should also see MSMQCoordinatedTransactionDispenser.

In this appendix

- *The MSMQ Enterprise and Its Sites*
- *MSMQ Server Properties*
- *Connected Network Properties*
- *Queue Properties*
- *Message Properties*

Appendix B

Exploring the MSMQ Objects

In earlier chapters, we discussed some general details about MSMQ's objects. We outlined the components necessary to deploy an application based on MSMQ. Such objects include computers, queues, and connected networks, and each object has properties associated with it. The properties, in turn, describe the function of the object, but more notably they can manage the behavior of the object.

The front-end manager for overseeing our MSMQ operation is the MSMQ Explorer. As explained earlier, it provides the users of MSMQ with a graphical user interface (GUI) that outlines the current MSMQ infrastructure.

The MSMQ Enterprise and Its Sites

As shown in Figure B.1, the MSMQ Explorer provides a topology view of the sites and their connected MSMQ computers.

Figure B.1

MSMQ site expansion view.

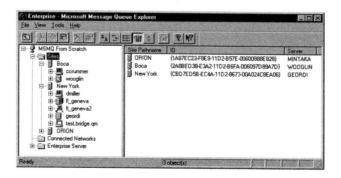

In Figure B.1, we have three sites (Boca, New York, and ORION). Under each site, we can expand the site to reveal its underlying computers. Each computer has a specific function and is carefully planned and installed with the correct infrastructure deployed for the business need.

Notice the icon that is associated with the computer. Each icon represents a different computer within the MSMQ infrastructure. Figure B.2 provides a reference point for the MSMQ icons.

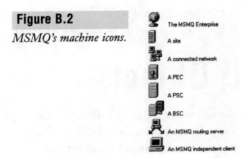

Figure B.2

MSMQ's machine icons.

The MSMQ Enterprise

A site

A connected network

A PEC

A PSC

A BSC

An MSMQ routing server

An MSMQ independent client

Between the Boca and New York sites, all the available MSMQ machines are deployed:

- wooglin——Primary enterprise controller (PEC)
- geordi—Primary site controller (PSC)
- fl_gevena—Backup site controller (BSC)
- fl_gevena2—Routing server (RS)
- ccrummer/dmiller—Independent clients (ICs)
- test.bridge.qm—Foreign computer

Now that you have seen a full layout of MSMQ's computers, let's break them down and see what each object has to offer.

The MSMQ Enterprise

MSMQ needs to start somewhere. That somewhere is with the enterprise. The enterprise is the top layer in the hierarchy, and it provides a foundation for the construction of our MSMQ topology, meaning that all MSMQ objects must be affiliated with an enterprise. Before we get too far, let's see what is in the top of the chain.

Right-clicking on the Enterprise icon (MSMQ From Scratch) and selecting Properties will reveal its information. Figure B.3 displays what is available.

Figure B.3

*MSMQ Enterprise
General properties.*

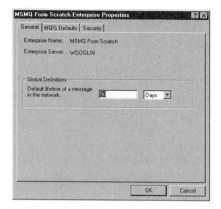

B

The first tab in Figure B.3 gives the general information about the MSMQ Enterprise: the name of the enterprise and the machine responsible for it (PEC/wooglin). The other snippet available is the global definition entry, which allows us to set a default value for the life span of a message. By default, messages that have not been received (destructively removed) from their queue within 90 days will be deleted. If this value is not acceptable to you, simply alter it to the desired value (in days or hours).

Figure B.4 shows the MQIS Defaults tab from which we can alter the replication values. The MQIS is replicated between MSMQ servers every *n* seconds. The values displayed represent inter- and intrasite replication.

Figure B.4

*MSMQ Enterprise
MQIS properties.*

Intersite replication is the action of information (queue creation or updates, addition of computers) being passed between MQIS on other sites. Intrasite replication is information being updated between MQISs within the same site.

Note Only new or updated information is replicated.

The final tab, Figure B.5, shows the information pertaining to security. The security that is provided under the enterprise is associated with the following items:

Permissions—Allow users to construct and manipulate objects within the entire enterprise

Auditing—Tracks who does what to what objects

Ownership—Allows users to take control of the enterprise

Figure B.5

MSMQ Enterprise Security properties.

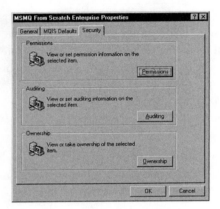

MSMQ Server Properties

As you are now aware, the PEC is the most important MSMQ server. It provides the foundation of our infrastructure and holds the master copy of the MQIS. The PEC can also serve as any of the other MSMQ servers (PSC, BSC, or routing server). The properties that are associated with the PEC also apply to the others.

General Tab

Right-clicking on the PEC (wooglin, in our example) and selecting Properties presents the general information about the server shown in Figure B.6.

When the MSMQ server properties are first enabled, the General tab is shown.

All MSMQ servers have similar properties; Table B.1 details which machines have which properties and explains how the values are interpreted.

Figure B.6

PEC's General properties.

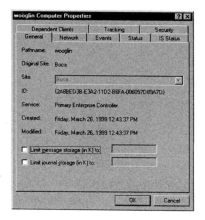

Table B.1   MSMQ Server Properties

Property	Description
Pathname	Specifies the machine name. This property will be the machine name prefix on the queue's pathname, representing the physical location of the queue.
Original Site	Specifies the site the machine was originally affiliated with. This property is used only with ICs.
Site	Allows a machine to be relocated to another site. This property is available only for ICs and extends the flexibility and portability of the IC.
ID	Gives the GUID for the object at hand. *GUID* stands for *Globally Unique Identifier.* This value allows each object (machine, queue, or message) to have a unique value for its entry in the MQIS. The GUID is automatically assigned with the creation of each object.
Service	Denotes the function or machine type of the computer.
Limit Message and Journal Storage	Limits the number of bytes for all the messages on all queues. Used as a control mechanism for allocating machines to contain only certain amounts of data. The entry allows users to specify total machine limits on all queues but does not enable them to select how big each message size can be. With machines running NT, messages can be no larger than 4MB. Windows 95/98 limits message size to 400K.

The majority of these properties are set when the server is installed, and cannot be altered by the administrator. The exception to this is the site name property when looking at the properties of an IC, and the message and journal size properties.

Network Tab

The next tab, the Network tab (as seen in Figure B.7), allows you to add, edit, or remove connected networks (CNs) associated with that computer. CNs are described further in the next section.

Figure B.7

PEC's Network properties.

Events Tab

The Events tab provides information extracted from the Windows NT Event Viewer. Figure B.8 displays examples of entries affiliated with the computer. It is filtered information pertaining to specific events associated with MSMQ. A link is also provided to invoke the full version of Event Viewer.

Figure B.8

PEC's Events properties.

This information is useful for identifying problems and for locating specific events associated with topology construction or application intervention. If further information is required, consider using the Auditing function located on the Security tab.

Status Tab

Status provides information concerning resources allocated to the machine. In Figure B.9 values are displayed for the computer's statistics. Such items include the total of all messages on all queues, byte counts, and established sessions (how many are currently connected to that computer). This information is provided via the Performance Monitor that is supplied with Windows NT. Again, you can launch the full version of Performance Monitor from a link.

B

Figure B.9

PEC's Status properties.

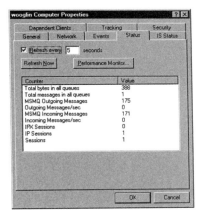

IS Status Tab

Both the IS Status tab, shown in Figure B.10, and the Status tab provide information that is related to the MQIS. Whereas the latter notes statistical information, the IS Status tab shows database replication information.

Dependent Clients Tab

Dependent clients (DCs) are essentially synchronous clients that require an established session with a server to perform MSMQ functions (RPC-based applications). The Dependent Clients tab shows all DCs that are currently connected to that server. This area is the only one that displays this information. DCs are not displayed in the common MSMQ Explorer.

Figure B.10

PEC's IS Status properties.

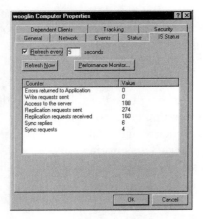

Tracking Tab

The Tracking tab in Figure B.11 monitors messages as they travel throughout the MSMQ network. Enabling a queue and specifying the types of messages to track are configured on this screen.

Figure B.11

PEC's Tracking properties.

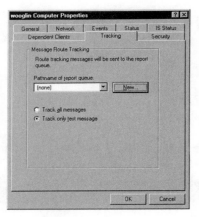

This feature is commonly used in new environments where you need to ensure that messages are traveling to their intended destinations and via the correct routing servers (if implemented).

If you create a queue via the tracking tab, the queue is defined with a label title MS Report Queue. All queues listed via the provided combo box are filtered on the Label property of the queue.

Security Tab

This is the same as the page shown in Figure B.5, and is the standard Windows NT object security panel.

Connected Network Properties

Within MSMQ, a *connected network (CN)* is a logical group of computers where any two of the computers can establish a direct network session with each other. The computers within a CN must support the same protocol and must be able to establish a network session. To test the connectivity between machines, issue a TCP/IP ping on the specific machine. For example, from a command prompt, enter: **ping <machine name or IP address>**.

B

Connected networks can span multiple sites. Computers can belong to several CNs, but all computers operating within the same CN must use the same protocol. CNs can support both Internet Protocol (IP) and internetwork packet exchange (IPX) protocols. Think of the CNs as a shadow of protocol usage. All clients using IP use one specific CN; all computers implemented on IPX use another CN.

The servers can belong to both CNs, providing routing capabilities between sites.

An additional feature of CNs is their capability to provide connectivity to other message queuing mechanisms. By creating a CN, you have the option of creating an IP, an IPX, or a foreign CN. The foreign CN provides the extension of MSMQ to other environments. In Figure B.12, you can see the two different CNs that are implemented. The Boca_CN CN provides connectivity to all MSMQ computers running the IP protocol. The MQS_CN CN provides connectivity to an external queuing product, in this case MQSeries. Refer to Chapter 14 for further the details on outside connectivity.

Figure B.12

MSMQ Connected Network Explorer view.

General Tab

Just like the other objects discussed, a CN has its own properties. Right-clicking the desired CN and selecting Properties will display something like Figure B.13. The General tab provides information of the GUID and protocol type.

Figure B.13

*MSMQ Connected
Network properties.*

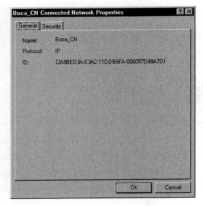

Queue Properties

The queue is the logical view of the physical data storage. A key feature of MSMQ is the capability to assure the delivery of our messages. The queue plays a very important role in fulfilling this demand. Chapter 1, "An Overview of Message Queuing and MSMQ," provided some basic information on the purpose of the queue and some different queue types. The following material provides a more detailed view of the queue and its properties.

General Tab

When you first display the properties of a queue (right-click on the queue), the General tab is shown; see Figure B.14. Table B.2 describes each property you see.

Figure B.14

*Queue's General
properties.*

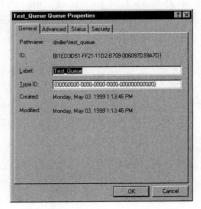

Table B.2   General Queue Properties

Property	Description
ID	GUID of the queue object.
Label	Application-defined value that aids in queue selection; provides a level of qualifying a queue in a selection process. For example, if all print queues have a specific TypeID, you could use Label to determine floor number and/or location of all the queues.
TypeID	User-defined property that can provide a level of qualification. A GUID is a typical TypeID. Use guidgen.exe to provide a unique value for this entry. TypeID and Label can be used in combination to determine a queue selection.
Create Date/Time	Date and time the queue was created; read-only.
Modified Date/Time	Date and time when the queue was last modified.

Advanced Tab

The next tab, as shown in Figure B.15, displays the advanced features of the queue. Table B.3 describes each property you see.

Figure B.15

Queue's Advanced properties.

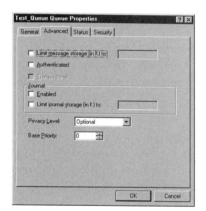

Table B.3   Advanced Queue Properties

Property	Description
Limit Message Storage	User-defined entry that sets the quota for total message accumulation. Although you cannot dictate a queue's maximum message size, you can limit the queue's total messages (in kilobytes). By default, the queue is only restricted by drive space.
Authenticated	Specifies whether the queue accepts only authenticated messages.

continues

Table B.3   continued

Property	Description
Transactional	Indicates whether a queue may be used to hold transactional messages. This property can only be set when the queue is created.
Journal Enabled	Indicates whether to enable source journaling, the process of storing a copy of an outgoing message.
Limit Journal Message Storage	Similar to the true message storage size, journal message storage limits the accumulation of journal messages.
Privacy Level	Specifies whether the queue accepts private (encrypted) messages, nonprivate messages, or both.
Base Priority	Specifies a single base priority for all messages sent to a public queue. Can be set to an integer value between –32768 and +32767 (default is 0). Applications can make use of this feature in combination with message priority. Note: Queue priority take precedence over message priority.

Message Properties

Just like all the objects discussed earlier in this appendix, messages have their own set of properties. In Figure B.15, a message has several properties associated with it. Message size (in bytes) has a limitation of 4MB on Windows NT and 400KB on Windows 95/98.

General Tab

Right-click on a message and select Properties to display the General tab, shown in Figure B.16. This tab contains the general properties of a message. Table B.4 shows the several important elements featured here.

Figure B.16

Message—General properties.

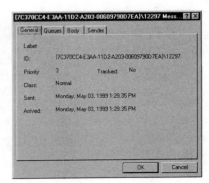

Table B.4   General Message Properties

Property	Description
Label	Similar to a queue's label, the message label is application defined and can provide values noting the message's function, type, or action to be taken.
ID	A GUID representing a unique identifier for this message. ID is created automatically when the message was successfully placed on the queue.
Priority	Allocated by an application, priority levels for messages can range from 0 to 7, with 0 as the default. An application can make use of priority if it needs to process messages that are more important ahead of other, less important messages. With the behavior of queue being first in, first out (FIFO), lesser priority messages could be ahead of more important data. Priority allows for the more important messages to be processed in a timelier manner.
Tracked	Indicates whether the message was tracked.
Class	Indicates message type. A message can be a normal MSMQ message, a positive or negative (arrival and read) acknowledgment message, or a report message. This property is set by MSMQ.
Sent	Send date and time of the outbound message.
Arrived	Date and time that the message was successfully written to the queue.

Queues Tab

Figure B.17 shows the Queues tab, and Table B.5 describes its properties.

Figure B.17

Message—Queue properties.

Table B.5 Queue Properties of the Message

Property	Description
Destination	Displays the intended queue name, using the direct format name.
Response	Displays the response queue (if defined), which notes the queue to be used for reply messages. This field is typically used in the request/reply model.
Administration	Notes the name of the queue to be used for administration-type messages, such as acknowledgments.

Body Tab

The Body tab displays the full content of the message. If the display looks unfamiliar, it may be in Unicode format. In addition, the screen gives the byte count of the message on the queue. Figure B.18 is an example of the Body tab.

Figure B.18

Message—Body properties.

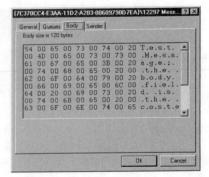

Sender Tab

The Sender tab represents information about the sending machine and application. Figure B.19 shows the details provided in the Sender properties screen, and Table B.6 describes them.

Figure B.19

Message—Sender properties.

Table B.6   Sender Properties of the Message

Property	*Description*
GUID	The GUID value is affiliated with the machine that sent the message. This value is equivalent to the GUID located on the specific machine's properties (discussed earlier this appendix).
Pathname	The name of the sending machine.
User	Displays the UserID of the sending application.
SID	Provides the security identifier of the sending UserID.
Authenticated	Denotes whether the message is encrypted.
Encrypted	Displays whether the message is encrypted.

B

Appendix C

In this appendix

- *API Test Program*
- *The Distributed Draw Program*

Introducing the MSMQ Samples

A set of demonstration programs is installed with MSMQ, and source code is included for them. However, because these programs are demos, they may not have all the error or validity checking of true application programs.

Assuming that you took all the default installation options, you can find the programs from the Windows menu—select Start, Programs, Microsoft Message Queue, Samples. The programs are API Test and Distributed Draw ActiveX Components. The source code for the programs can be found in …\Program Files\MSMQ\sdk\samples.

API Test Program

The API Test program allows you to create, locate, open, close and delete queues and send and receive messages. In Figure C.1, you can see the options available in the API Test.

Figure C.1

Sample program: API Test.

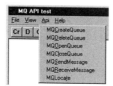

Follow this procedure to see the API program demonstrate MSMQ's functionality:

1. Create a queue. Your local machine name is the default in the Pathname field. Type in the queue name (that is, **testq**). A default label, API Test Queue, is displayed in the Label field.

2. Locate the queue. A list of available queues is displayed.

3. Open the queue for send access. Choose the queue from the drop-down list and check the box marked Send Access.

4. Send a message. Many options are available in the Send dialog box. Simply type a label and a body and send the message on its way.

5. Open another instance of the API Test application. Locate queues, open the test queue for receive access, and receive messages. The message details are displayed.

6. You can now send and receive messages between the applications.

To further demonstrate the power of asynchronous processing, try running the applications on different computers and disconnecting them at different times:

- If the queue is located on the sending machine, messages can be sent but not received without a connection. As soon as the connection is reestablished, the messages can be received.

- If the queue is located on the receiving machine, messages cannot be sent. Only messages sent prior to losing the connection can be received by the receiving application. (In a planned connectionless operation, the sending application would address the target queue by its direct format name, and then normal operation would continue.)

When you are done with the API tests, you can use them to

- Close the queue
- Delete the queue

The Distributed Draw Program

The Distributed Draw program demonstrates even more dramatically the power of an asynchronous connection between two computers:

1. Start Distributed Draw on one computer.

2. You are prompted for a name, which is used to create a queue on your computer.

3. Run Distributed Draw on another computer, using a different name.

4. In the Remote Friend field on the second computer, type the name you used for the first computer.

5. In the Remote Friend field on the first computer, type the name you used for the second computer.

Both computers (both instances of Distributed Draw) now have a queue on their own computer for receiving messages and have opened the other instance's queue to send messages to. Whenever you type or move the mouse, the result is sent in a message to the other application. A connection has been established, and the communication appears seamless between the two computers. You can demonstrate that the connection is, in fact, asynchronous simply by closing the instance of Distributed Draw on the second computer.

Continue to send messages from the first computer and then run the program again from the second computer. The messages are retrieved as soon as the correct queue is specified (the Remote Friend). In the meantime, you can also see the messages sitting on the queue. Start MSMQ Explorer and look for the queues created by Distributed Draw (named from the name you entered when you started the program).

Index

B

Get **FREE** books and more...when you register this book online for our Personal Bookshelf Program

http://register.quecorp.com/

 Register online and you can sign up for our *FREE Personal Bookshelf Program*...unlimited access to the electronic version of more than 200 complete computer books—immediately! That means you'll have 100,000 pages of valuable information onscreen, at your fingertips!

 Plus, you can access product support, including complimentary downloads, technical support files, book-focused links, companion Web sites, author sites, and more!

 And you'll be automatically registered to receive a *FREE subscription to a weekly email newsletter* to help you stay current with news, announcements, sample book chapters, and special events, including sweepstakes, contests, and various product giveaways!

 We value your comments! Best of all, the entire registration process takes only a few minutes to complete, so go online and get the greatest value going—absolutely FREE!

Don't Miss Out On This Great Opportunity!

QUE® is a brand of Macmillan Computer Publishing USA.

For more information, please visit *www.mcp.com*